ANCIENT INDIAN TRADITION & MYTHOLOGY

Translated by

A BOARD OF SCHOLARS

Edited by

G.P. Bhatt

VOLUME 52

ANCIENT INDIAN TRADITION AND MYTHOLOGY

Mahāpurāṇas *Translated into English*

Gen. Ed. Dr. G.C. TRIPATHI

Founder Eds. LATE J.L. SHASTRI and LATE G.P. BHATT

PUBLISHED VOLUMES

Vols. 1-4	ŚIVA PURĀṆA *Tr.* J.L. Shastri
Vols. 5-6	LIṄGA PURĀṆA *Tr.* J.L. Shastri
Vols. 7-11	BHĀGAVATA PURĀṆA *Tr.* G.V. Tagare
Vols. 12-14	GARUḌA PURĀṆA *Tr.* J.L. Shastri
Vols. 15-19	NĀRADA PURĀṆA *Tr.* G.V. Tagare
Vols. 20-21	KŪRMA PURĀṆA *Tr.* G.V. Tagare
Vols. 22-26	BRAHMĀṆḌA PURĀṆA *Tr.* G.V. Tagare
Vols. 27-30	AGNI PURĀṆA *Tr.* N. Gangadharan
Vols. 31-32	VARĀHA PURĀṆA *Tr.* S. Venkitasubramonia Iyer
Vols. 33-36	BRAHMA PURĀṆA *Tr.* J.L. Shastri
Vols. 37-38	VĀYU PURĀṆA *Tr.* G.V. Tagare
Vols. 39-48	PADMA PURĀṆA *Tr.* N.A. Deshpande
Vols. 49-71	SKANDA PURĀṆA *Ed.* G.P. Bhatt, *Tr. & Annot.* Shridhar Balooni & Pratosh Panda
Vols. 72-73	VĀMANA PURĀṆA *Tr. & Annot.* R.S. Shiva Ganesha Murthy
Vols. 74-76	GAṆEŚA PURĀṆA *Tr. & Annot.* Greg Bailey
Vols. 77-82	BRAHMAVAIVARTA PURĀṆA *Tr. & Annot.* G.P. Bhatt

PURĀṆAS UNDER PREPARATION

Viṣṇu Purāṇa • Harivamśa Purāṇa • Bhaviṣya Purāṇa • Matsya Purāṇa • Devī Bhāgavata Purāṇa • Kālika Purāṇa • Mārkaṇḍeya Purāṇa • Viṣṇudharmottara Purāṇa

THE SKANDA PURĀṆA

Part- IV

Translated and annotated by
DR. G.V. TAGARE

MOTILAL BANARSIDASS PUBLISHERS
PRIVATE LIMITED • DELHI

Reprint : Delhi, 2017
First Edition: Delhi, 1993

ISBN: 978-81-208-1082-2

MOTILAL BANARSIDASS
41 U.A. Bungalow Road, Jawahar Nagar, Delhi 110 007
8 Mahalaxmi Chamber, 22 Bhulabhai Desai Road, Mumbai 400 026
120 Royapettah High Road, Mylapore, Chennai 600 004
236, 9th Main III Block, Jayanagar, Bengaluru 560 011
8 Camac Street, Kolkata 700 017
Ashok Rajpath, Patna 800 004
Chowk, Varanasi 221 001

UNESCO COLLECTION OF REPRESENTATIVE WORKS—*Indian Series*
This book has been accepted in the Indian Translation Series of the UNESCO Collection of Representative Works, jointly sponsored by the United Nations Educational, Scientific and Cultural Organization (UNESCO) and the Government of India

MLBD Cataloging-in-Publication Data
The Skanda Purana (Part IV)
Translation and Annotated by
Dr. G.V. Tagare
Includes Index
ISBN: 978-81-208-1082-2
I. Hinduism II. Purana III. Skanda
IV. Tagare, Dr. G.V.

Printed in India
by RP Jain at NAB Printing Unit,
A-44, Naraina Industrial Area, Phase I, New Delhi–110028
and published by JP Jain for Motilal Banarsidass Publishers (P) Ltd,
41 U.A. Bungalow Road, Jawahar Nagar, Delhi-110007

PUBLISHER'S NOTE

The purest gems lie hidden in the bottom of the ocean or in the depth of rocks. One has to dive into the ocean or delve into the rocks to find them out. Similarly, truth lies concealed in the language which with the passage of time has become obsolete. Man has to learn that language before he discovers that truth.

But he has neither the means nor the leisure to embark on that course. We have, therefore, planned to help him acquire knowledge by an easier course. We have started the series of Ancient Indian Tradition and Mythology in English Translation. Our goal is to universalize knowledge through the most popular international medium of expression. The publication of the Purāṇas in English Translation is a step towards that goal.

EDITORIAL

This Part of the *Skanda Purāṇa* covers the whole of *Veṅkaṭācalamāhātmya* which is the first Section of the second Book, namely *Vaiṣṇavakhaṇḍa*. The mountain Veṅkaṭācala which is eulogized here is situated in Andhra Pradesh in the South, being an extension of the Eastern Ghats.

Out of the episodes narrated in this Section two are especially noteworthy, viz. those of Princess Padmāvatī and King Parīkṣit.

The first one is a longer narrative which culminates in the marriage of Padmāvatī to Śrīnivāsa. The story is interesting but what interests more is the revelation that Padmāvatī was really Vedavatī reborn, who, during the Lord's incarnation as Rāma, had served as a substitute for Sītā when Rāvaṇa abducted her. Rāvaṇa's intention had been anticipated by god Agni dwelling in the Agnihotra fireplace of Rāma in Pañcavaṭī and accordingly in order to frustrate the demon's attempt the god substituted Vedavatī from Pātāla, who resembled Sītā, for the latter and sent the real Sītā to Pātāla for keeping her under the protective custody of Svāhā, Agni's wife. As the narrative goes, Vedavatī in a former birth was sinfully touched by Rāvaṇa, which was expiated by her by committing self-immolation. She was then reborn to take revenge on Rāvaṇa and for her successful acting as Sītā she was rewarded by Lakṣmī (who had incarnated as Sītā) with the promise that she could marry the Lord incarnated as Śrīnivāsa on her rebirth as Princess Padmāvatī.

The narrative of King Parīkṣit is too well known to be gone into in detail. Parīkṣit belonged to the twilight period between the end by Dvāpara and beginning of Kaliyuga and had, under the influence of the latter, insulted a meditating sage named Śamīka by throwing a dead serpent over his shoulders, thus earning the wrath of the sage's son Śṛṅgin. Parīkṣit under Śṛṅgin's curse had to die of Takṣaka's bite on the seventh day. He could have been saved by Kāśyapa, a great physician and toxicologist, but for the fact that Takṣaka lured him away from his duty of saving a life by making to him a liberal gift of wealth. And here lies the relevance of the event for our age.

In recent years mercy killing/euthanasia has become a moot question. If a patient has lost all hope for his cure, is terminally ill, should he be saved from further suffering by injecting a fatal dose into his veins? What is legally and morally justified? Should he be allowed to live and wait for a natural and inevitable death, or should the doctors stop the unnecessary suffering by ending his life mercifully? In this Section of our Purāṇa a great sage Śākalya says that as long as the vital airs cling to the throat of a man about to die, it is our moral duty, it is most imperative that treatment to save him should be continued till the last moment. Any move to the contrary should not only be shunned but vigorously opposed. Śākalya calls that person as *Brahmaghātaka* who is competent to treat a person afflicted by poison or illness but does not save him, and equates him with a Brāhmaṇa-slayer, a drink-addict, a thief, a defiler of preceptor's bed and declares these as unpardonable sins having no way of expiation. Interestingly this section makes two other faults as well which people take rather lightly, unpardonable and having no expiation, and they are committing breach of trust and ungrateful conduct.

There is ample evidence here to show that at the time of this Purāṇa norms of religious and social conduct including rules of etiquette were very high and meant to be strictly adhered to. Their violation used to be stringently punished. Nowadays we seem to have become too lax in observing rules of right conduct and especially in our attitude towards women in general and brother's wife in particular, so much so that in certain regions and sections of population the latter is treated on a par with one's own wife, for which even social sanction sometimes exists. This Purāṇa opposes this and cautions by declaring that one who sexually approaches one's brother's wife has no course open to him for expiation. Even such insignificant looking acts as wishing, greeting, making obeisance were treated seriously and rules, do's and don't's, were elaborately laid down as is evident from vv 15-23 of chapter 22 of this Section.

G. P. BHATT

CONTENTS

ABBREVIATIONS

Common and self-evident abbreviations such as Ch(s)—Chapter(s), p—page, pp—pages, v—verse, vv—verses, Ftn—Footnote, Hist. Ind. Philo.—History of Indian Philosophy are not included in this list.

ABORI	*Annals of the Bhandarkar Oriental Research Institute*, Poona
AGP	S.M. Ali's *The Geography of Purāṇas*, PPH, New Delhi, 1973
AIHT	*Ancient Indian Historical Tradition*, F.E. Pargiter, Motilal Banarsidass (MLBD), Delhi
AITM	*Ancient Indian Tradition and Mythology* Series, MLBD, Delhi
AP	*Agni Purāṇa*, Guru Mandal Edition (GM), Calcutta, 1957
Arch. S.Rep.	Archaeological Survey Report
AV	*Atharva Veda*, Svādhyāya Maṇḍal, Aundh
BdP	*Brahmāṇḍa Purāṇa*, MLBD, Delhi 1973
BG	*Bhagavadgītā*
BhP	*Bhāgavata Purāṇa*, Bhagavat Vidyapeeth, Ahmedabad
Br	*Brāhmaṇa* (preceded by name such as Śatapatha)
BsP	*Bhaviṣya Purāṇa*, Vishnu Shastri Bapat, Wai
BVP	*Brahma Vaivarta Purāṇa*, GM, 1955-57
CC	*Caturvarga Cintāmaṇi* by Hemādri
CVS	*Caraṇa Vyūha Sūtra* by Śaunaka, Com. by Mahīdāsa
DB	*Devī Bhāgavata*, GM, 1960-61
De or GDAMI	*The Geographical Dictionary of Ancient and Mediaeval India*, N.L. De, Oriental Reprint, Delhi, 1971
DhS	*Dharma Sūtra* (preceded by the author's name such as Gautama)
ERE	*Encyclopaedia of Religion and Ethics* by Hastings
GP	*Garuḍa Purāṇa*, ed. R.S. Bhattacharya, Chowkhamba, Varanasi, 1964
GS	*Gṛhya Sūtra* (preceded by the name of the author such as Āpastamba)
HD	*History of Dharma Śāstra*, P.V. Kane, G.O.S.
IA	*The Indian Antiquary*
IHQ	*The Indian Historical Quarterly*

JP	*Purāṇa* (Journal of the Kashiraj Trust), Varanasi
KA	*Kauṭilya Arthaśāstra*
KP	*Kūrma Purāṇa*, Veṅkaṭeśvara Press Edn., Bombay; also Kashiraj Trust Edn., Varanasi, 1971
LP	*Liṅga Purāṇa*, GM, 1960; also MLBD, Delhi, 1981
Manu	*Manusmṛti*
Mbh	*Mahābhārata*, Gītā Press, Gorakhpur, VS 2014
MkP	*Mārkaṇḍeya Purāṇa*
MN	*Mahābhārata Nāmānukramaṇī*, Gītā Press, Gorakhpur, VS 2016
MtP	*Matsya Purāṇa*, GM, 1954
MW	M. Monier-Williams' *Sanskrit-English Dictionary*, MLBD, Delhi, 1976
NP	*Nāradīya* or *Nārada Purāṇa*, Veṅkaṭeśvara Press, Bombay
PCK	*Bhāratavarṣīya Prācīna Caritrakośa*, Siddheshwar Shastri, Poona, 1968
PdP	*Padma Purāṇa*, GM, 1957-59
PE	*Purāṇic Encyclopaedia*, V. Mani, English Version, MLBD, Delhi, 1975
PR or PRHRC	*Puranic Records on Hindu Rites and Customs*, R.C. Hazra, Calcutta, 1948
ṚV	*Ṛg-Veda*, Svādhyāya Maṇḍal, Aundh
Śat Br	*Śatapatha Brāhmaṇa*
SC or SMC	*Smṛti Candrikā* by Devanna Bhaṭṭa
SEP	*Studies in Epics and Purāṇas*, A.D. Pusalkar, Bharatiya Vidya Bhavan (BVB), Bombay
SkP	*Skanda Purāṇa*
SP	*Śiva Purāṇa*
VāP	*Vāyu Purāṇa*
VR	*Vālmīki Rāmāyaṇa*
VdP	*Viṣṇudharmottara Purāṇa*
VmP	*Vāmana Purāṇa*
VP	*Viṣṇu Purāṇa*
VrP	*Varāha Purāṇa*

SKANDA PURĀṆA

BOOK II: VAIṢṆAVAKHAṆḌA

SECTION I: VEṄKAṬĀCALAMĀHĀTMYA

Obeisance to Śrī Gaṇeśa

Henceforth begins Book II: Vaiṣṇavakhaṇḍa. There, Section I is Veṅkaṭācalamāhātmya[1] ('Greatness of Veṅkaṭācala').

CHAPTER ONE

Nārada's Vision of Yajñavarāha[2] *(Stationed on the Peak of Sumeru)*

1. In the holy forest called Naimiṣa[3] great sages, foremost of whom was Śaunaka, performed a *Satra* ('Sacrificial Session') of twelve years' duration for the protection of the world.

2. A sage of great intellect, named Ugraśravas,[4] a narrator

---

1. *Veṅkaṭācala or Veṅkaṭādri*—The Veṅgaḍam (Veṅkaṭam) of Vaiṣṇava Alvārs (Saints) is the name of the seventh ridge of the Tirupati Hill in the Chittoor District of Andhra Pradesh. It is situated at 13° 41″ North Latitude and 79° 24″ East Longitude. The hill is 2820 feet above sea level. It is an extension of the Eastern Ghats. The hill consists of seven peaks. These are supposed to be the seven hoods of Ādiśeṣa, the mythological serpent who supports the earth. The other six peaks (rather ridges) are designated as Śeṣācala, Vedācala, Garuḍācala, Añjanācala, Vṛṣabhācala and Nārāyaṇācala. The main deity Śrī Veṅkaṭeśvara is on the seventh ridge (Veṅkaṭācala).

2. *Yajñavarāha*—The Boar-incarnation of Viṣṇu is identified with the Vedic sacrifice. Some Vedic scholar composed a poetic description of the Divine Boar in Yajña-terminology. It was so beautiful that it was adopted by Purāṇa-writers (e.g. BdP I.i.5.9-23, VāP I.6.16-21, BmP 213.33-42, MtP 248.67-73), Smṛti writers like Viṣṇu 1.3-9 and even by Śaṅkara in his Com. on *Viṣṇu-sahasra-nāma* v. 118 on *Yajñāṅga*.

3. *Naimiṣa*—Usually identified with modern Nimsar at a distance of 20 miles from Sitapur and 45 miles NW of Lucknow. But V. V. Mirashi places it on Gomatī somewhere in Sultanpur area some 40 miles from Ayodhyā (*Purāṇa* X-1-34). The Naimiṣāraṇya on Dṛṣadvatī mentioned in VāP I.1-12 is not intended here.

4. Ugraśravas is not a direct disciple of Vyāsa. His father Romaharṣaṇa was so. The term 'disciple' is used loosely as a *Paraṁparā Śiṣya*. At the time

of (sacred) tales, son of Romaharṣaṇa and a disciple of Vyāsa, approached them.

3. Duly honoured and adored by them, Sūta, the most excellent one among *Paurāṇikas* ('persons well-verse in mythological tradition'), narrated that divine Purāṇa named Skanda.

4. He narrated in detail the account of creation, annihilation (of the universe), genealogy, histories of dynasties of kings, lineage of sages and the details of Manvantaras.[1]

5. On hearing the stories of the greatness and powers of the holy places those leading sages spoke to Sūta of perfect self-control with a desire to listen to the stories.

The sages said:

6. O omniscient son of Romaharṣaṇa, well-versed in the Purāṇic lore, we wish to hear about the greatness of the prominent mountains on the surface of the earth. O highly fortunate sage, tell us what are the important mountains.

Śrī Sūta replied:

7. Formerly on the banks of the river Jāhnavī (i.e. Gaṅgā) I asked Vyāsa, the most excellent one among great sages, this very question. He, the most excellent one of my preceptors, said to me:

Vyāsa said:

8-13. Formerly, in the divine Yuga, O Sūta, Nārada, the most excellent one among sages, went to the peak of Sumeru which is extremely resplendent on account of different kinds of gems and jewels. In its middle he saw the vast and divinely bril-

---

of SkP the Sūta became dignified as he is called 'Śrī Sūta'. He is called *Paurāṇika*, an office-bearer in *Kauṭilīya Arthaśāstra*. Probably an example of social mobility in the case of Ugraśravas.

1. These are regarded as the five traditional characteristics of a Purāṇa. They are also mentioned in AP 1.14, BSP I.2.4-5, GP I.215.14, KP I.1.12, VP III. 6.25. Amarasiṁha (5th cent. CE) has recorded these in his Lexicon (I.6.5). Although these characteristics have been unanimously accepted by Purāṇa-writers as essential parts of a Purāṇic Text, actually the Purāṇa Texts that have come down to us hardly conform to this definition.

liant abode of Brahmā. In the region to the north of it he saw an excellent Pippala tree (holy fig tree). It was a thousand Yojanas high and twice that in extent. At its root he saw a heavenly *Maṇḍapa* (hall) equipped (i.e. decked) with different kinds of gems and jewels. It was adorned with thousands of ruby-columns. There were clusters of necklaces of *Svastika* design made of *lapis lazuli*, pearls and other jewels. It was rendered splendid by means of divine *Toraṇas* ('ornamental arched doorways'). There were many kinds of birds and animals made of splendid gems and jewels of all the nine kinds. It had a big entrance made of topaz. The *Gopura* (the minaret or a lofty towered gate at the gateway) had seven storeys. It was rendered splendid by means of two panels of doors made of brilliant diamonds.

14. After entering it he saw a divine pearl-set platform within. The great sage climbed on to the lofty dais set with *lapis lazuli*.

15. In its middle he saw an exceedingly lustrous throne that was unequalled (in workmanship) and very high. It had eight brilliant legs and was studded with pearls.

16. In its middle there was a divine lotus lovely and splendid with a thousand petals. It was white and resembled a thousand moons in beauty and splendour. It sparkled exceedingly with its pericarp and filaments.

17. In its middle he saw a beautiful being in the form of a man as huge as the Kailāsa mountain. He had a brilliance of ten thousand full moons. He was seated within the lotus.

18. He had four arms and highly magnificent limbs. He had the splendid face of a boar. The excellent Puruṣa had a conch and a discus (in two hands) and held (the other two) in gestures of granting boons and immunity from fear.

19. He wore yellow garments. The Lord with long eyes resembling lotuses had a gentle face resembling the full moon. His lotus-like face had the fragrance of incense.

20. The sound of Sāman hymns issued from him. He was an embodiment of Yajñas.[1] The wooden sacrificial ladle (*Sruc*) constituted his snout. The *Sruva* (ladle) was his nose. He resembled the

1. Vide supra p. 1, fn 2. This is an echo of the Yajñavarāha description in other Purāṇas.

Milk Ocean. A crown enhanced the brilliant splendour of his face.

21. He had the Śrīvatsa mark on his chest. He shone with a splendid white sacred thread. His strong and broad chest projected forward shining brightly with the splendour of the Kaustubha jewel.

22. He was bedecked in divine ornaments of gold studded with excellent gems and jewels. He was as sparkling as the autumnal cloud overspread with clusters of lightning streaks.

23. With the sole of his left foot placed on a footstool he constantly shone brilliantly with ornaments like bangles, armlets, bracelets and ear-rings.

24. Day and night, he was attended upon by Brahmā and the leading sages, Vasiṣṭha, Atri, Mārkaṇḍeya, Bhṛgu and many others.

25-26. He was served and attended upon by Indra and other Guardians of the Quarters and groups of Gandharvas and celestial damsels. Nārada bowed down to the Lord of Devas and approached him. He eulogized Dharādhara ('the Uplifter of the Earth') with excellent passages from the Upaniṣads. Extremely delighted Nārada stood near the Lord.

The Arrival of Goddess Earth to the Presence of Varāha

27-29. In the meantime there arose the sound of the divine Dundubhi drum. Thereafter there came Goddess Earth accompanied by her friends. She was exceedingly brilliant with her robes in the form of the oceans abounding in gems and jewels. She bent under the weight of her breasts in the form of Sumeru and Mandara. She was dark in complexion like fresh leaves of Dūrvā grass. She was adorned in all ornaments.

30-33. She was accompanied by her friends Ilā and Piṅgalā. Then (Goddess) Earth scattered at the feet of Lord Śrī Varāha a (big) collection of flowers brought by them. Then she bowed down to the Lord of the Chiefs of Devas and stood there with palms joined in reverence. Śrī Varāha embraced that Goddess and placed her in his lap. With his mind exceedingly pleased the Lord enquired about the happiness and welfare of Earth.

Dialogue between Earth and Varāha

Śrī Varāha said:

34. O Goddess Earth, I established you on the delightfully pleasing head of Śeṣa. I placed the world (people) on you with the mountains as your assistants. Thereafter I came here, O gentle lady. Why have you come here yourself?

Earth replied:

35-36. You lifted me up from the nether worlds and made me stable and steady on the (head) of Ananta splendid with a thousand hoods, as if on a high pedestal studded with jewels and precious stones. O Lord, you placed the mountains capable of sustaining me as my assistants. O Puruṣottama, they are holy and identical with you. Now, O mighty one, tell me about the chief ones among them, who are my supports.

The Description of Śeṣācala's Excellence Among all Mountains

Śrī Varāha said:

37-41. O Vasundharā, the following mountains[1] are your supports: Sumeru, Himavān, Vindhya, Mandara, Gandhamādana,

---

1. VV 37-41 give a list important mountains. They are identified as follows:

Sumeru	Rudra Himalaya in Garhwal (De 196)
Himavān	The Himalayas
Mandara	A hill situated in Banka subdivision in Bhagalpur, Bihar (De 124)
Gandhamādana	(I) A part of Kailāsa on the southern side (De 60) (II) The northern parapet of the Hindukush System (AGP 91)
Śālagrāma	A hill in the Haimavatī region, near the source of Gaṇḍak
Mālyavān	Karakorum between Nīla and Niṣadha (De 123)
Pāriyātraka	The western part of the Vindhya range (De 149)
Mahendra	The range of hills from Orissa to Madura in Tamil Nadu (De 119)

Sālagrāma, Citrakūṭa, Mālyavān, Pāriyātraka, Mahendra, Malaya, Sahya, Siṁhādri, Raivata and the great golden mountain named Añjana, the son of Meru. These have been served (i.e. resorted to) by me, by groups of Devas and by those of sages.

O Mādhavī, I shall describe the chief ones among these accurately. Listen:

Sālagrāma, Siṁhādri and the leading mountain Gandhamādana—these excellent mountains, O Goddess, have occupied the quarter of Himavān (i.e. the north). O Vasundharā, I shall name the mountains famous in the south.

42. Aruṇādri,[1] Hastiśaila, Gṛdhrādri and Ghaṭikācala—all these excellent mountains are near Kṣīrā river.

43. To the north of Hastiśaila, five Yojanas (i.e. 60 km) away, is the river Suvarṇamukharī,[2] the most excellent one among all the rivers.

44. On its northern bank is the excellent lake named Kamala. On its shore dwells Lord Hari who bestowed boons on Śuka.

45. Kṛṣṇa, the destroyer of the agony of devotees, (is present there) along with Balabhadra. He is always propitiated by Vaikhānasas ('recluses') and groups of sages.

Malaya	Southern part of the Western Ghats south of Kāverī (De 122)
Siṁhādri	A part of the Himalayas
Raivata	Mt. Girnar near Junagarh in Gujarat (De 165)
Añjana (Giri)	The Suleiman range in West Panjab, Pakistan (De 8)

1. Aruṇādri or Aruṇācala, Tiruvannamalai in the South Arcot District, is 'The Fire-mountain' described in *Aruṇācala-Māhātmya*.

2. One of the most sacred rivers in South India. It rises in Agastyācala and falls into the southern sea. It flows through the North Arcot District with the sacred Śiva Kṣetra Kālahastī on its bank. It flows near Vṛṣabhācala and has Veṇā, Vāghurā and Kalyā as its tributaries.

46. In an excellent forest to the north of the lake named Kamala is the great abode of Vāsudeva named Śrī Veṅkaṭācala.[1] The forest was rendered splendid by Haricandana trees. It extended to two and a half Krośas (i.e. $2\frac{1}{2} \times 3 = 7\frac{1}{2}$ km) (i.e. its distance from the lake was $7\frac{1}{2}$ km).

47-48. The leading mountain was one Yojana high (12 km) and extended to seven Yojanas (84 km). O Goddess, it is golden and very long with ridges abounding in gems and jewels.

On that mountain the following always reside: groups of Devas beginning with Indra, leading sages beginning with Vasiṣṭha, Siddhas, Sādhyas, Maruts, Dānavas, Daityas, Rākṣasas and groups of celestial damsels beginning with Rambhā.

49. Nāgas, Garuḍas and Kinnaras perform penance there. The rivers there, occupied by these, yield merits on being visited. O Mādhavī, there are many divine lakes too here.

50-52. (A description of the pre-eminence of Svāmipuṣkariṇī among all the Tīrthas) Listen to the (following) most excellent ones among all the Tīrthas[2]: Cakratīrtha, Daivatīrtha, Viyadgaṅgā, Kumāradhārikātīrtha, Pāpanāśana, Pāṇḍavatīrtha and Svāmipuṣkariṇī. They say that these seven Tīrthas are the most excellent ones on the splendid Nārāyaṇagiri. The splendid Svāmipuṣkariṇī is the most excellent one among these.

---

1. Vide supra p. 1, fn. 1. Its other names are Vṛṣa or Vṛṣabha, Cintāmaṇi, Jñānādri, Tīrthādri and Puṣkarādri.

2. The following are the locations of Tīrthas *vis-a-vis* the Veṅkaṭeśa Temple:

Svāmitīrtha or *Puṣkariṇī*	:	is a tank near the Veṅkaṭeśvara or Tirumal Temple.
Cakratīrtha	:	This lies to the north-west of the Tirumal temple.
Daiva Tīrtha	:	This Tīrtha is a tank in the forest to the north-west of the Tirumal Temple.
Viyadgaṅgā or *Ākāśagaṅgā*	:	This lies two miles to the north of the Tirumal Temple.
Kumāradhārikā or *Kumāradhārā*	:	This lies six miles to the north-west of the Tirumal Temple.
Pāpanāśa Tīrtha	:	This is a low waterfall at a distance of three miles to the north of the Tirumal Temple.
Pāṇḍava Tīrtha	:	It lies about a mile to the north-east of Śrī Veṅkaṭeśvara Temple.

53. I dwell with you on the western bank of this. On its southern bank dwells Śrīnivāsa, the Lord of the universe.

54-55. O Earth having the oceans for your robes, it is on a par with all the Tīrthas beginning with Gaṅgā.

O Earth, Svāmisarovara (i.e. Svāmipuṣkariṇī) has attained the leadership of all the Tīrthas in the three worlds including both lakes and rivers. All the Tīrthas reside on this divine mountain in order to serve the sacred Svāmipuṣkariṇī. I shall mention their number to you.

56. There are sixty-six crores of Tīrthas on this excellent sacred mountain, O Vasundharā, and among them six Tīrthas are extremely prominent.

57. Tuṁba Tīrtha[1] is a great Tīrtha and is like the embryo of five leading Tīrthas. It dispels the fear of being in the womb (again) in the case of those who take their bath here, O excellent Earth.

Dharaṇī said:

58. O mighty one, six Tīrthas have been mentioned by you on the mountain. Tell me their greatness in proper sequence. O Uplifter of Earth, describe the merits acquired by men who take their bath therein.

Śrī Varāha said:

59-61. O Mādhavī, listen. I shall relate to you the greatness of Nārāyaṇādri (i.e. mountain Nārāyaṇa). Devas, sages, Yogins beginning with Sanaka and learned men called that mountain which is the abode of the Supreme Soul, Añjanādri in Kṛta Yuga. They called that mountain Nārāyaṇagiri in Tretā, and mount Siṁha in Dvāpara and Veṅkaṭācala in Kali.

62-63. A person who is a thousand Yojanas away, or who is in another continent, may bow down with great devotion in the direction of the pre-eminent mountain. He shall then be rid of all sins and shall go to Viṣṇu's region. I shall recount to you the greatness of the six Tīrthas on that (mountain) in a sequence.

1. Also called Tumburu or Phālgunī Tīrtha: This is situated ten miles to the north of the Tirumal Temple in a forest.

The Greatness of Kumāradhārā[1]

64-67. O gentle lady, listen attentively to the destroyer of all the sins. On this prominent mountain, O Vasundharā, there is a lake named Kumāradhārikā. It sanctifies all the worlds. When the Sun is in the Zodiac Aquarius, in the month of Māgha, on the great full-moon day conjoined with the star Maghā, a devotee shall take his holy bath in that lake at midday, in the place where Kārttikeya, the son of Pārvatī, born of Fire-god, worships Śrīnivāsa along with Devasenā.

O lady devoid of impurities, listen to his meritorious benefit. He shall attain, O Dharā, the mother of all the worlds, that benefit which one gets by taking one's holy bath regularly for twelve years in all the Tīrthas beginning with Gaṅgā.

68. He who makes a gift of food in that holy spot along with monetary gifts in accordance with his capacity, attains as much benefit as is mentioned in the case of the holy bath.

69-70. The person who takes his bath in the Tumba Tīrtha in the mountain-cavern when the Sun is in the Zodiac Mīna (Pisces), when it is the full-moon day associated with the Asterism Uttarā Phālgunī and in the excellent fourth *Prahara* ('watch of the day')—such a person is not born again in a womb, O Goddess.

The Greatness of Ākāśagaṅgā

71. When the Sun is in the Zodiac Meṣa (Aries) in conjunction with the Citrā star and it is a full-moon day, the devotee shall take his holy bath in the waters of Ākāśagaṅgā in the morning. He shall attain salvation.[2]

The Greatness of Pāṇḍava Tīrtha

72-74. When the Sun is in the Zodiac Vṛṣabha (Taurus) in the month of Vaiśākha, the devotee should take his holy bath in

1. This is regarded as the birth place of Kumāra Kārttikeya, Skanda or Subrahmaṇya. Hence the Tīrtha is named after him. Cf. Varāha Purāṇa (VrP) Part II, Ch. 1, vv 61-65; MkP Ch. 4.
2. For the auspiciousness of this occasion cf. VrP II.1.68-69.

the Tīrtha named Pāṇḍava at the hour of *Saṅgava* (i.e. three *Muhūrtas* after the dawn) on the following days: The *Tithi* should be *Dvādaśī* (twelfth) in conjunction with Sunday if it is the bright half or in conjunction with Tuesday if it is the dark half or, whether it be dark or bright half, on any Sunday in combination with Puṣya or Hasta star.[1] The man who takes bath thus shall not attain any misery here. He shall attain happiness in the other world.

The Greatness of the Holy Pool of Pāpanāśana

75-77. O lady of exalted fortune, the devotee should take his holy bath regularly in the Tīrtha named Pāpanāśana on the top of the prominent mountain on any of the following days: Whether it be bright half or dark half, *Saptamī* (i.e. seventh *tithi*) should be in conjunction with a Sunday or the star Puṣya or the star Hasta.[2] That excellent man shall be liberated from the sins acquired in the course of a crore of births.

The Greatness of Devatīrtha

78-83. Listen, O gentle lady, to the greatest secret. On the great mountain named Ananta, on the peak to the north-west of my divine abode, there is an exceedingly splendid lake in the cave of the mountain. It is called Devatīrtha. O gentle lady, I shall tell you the (appropriate) time of taking holy bath in that highly meritorious Tīrtha, (which is when there is) the combination of a Thursday with the Puṣya star, or of a Monday with the Śravaṇa star or on a Vyatīpāta day.[3] Listen to the merit of the person who takes holy bath on all these days. All his sins whether committed knowingly or unknowingly shall perish. This Tīrtha, i.e. Devatīrtha is exceedingly sacred. By taking his holy bath in Devatīrtha all his merits increase. He will be endowed

1. Cf. VrP II.1.70-71.
2. Cf. VrP II.1.72-73.
3. Cf. VrP II.1.74-80.

Vyatīpāta is an astronomical Yoga when the Sun and the Moon are in the opposite Ayana and have the same declination, the sum of their declinations being 180. (MW 1030A)

with sons and grandsons. He will attain a long life. At the end of his life he goes to heaven and is honoured in the world of the Moon.[1] One who makes a gift of food on that day (will attain the same benefit) as one who makes a gift of food throughout his life. O Goddess Vasundharā, a great secret has been disclosed to you.

Vyāsa said:

84. On hearing (these words) Goddess Earth became highly delighted in her mind. With pleasing words she eulogized the Uplifter of Earth, Varāha, who has none equal to him.

EULOGY OF VARĀHA BY GODDESS EARTH

Dharaṇī said:

85. Obeisance to you, O Lord of the Chiefs of Devas, O Acyuta, with the face of a Boar, O Lord resembling the Milk Ocean, O mighty one with adamantine curved teeth.

86. At the beginning of the Kalpa I have been lifted up from the waters of the ocean, O Lord, by you with a thousand arms. O Viṣṇu, I hold up the worlds.

87. O Lord shining with the sacred thread and many divine ornaments, O Lord adorned with divine gems and jewels, the wearer of exceedingly reddish robes.

88. Obeisance, obeisance (to you, O Lord) with lotus-like feet on a par with the rising Sun, O Lord with the curved teeth resembling the Crescent Moon, O Lord of great strength and exploit.

89. O Lord with limbs smeared with sandal paste of divine origin, having ear-rings made of heated gold, O Lord bedecked in golden armlets, shining with sapphire gems.

90. O Lord who had torn up Hiraṇyākṣa with the tips of adamantine curved teeth, O Lord of great strength with eyes beautiful like lotuses, O Lord fascinating with the sounds of Sāman hymns.

---

1. V.L. After death he attains heaven and is eulogized in the region of Indra.

91. O Lord with the Vedas as the crest jewel, O immanent soul of everyone, O Lord with enchanting exploits, O Lord, saluted by the Four-faced Lord (i.e. god Brahmā) and Śaṁbhu, O Lord with large eyes.

92. O Lord, the embodiment of all the lores, O Lord beyond the worlds, obeisance, obeisance. O infinite one, the embodiment of bliss, O Kālakāla (? Death unto the god of Death), repeated obeisance to you.

Departure of Lord Varāha along with Dharaṇī to Śeṣācala

93-95. After eulogizing the Lord thus Goddess Earth saluted him (falling) on his feet. On seeing her saluting the eyes of the Lord beamed with delight. He lifted up Goddess Earth with his arms and embraced her. He sniffed the face of Dharaṇī and placed her on his left lap. He then rode on Lord Garuḍa and went to Vṛṣabhācala. The Lord of the Earth was eulogized by the leading sages beginning with Nārada.

96. On the western bank of Svāmipuṣkariṇī, honoured by all the worlds, remains seated the Lord having the face of Boar. He is worshipped there by the leading sages, Vaikhānasas ('anchorites') of great magnificence, noble souls on a par with Brahmā.

Greatness of Veṅkaṭācala

Vyāsa said:

97. After seeing him, O Sūta, Nārada related it (to the sages) formerly. I heard this there in the assembly of sages.

98. O Sūta, you had asked about the greatness of the mountains that has been duly recounted by me accurately in the manner it was originally heard from Nārada.

The Benefit of (Listening to This) Chapter

99-100. O Sūta, he who reads (recites) this holy discourse of us both on piety and devotion in front of the Lord or in front of Brāhmaṇas or in front of all castes listening to it with great devotion, shall attain pre-eminence in the company of sons and grandsons.

101. All the persons who listen shall attain what is desired.

Sūta said:

102-103. Thus said the holy lord Vyāsa to me—Vyāsa who was attended to by the sages. O leading sages, everything has been recounted by me here in the same manner as has been heard formerly from my preceptor Kṛṣṇadvaipāyana.

On hearing these words of Sūta, they became delighted in their minds.

The sages said:

104. O Sūta, the greatness of the holy mountain named after the Lord of Serpents, Śeṣa, has been told by you. This mountain is the holiest among all the holy mountains on the earth. This greatness is destructive of sins. It yields the benefit of salvation.

105. Varāha accompanied by Dharaṇī went to mountain Vṛṣa. After reaching it what did he say to Goddess Earth? O highly intelligent one, recount it to us.

CHAPTER TWO

Propitiation of Śrī Varāha by Mantras

Śrī Sūta said:

1-3. O ye sages, listen to the ancient holy story. Formerly, in the Vaivasvata Manvantara, in the most meritorious Kṛta-yuga, the Lord of Earth, the Lord of Devas dwelt on the Nārāyaṇa mountain in the form of a Boar.

Accompanied by her friends and attendants, Dharaṇī (Goddess Earth) bowed down to the Lord whose eyes resembled red lotus and were longish. She then asked thus:

Dharaṇī asked:

4-6. O Lord of Devas, by which Mantra are you to be propitiated, whereby you will become delighted? Tell me that (Mantra), O Lord, which is a perpetual favourite of yours.

It should be the cause of all prosperity unto those who repeat it. It should bestow sons and grandsons. It should always grant imperial power and position. It should yield all desired things to those who wish for them. It should grant the attainment of your own region at the end. O Lord Varāha, the bestower of honour, with love towards me, tell (the Mantra) that is of this type (potency).

Śrī Sūta said:

7. On being asked by Earth thus the Lord said with pleasure and smile spreading over his face:

Śrī Varāha said:

8-9. Listen, O gentle lady, to the exceedingly great secret (Mantra) that causes prosperity immediately, that yields lands, sons etc. It should be kept as a great secret and should never be revealed. Further, it should be communicated to a devotee of well-controlled mind, who is willing to render service.

THE MANTRA: "OṀ NAMAḤ ŚRĪVARĀHĀYA DHARAṆYUDDHARAṆĀYA CA SVĀHĀ"[1]

10. "Oṁ obeisance to Śrī Varāha who lifted up Earth. Svāhā." This Mantra should always be repeated by one who wishes to be liberated. He should be a Fire-worshipper with his wife alive.

11-13. O Goddess Earth, this Mantra is the bestower of all Siddhis. Saṁkarṣaṇa is mentioned as its sage. I myself am the Deity. The metre mentioned is *Paṅkti* ('one with ten syllables in a foot'). Śrī is the *Bīja* ('seed') cited. One who takes instruction of

1. This is a Paurāṇika Mantra but it has been given the semblance of a Vedic Mantra by stating its seer-sage, deity etc. in vv 10–13, the total number of repetitions of this mantra and Homa (vv 12b-13a) and the *Dhyāna* (description of the deity to be meditated on) in vv 14-16 and its benefit (*phalaśruti*) in vv 20-24.

this Mantra from a good preceptor should repeat it four hundred thousand times. He shall perform *Homa* with rice cooked in milk along with honey and ghee.

Now I shall describe (the personality of Varāha for) meditation that causes mental purity.

14-16. O Earth having the oceans for your robes, the devotee shall meditate upon me accompanied by you seated on my left thigh. I shall be meditated as having the lustre of a pure crystal mountain with eyes resembling the petals of red lotus, the face of a Boar, gentle appearance, four arms and the crown. There is the mark Śrīvatsa on the chest. In the lotus-like hands a conch and a discus are held (with one making) the mystic gesture of granting immunity from fear. I wear reddish yellow robes. I am bedecked in red ornaments. I am stationed on a lotus over the body of Śeṣa lying on the middle of the back of the divine Tortoise.

17. After meditating thus the devotee shall always repeat the Mantra one hundred and eight times. He shall attain all desired objects. He will certainly attain salvation in the end.

18. O Dharaṇī free from impurities, what I was asked by you has been told by me. Henceforth, O lady of pure face, relate to me what is intended by you (in your mind).

The Achievement of their Objectives by Dharma and others Through the Varāha Mantra

Śrī Sūta said:

19-21. On hearing this Earth asked him once again: "By whom, O Lord, has this (i.e. recitation) been formerly performed and what benefit has been acquired by him?"

On being asked thus again Lord Śrī Varāha spoke thus: "O Goddess, formerly in Kṛtayuga the great Manu named Dharma obtained this Mantra from Brahmā and repeated it over this (very) mountain. He saw me, obtained the boon and attained my region.

22. On account of the curse of Durvāsas Indra was formerly dislodged from heaven. He worshipped me here, O Goddess, with this (Mantra) and regained his heaven.

23-24. Other sages too, O Earth, repeated this Mantra and attained the highest state (i.e. salvation). Ananta, the Lord of serpents, obtained this Mantra from Kaśyapa. He performed the *Japa* in Śvetadvīpa continent and he became a support to Earth. Hence, this Mantra should always be repeated by human beings seeking lands."

Śrī Sūta said:

25. On hearing this Goddess Earth became highly pleased. She asked the supporter of Earth (i.e. Śrī Varāha) once again:

Dharaṇī said:

26. When does Śrīnivāsa, the Lord of the universe, the pure Lord of Devas, come to the great mountain named Veṅkaṭa accompanied by Śrī and Bhūmi.

27. How does Janārdana become one who will be able to live in another Kalpa? O Lord Varāha, relate this to me. My eagerness is great.

CHAPTER THREE

Manifestation of the Lord to the Eyes of Everyone at the Request of Agastya[1]

Śrī Varāha said:

1. Well, I shall relate to you an ancient incident, O lady of excellent face. Listen to the meritorious episode, O great Goddess, along with the sequel and the future.

2-3. Formerly, O Goddess, in the Vaivasvata Manvantara in the first Kṛta Yuga, O sinless lady, Śrīnivāsa accompanied

1. This and the following chapters follow closely the story in VrP, Part II, Chapters 3 ff. The names Viyad or Ākāśa and Dharaṇī remind us of Vedic *Dyāvāpṛthivī* and the finding of a baby daughter from the bowels of the earth is similar to the 'birth' (finding) of Sītā by Janaka while ploughing the sacrificial place.

by Śrī and Bhūmi saw the great penance of Vāyu and came to the bank of Svāmipuṣkariṇī.

Śrīkānta ('the beloved of Śrī') Hari, desirous of doing what is pleasing to Vāyu, shall stay in this southern meritorious shore in the splendid palace ('*Vimāna*') named Ānanda.

4. Ever since then Hṛṣīkeśa constantly propitiated by Lord Kārttikeya shall abide in this palace till the end of the Kalpa but (be) invisible.

Dharaṇī said:

5-6. How will the invisible Lord Śrīnivāsa, the Lord of Devas occupying your right side, be visible to human beings? Tell, O Lord of Suras, how he is (to be) propitiated by people?

Śrī Varāha replied:

7-10. Agastya reached this place and visited the eternal Deva (Lord). He propitiated him for twelve years, delighting him again and again. He prayed for the presence of the Lord, "May Your Lordship be visible." Hṛṣīkeśa who was accompanied by Śrī and Bhūmi (said as follows), O Dharā:

The Lord said:

O celestial sage, for your sake I shall be visible to all the embodied beings, but this Vimāna will never be visible. Till the end of the Kalpa, O great sage, I shall be undoubtedly visible in this place.

On hearing those words the sage became delighted and returned to his hermitage.

11-12. Thereafter, the Four-armed Lord became visible to human beings and others. Later on he will sit in the Vimāna worthy of being meditated upon by sages (?), being propitiated by Skanda and always served by Wind-god. Thus a great deal of time elapsed along with several sets of four Yugas.

The Birth of a Son Named Ākāśarāja to Mitravarmā

13-20. The twenty-eighth cycle of four Yugas started, O Vasundharā. At the end of Dvāpara the Bhārata war took place.

and then Kali Yuga set in. Vikramārka and other kings, Śakas and Śūdras and others will pass away without knowing or realizing me, O lady of excellent face. Then the mighty warrior Mitravarman born of the Lunar race will become the king of Tuṇḍīra Maṇḍala (country round Kāñcī) and reside in the city of Nārāyaṇapura.[1] He will be supreme with great rise in good fortune. When that king rules over the earth righteously, the earth became (i.e. will become) productive of plenty of fruits without being cultivated. It was (i.e. will be) adorned with plenty of plants and vegetation. There was no natural calamity such as drought, too much of rain and the like. All the people were virtuous.

A charming daughter of the Pāṇḍya king was his wife. A son named Viyat (i.e. Ākāśa, Sky) was born to him. He was an ornament unto the whole race. His wife named Dharaṇī was born of the family of Śakas. Entrusting the kingdom to his care, the excellent king Mitravarmā went to a meritorious penance-grove near Veṅkaṭādri.

Padmāvatī Comes out of the Bowels of the Earth

21-23. The great king named Ākāśa became an emperor. He observed the vow of having only one wife. The king was mentally attached to Dharaṇī (his wife). He cleared the ground on the banks of the river Araṇī for the sake of a Yajña ('sacrifice'). When the surface of the ground was being ploughed by means of a golden plough, a girl was seen coming out of the ploughed land as he was scattering a handful of seeds. The girl was lying on a bed of lotuses. She was beautiful with all characteristic features.

24-25. She shone like a doll made of gold. On seeing her the king was struck with wonder. His eyes beamed like a full blown (lotus). Taking the child with him, he rejoiced in the company of his ministers saying repeatedly, "This is my daughter."

---

1. As the capital of the country Tuṇḍira or Toṇḍa Maṇḍala, it should have been identical with Kāñcī. But Nārāyaṇapura is on the bank of Araṇī—a river in Toṇḍa Maṇḍala (infra 5.46). And the path to it from Veṅkaṭādri (infra 5.38-46) confirms its being different from Veṅkaṭādri.

An ethereal voice then spoke to him:

26-28. "It is true. This is your own daughter. Bring up this excellent-eyed girl." Then delighted in his mind the king entered his city calling the queen Dharaṇī. He spoke thus: "Look at this girl granted by the Lord to me. She has come out of the earth. Since we are childless, this girl shall certainly be our daughter." After saying this, king Viyat (Ākāśa) handed over the child to the queen.

Birth of a Son Named Vasudāna to King Ākāśa and His Wife Called Dharaṇī

29-31. As soon as the child entered the abode, queen Dharaṇī conceived. King Viyat was extremely pleased on seeing the lady with beaming glossy eyes. He said: "O lady with splendid eyebrows, the creeper in the form of the continuity of my race has borne fruit."

Then at the proper time queen Dharaṇī with lotus-like eyes gave birth to a son in a splendid Muhūrta when five Planets were in their ascendant position and the Sun was in the Zodiac Aries.

32. On the day of his birth divine drums were beaten. A shower of flowers fell on the abode (i.e. palace of the king). A gentle breeze pleasing to the touch blew.

33. To the persons who came to inform and congratulate him on the birth of the son the king gave as gift everything he had except the royal Umbrella and the Chowries.[1]

34. He made a gift of a crore of tawny-coloured cows. More than a hundred bulls were gifted. On the auspicious twelfth day he performed all the post-natal holy rites. The boy was named Vasudāna.

Śrī Varāha said:

35. O gentle lady, the charming son of Ākāśa named Vasudāna grew up everyday like the crescent moon in the bright half of a month.

---

1. These are royal insignia which a ruling monarch is prohibited to gift.

36. The sacred-thread investiture was duly performed. He was educated and trained by preceptors who had mastered the Vedic lore. He learned from his father the wielding of weapons and missiles along with their Mantras.

37. He learned the science of archery consisting of four divisions along with their ancillary subjects and subsidiary activities. Thanks to that powerful son, the father became extremely invincible to enemies.

38. He was as free from mud and stain as the sky in Summer along with the Sun. He was unbearable to look at like the sky at midday during the month of Vaiśākha.

CHAPTER FOUR

Nārada Approaches Padmāvatī

Dharaṇī said:

1. The name of that son of Viyat was mentioned by the Lord (i.e. you). What name did he give to that daughter (who was) not born of a womb?

Śrī Sūta said:

2. On being asked thus, Śrī Varāha, the Lord of the universe, said again:

Śrī Varāha said:

3-6. The intelligent king Ākāśa, on seeing that girl lying on a lotus, called that daughter of the earth by the name Padminī.

She attained the prime of youth. She was once sporting about in a garden reverberating with the sounds of parrots and cuckoos. Nārada, the excellent sage, came there by chance. On seeing her who appeared like the goddess of the forest Nārada was surprised and he spoke thus:

Nārada said:

7-8. Who are you, O timid girl? Whose daughter (are you)? Show me your hand.

On being asked thus that girl of fascinating limbs introduced herself to the sage: "O Brāhmaṇa, I am the daughter of King Viyat. Tell what (good) marks I have (on my palm etc.)." On being requested thus Nārada, the excellent sage, said:

The Physical Marks of Padmāvatī as Read by Nārada

Nārada said:

9. Listen, O lady of charming face; I shall tell your distinctive features. Your feet are good; O lady of excellent eyebrows. They are like red lotuses with (soft) petals.

10. The toes of the feet are red and straight and even, having red and elevated (vault-like) nails. The ankles are uniform and concealed; the splendid shanks are devoid of hair.

11. The knees are equal and exceedingly smooth and shining. The thighs are equal and gradually thick; the buttocks are large and stout and the loins are thought-provoking.

12. The navel is circular and deep; both the sides are thick; the middle is fascinating due to the three folds of the skin shining with curly hair.

13. The breasts are plump, thick-set and protruding with the nipples sunk within. Your hands have the lustre of red lotus with the lotus-line (on the palm). They are tender with straight and even fingers with excellent red joints when placed together; there is no space left in between the fingers.

14. The nails of the hands are like the beaks of a parrot. Your hands shine thereby. Your arms are long and delicate like the stalk of a flower, O gentle lady.

15. Your back appears like the altar; the middle is tender, delicate and straight. The neck is red and long, O splendid lady, and the shoulders stoop downwards.

16. The face is always pleasant and has the lustre of the moon devoid of its black spot; the cheeks are like a golden mirror, shining brilliantly with ear-rings.

17-19. O lady of splendid face, your nose has the shape of a flower of gingelly plant. Your forehead is exceedingly charming, resembling the spotless moon on the eighth day (of a fortnight). It is rendered more splendid by the dark forelocks. Your head has the shape of a regular circle. It has smooth long glossy tresses. Your face shines with your lips like the Bimba fruit (Momordica Monadelpha). The teeth sparkle when you smile. This is my definite conclusion that your face will be befitting Viṣṇu.

20. Your navel has a turn to the right like an eddy in Gaṅgā. You look like Lakṣmī born of the Milk Ocean.

Śrī Varāha said:

21. After saying thus and after being worshipped by them Nārada vanished. On hearing this her friends and attendants spoke to their friend Padminī:

22-24. "It is the advent of spring season. Let us go to the park for gathering flowers. *Karṇikāras* (Pterospermum acerifolium), *Cūtas* (Mango Trees), *Campakas*, *Pāribhadrakas* (Erythrina fulgens), *Palāśas* (Butea frondosa), *Pāṭalas* (Trumpet flowers), *Kundas* (Jasmine), and *Raktāśokas* (Red Aśoka) have blossomed. *Padminīs* (Lotus flowers), *Sindhuvāras* (Vitex negundo), *Mālatīs* (Jasmine), *Yūthikā* creepers (Jasminum auriculatum), *Kahlāras* (white esculent water-lily), *Karavīras* (Oleanders) are vying with one another in blossoming. Let us gather flowers in this park that is very pleasant and charming."

Departure of Padmāvatī to the Flower-Park along with Her Friends and Attendants

25. After saying this, they went to the park accompanied by the daughter of Ākāśa. They wandered here and there gathering flowers.

26-27. They saw a certain lordly elephant. He shone brilliantly with his two white and sparkling tusks. He was resplendent with two streams of ichor flowing from his broad cheeks. He was lofty with dust particles (scattered all over the body). He was accompanied by herds of cow-elephants. With a hissing of the tip of his tongue he sprayed his own face with waters coming out of his trunk.

28. On seeing him they became frightened and resorted to a tree (for refuge). In the meantime they immediately espied an excellent horse.

Śrīnivāsa's Arrival at the Flower-Park in the Course of Hunting

29. The horse was as white as the spotless moon. It was well-adorned with gold trappings and outfit. It was as lofty (and bright) as the autumnal cloud with glittering streaks of lightning.

30. On the horse they saw a dark-complexioned man having the splendour and features of Madana (i.e. god of love). His eyes had the shape of lotus-petals and they extended as far as his ears.

31. A brilliant blue crest tied with a silk cloth of very fine texture (adorned his head). He was adorned with ear-rings sparkling with rubies and jewels.

32. He held a divine Śārṅga bow covered with gold and studded with gems. With his other hand he held a golden arrow.

33. His waist shone with the hips covered with a yellow silk cloth. He was resplendent with bejewelled bangles, armlets and waist-band.

34. A curl of hair with a right twist shone on his broad chest. He was charming with a golden sacred thread shining over his shoulder.

35. He had been speedily chasing a wolf. On seeing him the maidens were struck with wonder. They stood there itself.

36. On seeing him seated on a horse the lordly elephant bowed down his head, lifted his trunk, turned back and went to the forest trumpeting.

37. When the elephant had gone back, the horse-rider came there looking for the wolf to the presence of those girls plucking the flowers.

Dialogue between the Lord and the Maidens

38-39. Approaching them, the rider on the horseback said:

"Did an animal called wolf come this way? Was it seen by you all? Tell me, O girls."

Śrī Varāha said:

40-42. The girls replied to him: "Nothing was seen by us. Why have you come to our park wielding an excellent bow. O leader of hunters, none of the animals living here should be killed. Go away quickly from this park which is in the protective jurisdiction of King Ākāśa."

On hearing the words of those maidens he got down from the horse.

43. "Who are you all? Who is this lotus-like maiden? She has excellent magnificence. All her limbs are fascinating. Her breasts are plump and protruding. Tell me. After hearing the same I shall go back to my abode in the mountain."

44. On hearing these words of his the friend and attendant of Padmāvatī urged by the daughter of Dharaṇī said to the hunter, a resident of the mountain:

45. "This is the daughter of King Ākāśa. She was born out of the bowels of the earth. O hero, she is our leader and her name is Padminī.

46. Tell us, O youth of handsome features, what is your name? Whose son are you? What is your caste? Where is your residence? Why have you come here?"

On being asked thus he replied to them with a smile on his lotus-like face:

47. "Those conversant with ancient traditions say that our family is that of the Sun. Our names are innumerable. They sanctify learned men.

48. By colour and name the ascetics say that I am Kṛṣṇa. My discus instills fear in the minds of the enemies of Suras and those who hate Brāhmaṇas.

49. On hearing the sound of my conch enemies become confounded. Even among the immortal beings there is no bow equal to mine.

50-52. They call me the lord of heroes, residing in Veṅkaṭādri. It was from the ridge of that mountain that I surrounded (i.e. accompanied) by my Niṣāda followers have come for hunting, riding on a horse, to your park. A certain animal moving rapidly like the wind has been pursued by me. It went away somewhere. Unable to see it I have now seen this maiden of exalted magnificence. I have come here with love. Can this maiden be obtained by me?"

53-54. On hearing these words of Kṛṣṇa they became infuriated and said: "If King Ākāśa sees you, he will bind you with fetters and take you away. Before this happens go quickly to your own abode."

Threatened by them thus, he mounted the swift horse. Accompanied by all his followers, he went back to the mountain quickly.

CHAPTER FIVE

Śrīnivāsa Enchanted on Seeing Padmāvatī

Śrī Varāha said:

1-3. On reaching the divine abode he got down from the excellent horse. Saying "You all may take rest" he dismissed all the Devas (who had assumed) the forms of hunters along with their attendants. He then entered the hall set with jewels. Climbing the flight of bejewelled stairs, he entered the five chambers one by one and after going beyond all the five chambers he reached the abode of pearls. Hari who had become exhausted and worried lay down on a swinging couch exquisitely inlaid with the nine different precious stones.

4-5. He went on recollecting that maiden of longish eyes with slender waist having the lustre of the interior of a lotus, with plump breasts and lotus-like face resplendent with smiles. He considered her the daughter of the Milk Ocean herself, the splendid lotus-born deity Lakṣmī. With his mind dwelling on her Lord Śrīnivāsa fell into a swoon.

BAKULAMĀLIKĀ'S ADDRESS TO SWOONING ŚRĪNIVĀSA

6-9. Then at midday the female attendant Bakulamālikā prepared divinely excellent meal having good flavour. It was exquisitely splendid and befitting gods. There were excellent side dishes,[1] pure rice, rice cooked in milk, rice mixed with jaggery, pudding made of green gram and rice etc. There were five different *Apūpas* (deep-fried pies), *Pūrikās* (deep-fried pancakes) and *Vaṭakas* (pulse-cakes fried in oil). Then she hastened to meet the Lord. She was accompanied by (three other attendants named) Padmāvatī, Padmapatrā and Citrarekhā.

She asked all those excellent maidens to wait at the entrance to the Lord's (abode). Bakulamālikā alone went near him.

10-11. After going near the Lord she saluted him with great devotion. On seeing the Lord lying helpless on the couch inlaid with gems, she massaged his feet. Finding him lying with his eyes closed deeply engrossed in thought about something, she smiled and spoke to him thus:

12. "Get up, O Lord of the Chiefs of Devas. Why do you lie down, O Puruṣottama? Excellent food has been got ready, O Lord. Come to take your food, O Mādhava.

13. Why do you lie down like one agonized and distressed? You are the destroyer of the agony and distress of all the worlds. What has been seen by you in the forest, O Lord, as you were ahunting?

14-15. Your plight, O Lord of large eyes, seems to be like that of a love-lorn man. Who was seen, a Deva maiden, a human one or a daughter of a serpent (Ahi)? O Lord of inconceivable soul, tell me about that girl who has captivated your mind."

Śrī Varāha said:

16. On hearing these words of hers, the Lord heaved a deep sigh. As he sighed thus, Bakulamālikā spoke to him affectionately:

17. "Who is that maiden so attractive even unto you, O Puruṣottama?" Hṛṣīkeśa spoke to her: "I shall tell all the facts. Listen."

1. The dishes are all vegetarian and the varieties of rice-preparations etc. are still popular in the country round Veṅkaṭādri.

The Reason for Marriage with Padmāvatī as told by Śrīnivāsa

The Lord said:

18. Formerly, in the auspicious Tretā Yuga, I killed Rāvaṇa. At that time the girl Vedavatī rendered assistance to Śrī (Sītā).

19-20. Lakṣmī appeared from the land of Janaka in the form of Sītā. In the Pañcavaṭī forest, when I went away to kill Mārīca, my younger brother too followed me on being urged by Sītā. In the meantime the king of Rākṣasas came there to abduct Sītā.

21-23. Fire-god present in the (place of) Agnihotra sacrifice knew (i.e. anticipated) the attempt of Rāvaṇa. He took the real Sītā to Pātāla and entrusted her to (his wife) Svāhā. There was a splendid lady named Vedavatī. Formerly, she was touched by the same Rākṣasa (but not molested). Yet she cast off her body in fire. In order to kill Rāvaṇa she was created once again with a form similar to that of Sītā. It was she who was abducted by Rāvaṇa and kept in custody in Laṅkā.

24-26. Afterwards when Rāvaṇa was killed, she entered fire once again. Agni handed over Lakṣmī, my Jānakī, who had been kept in her protective custody by Svāhā and told me about the attendant accompanying Sītā: "O Lord, this is Vedavatī who did what was pleasing to Sītā. For the sake of Sītā she remained in the abode of the Rākṣasa as one imprisoned by him. Hence, delight her with a good boon along with Śrī."

27-28. On hearing these words of Fire-god, the splendid (genuine) Sītā told me: "O Lord, this Vedavatī has always done everything pleasing to me. Hence she is a great devotee of the Lord. Hence, O Lord, choose her (as wife)." I replied:

29-30. "O goddess, I shall do so in the twenty-eighth Kaliyuga. Till then let her stay in the world of Brahmā and be adored by Devas. Afterwards she will become the daughter of Earth and (the adopted) daughter of (king) Viyat."

Thus that beautiful lady had been formerly granted boons by me and by Lakṣmī.

31-32. She is born of Earth in the city of Nārāyaṇapura. The chaste lady is on a par with Lakṣmī. She has eyes like lotus. She has been granted boons by Padmā (Lakṣmī). Today that charming lady was seen by me as I was hunting at that place. She was plucking flowers along with her friends and attendants who befitted her.

33-34. It is impossible to describe her beauty by me even in a hundred years. As in the case of Lakṣmī, if my contact with her today becomes feasible, my life will be steady. Take this to be the truth.

Departure of Bakulamālikā to the City of King Viyat

35. O Bakulamālikā, you go there. After seeing that girl, O Bakulamālikā, know whether the blemishless, long-eyed girl of lotus(-like) eyes is suitable to me on account of her beauty and gracefulness.

36-37. After saying this, he swooned once again. Bakulā said to him: "O Lord of Devas, I shall go hence to the place where that charming lady of yours lives at present. Tell me the way, O Lord of Ramā, whereby I shall have to go to her."

On being told thus the Lord of Ramā said to Bakulamālikā:

38-46. "O highly fortunate lady, go along this way where there is the cave of Śrī Nṛsiṁha. Get down from this beautiful mountain along that way.

After reaching the hermitage of Agastya visit the Liṅga named Agastyeśa worshipped by him on the banks of Suvarṇamukharī.

Enjoying the sight of Suvarṇamukharī with (its wonderful) ripples and waves, go along its bank till you reach the forest of the Brāhmaṇa Sage Śuka.

There is a holy lotus-pond there named Padmasaras. It is full of lotuses. Take your bath there and bow down to the excellent sage Chāyā Śuka who performs penance on its banks. Bow down to Kṛṣṇa accompanied by Balarāma always propitiated by Sage Śuka, O excellent lady.

Kṛṣṇa has pure yellow robes and he is dark in complexion like the gem sapphire. Balabhadra is white in complexion and is depicted as one about to go on a pilgrimage, repeating Mantras with uplifted hands holding a pearl necklace and wearing sandals. Bow down to Balabhadra.

From this lake, O lady of excellent face, you may take a golden lotus. After crossing Suvarṇamukharī and passing through forests and gardens, you will reach the banks of Araṇī. You may take rest in the middle of the forest. You will certainly be struck with wonder on seeing Nārāyaṇapurī.

47-55. In the parks and gardens you will see many trees[1] in full bloom laden with fruits such as Panasas (Jack trees), Āmras (Mangoes), Śirīṣas (Acacia Sirissa), Kundas (a variety of Jasmine), Tindukas (Diospyros embryopteris), Pāṭalas (Trumpet flower), Punnāgas (Calophyllum Inophyllum), Nāgaravanas (groves of Euphorbia Antiquorum), Rasālas (Bread fruit trees), Aṅkolas (Alangium Hexapetalum), Caṁpakas, Bakulas (Mimusops Elengi), Āmalakas (Emblic Myrobalan), Sālas (a variety of resin producing tree), Tālas (Palms), Hintālas, Padmakas (Cerasus Puddum), Jaṁbū (Rose apple), Niṁba (Margosa), Kadaṁba (Nauclea Cadamba), Elā (Cardamum), Pippalī (Long pepper), Madhukas (Bassia Latifolia), Arjunas (Terminalia Arjuna), Priyaṅgus (Aglaia Odorata), Hiṅgu (Asafoetida), Kharjūra (Date palms), Māyūra (Ligusticum Ajwaen), Aśoka, Lodhrakas (Symplocos Racemosa), Aśvattha (Holy fig tree), Uduṁbara (Ficus Glomerata), Plakṣa (Ficus Infectoria), Badarī (Jujube tree), Bhūrja (a kind of birch Betula Bhojpatra), Kīcaka (Bamboos), Ciñcā (Tamarind), Kiṁśuka (Butea frondosa), Mandāra (Erythrina Indica), Śālmalī (Silk cotton), Bījapūraka (Citrus Medica), Pūga (Betelnut tree), Nāraṅga (Orange), Likuca (Artocarpus Lacucha) and Nārikela (Coconut-palms)—all these in clusters and groves.

There are the flowering plants such as Mallikā, Mālatī, Kunda, and Yūthikā (all these varieties of Jasmine) as well as Ketakī (Pandamus odoratissimus). The parks abound in Karavīra (oleander) and lotuses. They shine with royal plantain trees.

The parks and gardens are thronged with peacocks, parrots, herons, vultures and Sārasa birds.

It echoes with the humming sounds of bees. Seeing all these on the banks of the river, you will get great delight.

Thereafter, you go by the north-east path to the city on a par with Indra's city. It is encircled by the river named Araṇī and is

1. The list of trees is repeated whenever a forest is to be described.

as if encircled by Gaṅgā. After going to the city of King Ākāśa, do the needful."

Śrī Varāha said:

56. After ordering that attendant named Bakulā thus and bidding her farewell, the Over-lord of Suras accompanied by Śrī lay down on his white splendid bed.

57-62. After bowing down to the Lord of the Chiefs of Devas, the attendant Bakulamālikā mounted on a red horse like the berry of *Abrus Precatorius* in shape and size. She went through the path indicated before seeing various kinds of animals such as elephants in rut as huge as mountains and adorned with white tusks. They were accompanied by herds of cow-elephants. They were eager to seize even clouds.

She saw lions resembling white clouds followed by herds of lionesses, tigers, bears, rhinoceroses, eight-footed Śarabhas, Gavaya oxen, deer, antelopes, jackals, the Priyaka species of deer, rabbits etc. She saw Sārasa birds and peacocks and wild cats.

She saw wolves, parrots, boars and many birds of excellent ability to produce nice sounds.

Seeing these different things and getting thrilled frequently, she reached the western bank of Araṇī that was full of trees.

63-64. After getting down from the red horse near the deity Agastyeśa, she visited Agastyeśvara, the Liṅga that was worshipped well by Agastya. After taking bath and having had a drink (to quench the thirst) she took rest on the bank of the river.

Words Addressed to the Attendants and Friends of Padmāvatī Present in the Divine Garden by Bakulamālikā

65-66. Some maidens came there to the presence of the deity from the royal abode. Seeing those attendants and friends of Padmālayā, Bakulamālikā approached them and asked them in course of a general talk:

Bakulamālikā said:

67. O young maidens, who are you? Tell me. You have wonderful ornaments and garlands. Wherefrom have you come

here? O ladies with faces devoid of impurities, what is your business here?

68. On hearing her words they said smilingly: "Listen attentively, O gentle lady. We shall recount it now."

CHAPTER SIX

Marks of Viṣṇu's Devotee

Detailed Information about Padmāvatī Reported to Bakulamālikā by the Attendants and Friends

The young maidens said:

1. We are females from the inner apartment of King Ākāśa. We are the friends and attendants of Padmālayā, the daughter of that king.

2. Some time back we went inside the forest (park) with the princess at the head. We were eagerly gathering flowers for the princess.

3-6. While we were seated at the root of a tree we saw a man dark in complexion like a sapphire. His chest was (as if) a temple of the goddess of glory and fortune. A gentle smile spread on his face. He had a pair of beautiful, plump, muscular and long arms. He wore a well-washed yellow cloth. He had golden arrows and a golden bow. He wore a gold crown. He was adorned with necklaces, armlets and other ornaments. Our friend Padmālayā, a lady with lotus-like eyes and a body resembling molten gold, saw him and blurted out, "Look, look (there)". Even as we were watching him, he vanished immediately.

7-8. Our friend swooned. She was then brought to the royal palace (while still in swoon).

Questions put to the Astrologer by King Viyat Regarding Padmāvatī

On seeing his daughter unwell the king consulted an astrologer:

"O prominent Brāhmaṇa, O sage, describe the effects of transits of various Planets on my daughter."

9-12. The Brāhmaṇa (who was) equal to Bṛhaspati (the preceptor of gods) (in intelligence), thought within himself (the positions of) the Planets and said: "All the Planets are favourable to your daughter, O excellent king. But the stable (?total) effect of the Planets is slightly confusing, O King."

Again the intelligent (Brāhmaṇa) pondered over the time of the question. He calculated the *Chāyā* (length of the shadow of a gnomon) and the *Liṅga* (Planetary position) and thought over the effects thereof and said: "The Moon who is the overlord of the *Lagna* is in the *Lagna*. Bṛhaspati (Jupiter) is in the *Kendra* (Centre). The diurnal bird is asleep. The *Praśnapakṣin* (the bird of astrological inquiry) is in the kingdom(?). O King, listen to its effect. There will certainly be normal health (in her case).

13. An excellent man has come towards the girl. Your daughter has swooned at his sight. She will be united with him.

14. A certain maiden deputed by himself will come. The words she will be uttering shall be conducive to your welfare and prosperity.

15-17. Carry out (her suggestion), O great King. It is the truth and nothing but the truth that I am saying. Further, I shall suggest another thing that will fulfil all her desires and is destructive of all ailments. Carry it out. It is conducive to the happiness of your daughter. Ask Brāhmaṇas to perform the holy bathing rite of Agastyaliṅga." After saying this to the king the astrologer returned to his house.

Brāhmaṇas are Deputed for the Worship of Agastyaliṅga in Accordance with the Suggestion of the Astrologer

18-22. King Ākāśa invited Brāhmaṇas well-versed in the Vedas, welcomed and honoured them and requested them thus:

"O Brāhmaṇas, go to the temple and perform the holy rite of grand ablution of Śambhu with recitation of Mantras."

After allowing them (to go), O splendid lady, he called us and said: "O girls, gather together all the essentials for the great ablution." On being commanded thus by the king himself we went to the temple. Now tell us, O fair lady, about your sudden visit. Whence do you hail? Where do you wish to go? On whose errand? You seem to have come here from the world of Devas riding on this divine horse."

Śrī Varāha said:

23. On being asked thus by them the delighted Bakulamālikā spoke these sweet words enhancing the delight of those girls:

Bakulamālikā replied:

24-25. I have come from Śrī Veṅkaṭādri. My name is Bakulamālikā. I have come riding on this horse with a desire to see (Queen) Dharaṇī. Will it be possible to see the gentle lady there in the palace?

On hearing these words of hers those maidens of the king said:

26-31. "O splendid lady, you will see Dharaṇī along with us." On being told thus by them she accompanied them to the palace of the king.

THE REPLY OF PULINDINĪ TO THE INQUIRIES MADE BY DHARAṆĪ

While the ladies were on their way, Dharaṇī saw a Pulindinī[1] (i.e. a woman of the Pulinda tribe) coming along the street. She was adorned with the berries of Abrus Precatorius (Guñjā) and shells. An infant of sucking age was kept tied to her back by means of the end of her cloth. She was heard proclaiming in the street thus: "Listen all of you; I speak the truth. I will tell past, present and future."

With pure smile (on her face) Dharaṇī called her. She ordered for a golden winnowing basket and placed pearls in it. She made them into three heaps of three *Prastha* measures and placed the

1. The whole episode of consultation with a woman of Pulinda (Forester) tribe is textually similar to a great extent to the one in VrP II (Uttara) 6.28 ff. The method of selecting a particular heap as the basis of the prediction is the same. Such belief in tribal women is still common to uneducated women even in Maharashtra.

whole thing in front of her. Thereafter Queen Dharaṇī asked her, "O Pulinda woman, tell me the truth, future or past." After saying this she stood by.

32-33. She told her about what she had been thinking in her mind. "O graceful lady, speak straight away if it was the middle heap that was thought of by you." Dharaṇī, the beloved queen of the king, said, "*Oṁ* (Yes)."

Dharaṇī said:

The heap has been said. Predict the effect. I shall give you a heap of money.

Pulindā said:

34-36. I shall speak the truth. O lady of excellent eyebrows, give some food to my child.[1]

On being requested thus Dharaṇī took some food in a golden vessel and handed it over to the Pulindinī and said, "Tell me the truth." The young woman received the food along with milk and fed the child with it.

Then the lady with excellent eyebrows spoke the truth: "It was due to the arrival of a man that the body of your daughter has withered away and become emaciated, O timid lady. Since she is not able to see his face once again, her body has become scorched. She is afflicted by the arrows of Cupid.

37-42. It was the Primordial Lord of Devas himself who came from Vaikuṇṭha. Hari, the bestower of whatever is desired by devotees, sports about on the peak of Śrī Veṅkaṭādri on the banks of Svāmipuṣkariṇī. He assumes the forms and features of the god of Love. He is the Supreme Bliss. He wields Māyā. He is the Lord of Ramā. He sports about along with Śrī.

(One day) riding on his horse and roaming about in the forest, O Queen, he came to the park and saw your daughter. On seeing her as (beautiful as) Ramā he came under the control of the god of Love. The Lord will be sending his attendant Lalitā

1. Unfortunately the tragic condition, want of food etc., of these tribals, has not changed since the days of the SkP.

to your presence. On being united with him like Ramā she will enjoy herself for a long time. These words of mine are true. See this today itself, O Princess! Give some (more) food to my son." After saying this, the Pulindinī kept quiet.

43-46. Once again she gave her ample food and dismissed her. When the Pulinda woman had gone away, the uncensured (i.e. praiseworthy) lady got up from the courtyard and entered the splendid inner apartment. It was there that her daughter Padmālayā was seated surrounded by her own attendants and friends.

She went near her daughter who was sick with love (and said), "What shall I do for you, daughter? O splendid girl, what is the object that is most pleasing to you?" On being asked thus by her mother, the wise and virtuous girl spoke slowly:

47-49. "O Mother, my mind is attracted towards that object alone which is comely and pleasing to the eyes and to the minds of good people in the world; which Brahmā and others are desirous of seeing; which is very great and omnipresent; which is the most resplendent among all resplendent things; which is the deity unto all the Devas; which can be attained here by good people and devotees and never by non-devotees. It bestows all desired things on devotees. O mother, let that be sought after."

Śrī Varāha said:

50. On hearing this Dharaṇī asked her daughter once again, "Describe the characteristic marks of the devotees by whom, O girl of beautiful eyes, that can be attained."

The Characteristic Marks of the Lord and Devotees of the Lord as Related by Padmāvatī

Padmālayā said:

51-54. Listen to the marks of the devotees attentively, O Mother. It is a secret, O Dharaṇī. They have permanent marks of conch and discus on the pair of arms.[1] Their special characteristic is *Ūrdhvapuṇḍra* (sectarian mark in a vertical V-like

1. It is a common practice of Vaiṣṇavas (followers of Rāmānuja as well as of Madhva) to stamp their bodies with Viṣṇu's weapons. The Ūrdhvapuṇḍra

form) with a gap in the middle. Others have twelve such *Puṇḍras* on the forehead, heart, neck, belly, two sides, two elbows, two arms, back and back of the neck. When they apply the mark they recite the twelve names beginning with 'Keśava' and ending with 'Vāsudeva' and say 'Obeisance to you'. When they apply it on the head, they say 'Vāsudeva'.

55. I shall tell their observances which are really fascinating. Listen, O Mother. They engage in reciting the Vedas regularly. They perform all the Vedic rites.

56. They speak the truth, O gentle lady. They are never jealous of or malicious to others. They do not insult others. They never take away other people's possessions.

57. Know those people to be Vaiṣṇavas ('devotees of Viṣṇu') who never remember, see or touch the beautiful wives of others.

58. They are kind and merciful to all living beings. They are always engaged in what is beneficial to all living beings. They always sing about the Lord of Devas. Know these to be devotees (of the Lord).

59. They are contented with whatever they have. They are faithful to their own wives. They are devoid of attachment, fear and anger. Know them to be the devotees and followers of Viṣṇu.

60-64. One who is endowed with qualities like these must have the (indelible impressions of) five weapons made by his father or preceptor or any other honourable gentleman. The learned devotee shall kindle fire in accordance with the injunctions in his own *Gṛhyasūtra*. He should offer sixteen *Āhutis* (oblations) reciting the Mantras of the discus etc., first with the original Mantra, then with the *Puruṣasūkta* and one hundred and eight times with the excellent Mantra of *Jātavedas*. After performing the *Homa* with *Mahāvyāhṛtis* (i.e. the great utterances, viz. Oṁ Bhūḥ Bhuvaḥ Svaḥ) he should heat the discus etc. The learned devotee then shall bear the impressions when they have been heated well by the preceptor and the heat can be borne.[1] The

---

is characteristic of the followers of Rāmānuja. From this mention it seems that the author probably belonged to that sect.

1. The practice of branding one's body with the heated metal seals with the marks of the discus, conch, mace etc. is still found among orthodox

impressions shall be received like the Mantras. The conch should be imprinted on one arm, the discus on the other, the Śārṅga bow with the arrow on the head, the mace on the forehead and the sword on the heart (chest).

65-68. These five impressions should be borne by the devotees of Viṣṇu desirous of salvation or the impressions of conch and discus shall be borne on both the arms. They must be of good shape and clear. Those who have impressions like these are known as devotees and followers of Viṣṇu. The Supreme Brahman can be realized only by them endowed with good conduct. My love is for him alone. My mind yearns to obtain him. O Mother, except Viṣṇu, I do not desire anyone else. I remember the dark-complexioned Viṣṇu. I speak about Hari, Acyuta. I sustain my life thereby alone. Let the means of being united with him be thought of.

Śrī Varāha said:

69. After saying this to her mother the lotus-faced lady became dejected and stopped speaking. On hearing her words, the mother thought, 'How should Viṣṇu be propitiated?'

Arrival of the Friends and Attendants (of Padmā) Near Dharaṇī Along with Bakulamālikā

70-73. In the meantime the girls accompanied by Bakulamālikā came to see Dharaṇī after worshipping Agastyeśa.

She fed the visiting Brāhmaṇas heartily with good food after duly worshipping them. She gave them monetary gifts in full along with garments and ornaments. She received their blessings for the purpose of achieving the desired objectives.

After bidding farewell to all those Brāhmaṇas she asked her young maidens, those high-minded attendants who had come back after worshipping Agastyeśa.

---

followers of Madhva. Their procedure does not include the Śārṅga-bow impression but they have the name-seal (*nāma-mudrā*) instead. The MS of *Tapta-mudrā-vidhāna* at Rāghavendra Svāmī Maṭh at Miraj (in Maharashtra) prescribes Paurāṇic verses describing the particular weapon (e.g. discus, mace) for recitation before branding, as 'mantra'.

CHAPTER SEVEN

Preparations for the Marriage of Padmālayā (Padmāvatī)

Information about Śrīnivāsa as Reported by Bakulamālikā to Queen Dharaṇī

Dharaṇī said:

1. Tell me, who is that excellent maiden? Where did she come into contact with you? Why has she come here? She appears to me to be worthy of veneration.

The girls replied:

2-5. O Queen, this is a divine lady. She has come to see you. She came into contact with us at the temple in the presence of Śiva. On being questioned, she said that she had come to see Your Highness. "Is it possible to see the queen conveniently at the palace by me?" When we were asked by her thus we said, "Be pleased to come with us. We are the servants of Dharaṇī. We are going to the palace."

On being told thus, O Queen Dharaṇī, she has approached you. Let her be asked by Your Highness, "What for have you come here?"

Śrī Varāha said:

6-7. On hearing their words thus Queen Dharaṇī asked her:

Dharaṇī said:

O gentle lady, where have you come from? What can be done by me for you? Tell me the truth. I shall try to help you to achieve the purpose of your visit.

Bakulamālikā said:

8-12. I have come from the mountain Veṅkaṭādri. My name is Bakulamālikā. Our Lord Nārāyaṇa dwells on the mountain Śrīveṅkaṭācala.

Once he mounted his horse as white as a swan and as quick as the mind and went for hunting. In the splendid season of spring he was roaming about in the forests of the king near the mountain Veṅkaṭādri. He saw on his way deer, elephants, lions, a variety of ox called *Gavaya*, the eight-footed animal Śarabha, Ruru deer, parrots, partridges, swans and other types of birds in the forest. The excellent god pursued a lofty leader of elephants, shedding ichor profusely and accompanied by cow-elephants.

Performance of Penance by King Śaṅkha at Svāmitīrtha at the Instance of Śrīnivāsa

13-15. After going from forest to forest he came near King Śaṅkha who was engaged in penance on Bṛhacchaila after installing Janārdana accompanied by Śrī and Bhūmi and worshipping him constantly with great devotion.

There is an excellent and sacred lake named Śaṅkhanāgabila. When he came near the bank of that lake, he got down from his horse. Assuming the attire of a king, he went near the excellent King Śaṅkha and asked him:

16-21. "What is it that you are doing, O excellent king, at the foot of this mountain Śeṣa?"

Śaṅkha replied:

I am the son of King Śveta. I belong to the land of Haihaya. For the propitiation of Mahāviṣṇu I performed all types of sacrifices here. I became dejected and frustrated because I could not get the vision of Mahāviṣṇu, O Prince. At that time a divine voice destructive of all worries spoke clearly:

"O king, I will not become visible to you here. Listen to my words. Go to Nārāyaṇādri and perform penance."

So I left my land. Here, O king, I propitiate the inconceivable Lord of Śrī after installing (him). I propitiate him by means of penance. Thanks to the blessings of Agastya, I worship him daily in accordance with the injunctions.

On hearing these words of his the Lord said with a derisive laughter:

22-25. "Go to Nārāyaṇādri. Why do you stay at the foot of this (mountain). Climb the mountain along this path and bow down to Viṣvaksena stationed on the western peak in the form of a boy at the foot of a *Nyagrodha* tree (Indian fig tree). Go to Svāmipuṣkariṇī and take bath there. O prince, you will see a *Valmīka* (anthill) and an *Aśvattha* (holy fig tree) there on the western bank. Perform your penance in between those two. A certain white boar roams about in this anthill. But it is visible only to the meritorious, O king."

Śrī Varāha (? Bakulamālikā) said:

26-27. After commanding him thus, the Lord mounted his horse and went for hunting. O lady of excellent eyebrows, he wandered from forest to forest and reached the river Araṇī. Getting down from his horse, he walked about on its excellent bank. The gentle breeze coming from the extremities of the forest, which was cool due to its blowing over lotuses and Kahlāra flowers, dispelled his fatigue and thus served Puruṣottama.

28-30. The trees served him by throwing showers of flowers. Thus the Lord was wandering amongst the trees heavily laden with blossoms and bending low. He was in search of a lordly tusker. He saw those well-dressed beautiful girls plucking flowers like streaks of lightning among clouds. He saw a young maiden among those girls. She had golden complexion. She was as exceedingly charming as Lakṣmī. The Lord became attached to her in his heart.

31-35. Desirous of getting her he asked those girls, "Who is this girl?" The man was told by them, "O mighty one, this is the daughter of King Viyat."

On hearing these words of theirs he mounted the horse and returned speedily to his abode, the beautiful mountain.

After reaching his abode on the banks of Svāmipuṣkariṇī the Lord sent for me and said, "Well Bakulamālikā, go to the city of King Viyat, dear friend, and enter the inner apartment. Go to his wife Dharaṇī. After enquiring about her health and welfare request for her beautiful daughter Kamalālayā (Padmālayā). O beautiful woman, return immediately after getting the approval of the king."

36. I have been ordered by the Lord thus, O Queen, and so I have come to your abode. What is suitable in this connection may

be done (by you) along with the king accompanied by (the council of) his ministers.

37. Consult your daughter and let the reply be given.

Decision of Dharaṇī and Others about the Marriage (of Padminī) at the Instance of Bakulamālikā

Śrī Varāha said:

38-39. On hearing her words the queen became delighted. She called King Ākāśa and both of them went to Kamalālayā. In the midst of the assembly of ministers the queen repeated the words of Bakulamālikā. On hearing them the king became delighted and spoke to the ministers and the priests:

King Ākāśa said:

40-44. This girl is not born of a womb. Kamalālayā is divine and highly fortunate. She has been sought by the Lord of Devas residing on Veṅkaṭādri. My desire is fulfilled today. Tell me whether it (the proposal) is acceptable to you.

On hearing the excellent words of the king all the ministers became delighted. They said to King Viyat:

"We are satisfied and happy, O great King. Your family will become the highest of all. Your matchless daughter will sport about along with Śrī. Let her be given to the Śārṅga-wielding Lord of Devas, the Supreme Soul. This spring season is glorious. Let the auspicious rite be performed quickly.

45-46. Let Dhiṣaṇa (Bṛhaspati, the preceptor of gods) be called and the auspicious hour for the marriage be fixed."

Confirmation of the Exact Auspicious Time for Marriage as per Advice of Bṛhaspati

Saying "so be it" the Lord of men called Bṛhaspati from the world of Suras and asked him about (the hour) for the marriage of the girl and the bridegroom.

The King asked:

47. The native star of the girl is Mṛgaśīrṣa; that of the Lord is Śravaṇa. Let the conjunction of these two be considered.

48-49. On hearing it Dhiṣaṇa said: "The star Uttarāphālgunī suits both of them for the increase of their happiness. It is declared so by the divine astrologers. Let their marriage be celebrated on the Uttarāphālgunī day." He said, "Let it be celebrated duly in the month of Vaiśākha."

Śrī Varāha said:

50-52. The king honoured Dhiṣaṇa duly and bade him farewell. He then said to the lady messenger, "O splendid lady, go to the abode of the Lord. Intimate to the Lord of Devas, O lady of holy rites, that the wedding shall be in the month of Vaiśākha. Let him be pleased to come here after making all arrangements for the marriage."

Thereafter, he sent Śuka, one of the favourites of the queen, as a messenger along with her. He sent his son Vāyu to bring Indra and others.

Decoration of the City by Viśvakarmā and Others

53. He called Viśvakarman and employed him in the job of decorating the city. He did it within a moment.

54. Indra discharged a shower of flowers. Groups of celestial damsels danced. Dhanada (Kubera) filled that abode with wealth, foodgrains etc.

55. Yama made the men on the earth free from sickness. Varuṇa filled (the place) with clusters of jewels and precious stones such as pearls etc.

56. After making arrangements for everything Devas went to Vṛṣācala.[1]

Bakulamālikā Accompanied by Śuka Comes to Śrīnivāsa

Śrī Varāha said:

57-59. Then Bakulamālikā accompanied by Śuka mounted a horse and went ahead. She reached Śrīveṅkaṭādri and got down

1. A hill on the northern side of Suvarṇamukharī.

from the horse near the abode of the Lord. Accompanied by Śuka she went inside and met the bright-eyed Lord seated on a jewel-set throne along with Śrī.

After bowing down she said with great delight: "O Lord, the mission has been duly accomplished there. Here Śuka has along with me to announce the auspicious tidings.

Śuka's Announcement of the Decision about the Marriage of Padmāvatī to Śrīnivāsa

60-65. On being commanded by the Lord to speak out Śuka bowed down and spoke:

Śuka submitted:

The daughter of Dharaṇī says to you: "O Mādhava, accept me. I speak out (i.e. repeat) your names. I always remember your person. O Lord of Ramā, your symbols are worn on arms and other limbs (by me). I worship your devotees who have undergone the five consecratory rites. I perform every holy rite only to please you, O Slayer of Madhu. I am obedient to my parents. I carry on all my activities for ever. O Lord of Devas, be pleased to shower your grace. Accept me, O Mādhava." So submits the daughter of Dharaṇī stationed on the lotus.

On hearing the words of Śuka pleasing to himself, Hari said:

Śrī Bhagavān said:

I shall come there along with Devas in order to celebrate the marriage. O Śuka, go and tell her that the Lord has said thus.

Padmāvatī Wears the Garland of Śrīnivāsa Handed over to Her by Śuka

66. After hearing the utterance of the Lord and taking the garland of sylvan flowers given by the Lord with him, Śuka hastened to the daughter of King Viyat.

67. He handed over the garland of basil, rendered fragrant by means of musk, to the gentle lady and told her the auspicious words of the Lord.

68. On hearing them and accepting the garland with head bowed down the daughter of Earth placed it on her head. Eagerly awaiting the arrival of the Lord she adorned herself with proper ornaments.

69-72. King Viyat joyously and eagerly invited Indu (Moon-god) and said:

"O king, let cooked rice of various tastes be prepared. Let the *Paramānnam* (Supreme Cooked Rice) fit to be offered to Viṣṇu, be prepared. It should be one approved by Devas, sages and the human beings. Let the four kinds of foodstuffs with good flavour be prepared by means of your nectarine rays, O Sudhākara."

After making every arrangement like this he waited for the arrival of the Lord. He seated himself in the assembly with delighted mind. The king was accompanied by Dharaṇī who had adorned her daughter adequately.

CHAPTER EIGHT

The Marriage of Śrīnivāsa and Padmāvatī

Lakṣmī and Others Adorn Śrīnivāsa for the Marital Rites

Śrī Varāha said:

1-3. Thereafter the Overlord of Devas called the beautiful lady Lakṣmī and said: "O graceful lady of beautiful eyes, tell me what should be done for the marriage. O Ramā, command your attendants. Do everything pleasing.

On hearing the words of Kṛṣṇa Śrī called her attendants and friends and directed them. On being commanded by Śrī the attendant, Prīti ('Pleasure'), took up the sweet-scented oil. Śruti ('Vedas') took up the silk cloth and stood waiting in the presence of the Lord.

4. Smṛti ('Code of Law') joyously brought the ornaments.

Dhṛti ('Fortitude') held the mirror and Śānti ('Quiescence') held musk.

5. Śrī ('Bashfulness') stood in front of Hari carrying the unguent Yakṣakardama.[1] Kīrti ('Fame') held the golden head-band and gem-set crown.

6. At that time Indrāṇī held the umbrella, Sarasvatī held a chowrie and Gaurī held the other chowrie. Jayā and Vijayā held the fans.

7-9. On seeing them coming Śrī got up immediately. She took the scented oil and applied it onto the Lord from head to foot. After rubbing and shampooing the body of the Lord with scented perfumes and powders Ramā performed the ablution of Hari. A hundred golden pots filled with the waters of the celestial Gaṅgā and other holy rivers were brought by elephants. The waters were rendered fragrant by means of camphor etc. Ramā took the pots one by one and performed the rite of ablution of Hari.

10-11. She fumigated the tresses of hair by means of incense and when they became dry, she tied them. After anointing the body of the Lord with gold-coloured scents Indirā (Lakṣmī) tied the blue silken robe on his waist along with the waistband. She adorned him with coronets and other ornaments.

12. Bejewelled rings were put on all the fingers. Dhṛti showed the mirror in front of the Lord.

13. Looking into the mirror the Lord of Devas applied the Ūrdhvapuṇḍra (vertical V-like sectarian mark) himself. Afterwards the Lord got on the back of Garuḍa along with Lakṣmī.

Departure of Śrīnivāsa to the City of King Viyat along with Brahmā and Others

14-15. Then he proceeded towards Nārāyaṇapurī accompanied by Brahmā, Īśa, Varuṇa, Yama, Yakṣeśa, Vasiṣṭha and other eminent sages, Sanaka and other Yogins as well as devotees and loyal followers of the Lord. The chieftains of Gandharvas sang. The groups of celestial damsels danced.

1. It is an ointment or perfumed paste consisting of camphor, agallochum, musk, sandalwood and Kakkola. MW 838b.

16. The divine Dundubhi drums were sounded then in the presence of the Lord. Reciting the *Svasti Sūktas* (Hymns of Benediction) the sages followed him.

17. Accompanied by the groups of Devas and Viṣvaksena and other attendants, followed by Bakulamālikā and other attendants and chaperons seated in chariots, the Lord reached the well-decorated city of King Ākāśa.

The Place of the Wedding of Padmāvatī

18-19. On seeing that the Lord had arrived, they made the bride sit on the elephant Airāvata and took her round the city. When King Ākāśa saw her come back to the entrance of ornamental gateway, the bride and the bridegroom were brought together. The King stood facing Lord Keśava along with his kinsmen.

20-22.[1] Viṣṇu took off the wreath of flowers from his neck with his hand and smilingly put it over the shoulders of Kamalā (Padmāvatī). She then took a garland of jasmine flowers and placed it round his neck. This (exchange of garlands) they repeated three times and then got down from the vehicles. They stood (or sat?) over the pedestal for a short while. Then Hari and the daughter of Earth entered the auspicious (marriage) chamber accompanied by the groups of Devas beginning with Brahmā.

23-26. The Lotus-born Lord (Brahmā) performed all the religious rites connected with the wedding beginning with the tying of *Māṅgalyasūtra* ('the thread of conjugal felicity') and ending with *Lājā Homa* (Homa with parched grains) along with the soaking of pulses for germination. After directing them to observe the *Vratas* the kinsmen took Kamalā and Hari to the bed-chamber. On the fourth day the Four-faced Lord concluded all

---

1. VV 20-26 describe the formalities of the marriage ceremony then in vogue, as follows:
   (i) Mutual exchange of garlands by bride and bridegroom at the entrance.
   (ii) Religious rites starting with tying the Māṅgalyasūtra and ending with Lājā Homa and soaking pulses for germination.
   (iii) Observance of *Vrata* for the first four days.

the holy rites. They took leave of King Viyat and made Lord Hari sit on Garuḍa accompanied by both the goddesses. They then proceeded ahead along with Devas. The party reached Vṛṣabhācala to the accompaniment of the sounds of the divine Dundubhi drums. The groups of Devas headed by Brahmā eulogized the Lord of the Chiefs of Devas.

27-28. The groups of sages including Śuka and others eulogized Puruṣottama. Even as he was being eulogized, the Lord entered the hall studded with jewels. There he sat on a throne accompanied by Ramā and the daughter of Earth (Padmālayā).

The Gifts and Presents made by King Viyat to the Bride and the Bridegroom

29. Accompanied by Mahendra and other Suras King Ākāśa began to make the gifts and presents to delight his daughter and Viṣṇu.

30-35. Rice grains were kept in huge pots of gold. There were many vessels of green gram and hundreds of ghee pots. There were thousands of milk pots and many pots of curds. There were divine mangoes, plantains and coconut fruits. There were emblic myrobalan fruits, ashgourds and royal plantains, jack fruits and citrons. There were jars filled with sugar.

Gold, jewels and pearls were in plenty. There were a crore of silk clothes. Thousands of men and women slaves were presented and crores of cows too.

He gave ten thousand horses white in colour like swans and the moon. There were more than a hundred elephants perpetually in their rut. He gave Viṣṇu, Śrīnivāsa, four thousand women experts in dance and music to serve in the inner apartment. After making all these gifts the king stood in front of the Lord (awaiting further instruction).

By the Favour of Śrīnivāsa King Viyat Attains the Boon of Devotion (to the Lord)

36-39. On seeing all these in the company of both the queens Hari, Veṅkaṭeśvara, became highly pleased and he said to the king, his father-in-law:

"Choose your boon, O king, my Sire, from me whatever you desire." On hearing these words of the Lord of Śrī King Viyat said to the Lord: "O Lord, grant me (the boon of) an unswerving service and loyalty to you. Let my mind rest in your lotus-like feet. Let there be devotion to you."

Śrī Bhagavān replied:

40-42. O eminent king, what you have said will take place fully.

Return of Brahmā and Others who had come for Marriage Festival to their Respective Residences

After granting him the boon and honouring him befittingly Hari duly honoured Brahmā, Īśa and all other Suras suitably and allowed them joyously to go back to the heavenly world. After all of them had gone the Lord sported about on the banks of Svāmipuṣkariṇī as before. He was accompanied by Śrī and the daughter of Earth. There in his divine abode he is seated, being honoured by Guha.

CHAPTER NINE

The Story of Hunter Vasu[1]*: The Greatness of Padmasaras*

Dharaṇī said:

1-2. In Kali Yuga, O Lifter of Earth, O my darling, by whom are you seen? By whom is your *Vimāna* (Temple) made on this mountain? By whom is Śrīnivāsa of graceful and charming features seen? Relate this, O Lord, out of love for me. I am eager to hear.

1. Though the chapter tells the story of Vasu, a Niṣāda, Raṅgadāsa, a Śūdra and Prince Toṇḍamān, it indirectly records the Brahminization

Śrī Varāha said:

3-8a. I shall (fore-)tell what is going to happen. Listen, O gentle lady, to what I say.

There was a hunter named Vasu on this holy and meritorious mountain. He was a devotee of Puruṣottama. He was keeper of a forest of Śyāmāka. He used to cook Śyāmāka rice. After pouring honey into it he used to offer it as *Naivedya* to the Lord of Devas accompanied by Śrī and Bhūmi. The wife of that devotee was a splendid lady Citravatī. She gave birth to an excellent son named Vīra. Vasu (lived happily) in the company of his son and wife who was highly devoted to her husband. On a certain day he entrusted his son with the duty of protecting Śyāmāka and went deep into the forest along with his wife in search of honey. He moved quickly with a desire to look out for beehives.

8b-11. The boy took cooked Śyāmāka grains, fried them in fire, ground them and offered them to the Lord of Śrī at the root of a tree. This food offering Vīra consumed joyously.

In the meantime Vasu also returned with honey. On seeing that the Śyāmāka grains had already been consumed he threatened his son. He raised up his hand with a sword in it to slay him.

---

of tree worship of the simple hill tribe, Niṣādas (probably the present Kuruvas), into that of Veṅkaṭeśa. Their usual *Naivedya* to the tree-god was Śyāmāka (boiled) rice mixed with honey (vv 4-5). It was offered at the root of the tree (v 9). It was a Tamarind tree. The Lord had prohibited Raṅgadāsa from cutting down the Tamarind tree (v 31), for the Tamarind tree is Viṣṇu's abode and the Campaka, that of Lakṣmī. The Bilva tree has a special place of honour with Śrīnivāsa as he manifested himself under a Bilva tree (vv 77-78). Bilva leaves are used in the worship of Veṅkaṭeśa (v 108). A temple was built there of Veṅkaṭeśa and of Lakṣmī by a Pallava Prince called here Toṇḍamān (which is really the name of the country around Kāñcī).

The evolution of god Viṭṭhala of Pandharpur in Maharashtra is also on similar lines.

As noted by Dr. N. Ramesan, *The Tirumal Temple*, Ch. 3, the age of Pallavas constitutes the first important landmark in the history of Toṇḍamaṇḍalam. (In the text the name of the region is transferred to the Prince.)

The Lord's Address to Vasu who was Intent on Killing His Son

12-14. Viṣṇu who was present in the tree then caught hold of the sword with his hand. In order to see by whom the sword had been seized he looked in the direction of the tree and saw the Lord holding the conch, discus and iron club with half of his body seen mounted on the tree. Vasu cast off the sword and bowing down to Keśava said to him: "Why is this act being done by you, O Lord of the Chief of Devas?"

Śrī Bhagavān replied:

15-16. O Vasu, listen to my words. Your son is devoted to me. He is a greater favourite of mine than you. So I became visible to him. I am present everywhere on the banks of lake Śvāmisaras.

On hearing the words of the Lord thus Vasu became delighted.

Arrival of Raṅgadāsa at Śrī Śeṣācala for the Worship of Śrīnivāsa

17-21. In the meantime (a devotee named Raṅgadāsa) came to this place from Pāṇḍya territory. Though he was a Śūdra, he was endowed with great devotion to Viṣṇu ever since his childhood.

He reached Nārāyaṇapurī and bowed down to Śrī Varāha. There he heard that Śrīnivāsa, the self-born Lord worshipped by the Lords of Devas, was staying on Veṅkaṭādri. On hearing about it he started from that place. He reached (river) Suvarṇamukharī and had his holy bath therein. He crossed it and took bath in the lake named Kamalā, the lake that yields merit. He bowed down to Lord Kṛṣṇa who was installed on its banks along with (Bala) Rāma. Thereafter he went to the forest abounding in herds of elephants. Gradually he came to Śeṣādri and saw the spring and the mountain-torrent.

22-26a. Having reached near it he went to Śiva worshipped by the tawny-coloured cow. The holy Tīrtha in front of it is Cakratīrtha. It is very deep and destructive of sins. After taking his bath there he went to Veṅkaṭādri slowly in order to propitiate the Lord, where he was joined by an anchorite who was proceeding to Veṅkaṭādri for performing worship. Raṅgadāsa, a boy of twelve years, climbed (the mountain), reached Svāmipuṣkariṇī and took his holy bath with great devotion. He visited the lotus-eyed Hari accompanied by Śrī and Bhūmi staying at the root of a tree in the middle of the forest on the banks of Svāmipuṣkariṇī. (There) the Lord had been worshipped by the sage and anchorite Gopīnātha.

26b-28. He saw Garuḍeśāna (Lord Garuḍa) of splendid yellowish blue colour, stationed in the sky with his wings spread over the head of the Lord like a canopy. He was attended upon by the conch, discus, iron club and sword standing nearby. Behind them he saw (the bow) Śārṅga as well as the arrow.

Construction of a Divine Park, Pavilion etc. by Raṅgadāsa in Honour of Śrīnivāsa

29-34a. On seeing Śrīnivāsa thus Raṅgadāsa was much surprised. He thought, 'I shall make a park for this Lord.' Taking this decision in his mind thus, the intelligent devotee stayed at the root of the tree. He made the Vaikhānasa prepare the *Naivedya* offering to Viṣṇu everyday.

After clearing the terrible forest gradually he cut off the trees at the sides. On being commanded by the Lord he avoided cutting two trees resorted to by the Lord himself, viz. the *Ciñca* (Tamarind) tree that was the place of residence of the Lord and the *Campaka* tree of Ramā. Then he built a wall of stones on the ground all round the Lord.

He made flower gardens all round the wall outside. He planted all the flowering creepers and shrubs of Mallikā, Karavīra, lotus, varieties of jasmine (Mandāra, Mālatī) etc. as well as groves of basil plants and Campakas.

34b-38. He got a well dug up there and made the parks and gardens flourish with its waters. He plucked and gathered flowers from the parks and wreathed them into garlands himself. After making garlands of variegated colours, he handed them to the priest worshipping there. The priest used to take those garlands and tie them round the head and shoulders of Lord Śrīnivāsa accompanied by Śrī and Bhūmi.

Thus that liberal-minded devotee remained there rendering service to the Lord. Staying thus he spent about seventy years. Raṅgadāsa, the noble-souled devotee, gathered flowers and served the Lord for such a long period.

Raṅgadāsa Forgets his Duty of Serving the Lord on Seeing the Amorous Sports of a Gandharva

39. A certain Gandharva came to that park in order to bathe in the lake in the company of youthful maidens of royal Gandharva families.

40-44. He had left his aerial chariot in the sky and carried on his amorous aquatic sports.

Observing him sporting about in the lotus-pond along with the beautiful girls this Śrīraṅgadāsa forgot his duty of wreathing the garlands. Though he had perfect control over his sense organs, he had an emission of the semen virile on seeing their sports.

Even as Raṅgadāsa was watching, that Gandharva youth rose up from the lake, smilingly covered himself with the divine robes and got into the charming aerial chariot along with those lovely ladies. Then he went back to the abode of Dhanada (i.e. Kubera).

When the king of Gandharvas departed, Raṅgadāsa who had been under delusion, felt ashamed. He left off the garlands, took bath in the lake and fetched more fresh flowers. Then he went to the temple slowly.

45-46. On seeing him arrive after the period of worship was over the Vaikhānasa asked him, "Friend, why are you late in coming? The garlands too have not been wreathed by you. What were you doing in the park?"

Śrī Varāha continued:

47. On being asked thus Raṅgadāsa did not speak anything because of his shame. As Raṅgadāsa remained ashamed, Madhusūdana spoke to Raṅgadāsa:

Śrīnivāsa's Words to Raṅgadāsa who was Ashamed on Recollecting his own Condition

Śrī Bhagavān said:

48-52. Why are you ashamed, O Raṅgadāsa? You have been deluded by me. Indeed you are one who has conquered his lust. O highly intelligent one, have courage. You will become a king on the surface of the earth like the Gandharva king. You will always be devoted to me. After enjoying all great worldly pleasures you will construct outer walls and pavilions for me then. I will be extremely delighted and will grant you salvation. You render service unto me here itself till you cast off the mortal body. It is thus that my devotees who are desirous (of pleasures) will get salvation.

After saying this Lord Viṣṇu did not say anything else. On hearing this Raṅgadāsa made that garden more splendid.

The Story of the King Named Toṇḍamān

53-57. That intelligent (devotee) served and worshipped the Lord for more than a hundred years and then went to heaven. He was born in the great Lunar race and became well-known as Toṇḍamān. The hero was the son of Suvīra and Nandinī.

He was extremely intelligent. He had Devotion to Viṣṇu engendered in him even at the age of five. He was a mine of many good qualities such as good behaviour, heroism, boldness, virility etc. He married Padmā, the charming daughter of the Pāṇḍya (king). Afterwards the king married a hundred girls of different lands in *Svayaṁvara* ('Self-choice') type of marriage. He sported about like the Lord of Devas living in Nārāyaṇapura on the earth. He obtained permission from his father to go for hunting. Thc son of leonine valour went near Veṅkaṭādri for hunting.

King Toṇḍamān goes to Śrī Śeṣācala for Hunting

58. He was moving about on foot accompanied by his attendants, when he saw the leader of a herd of elephants. He was in the rut, shedding ichor profusely.

59-62. On seeing him he was surprised and he pursued him in order to catch him. He crossed Suvarṇamukharī and bowed down to Śuka, the excellent Brahmarṣi. After being permitted by him, he went from forest to forest.

He then saw goddess Reṇukā who was stationed in the form of an anthill. She is the bestower of desired things on favourite devotees. She stayed in the divine garden always accompanied by her attendants. She was adored even by Devas. Toṇḍamān bowed to her and then went to the west.

The Story of the Parrot of Five Colours Staying Near Śrīnivāsa

63. He saw a parrot of five colours and pursued it with a desire to catch it. The parrot quickly flew towards the mountain chirping out *Śrīnivāsa*! *Śrīnivāsa*!

64. Closely following it the king too climbed the lord of the mountains, observing closely the different caves and crevasses and the peaks all round.

65. Searching for the parrot he came to the Śyāmāka field. He did not see the excellent parrot but saw the keeper of the forest.

66. Welcoming hurriedly the king who was coming towards him, he humbly bowed down to him and stood by with palms joined in reverence.

67-68. Toṇḍamān too duly honoured the forester and asked him: "Did any parrot of five colours come here? Was any such parrot seen by you? Where must have it gone chirping *Śrīnivāsa*! *Śrīnivāsa*! O forester?"

The forester replied:

69. That five-coloured (parrot) is a permanent favourite of Śrīnivāsa and remains at his side always. It has been brought up by Śrī and Bhūmi.

70. It stays always in the presence of the Lord on the banks of Svāmipuṣkariṇī. That glorious parrot cannot be caught by anyone.

71. After sporting about as it pleases on this excellent

mountain, at the end of the day it invariably comes back to the Lord and remains near him.

72-75. O Prince, I shall now go to propitiate that Lord. Be pleased to take rest at the foot of this tree till I return. You can happily play with this son of mine.

The king said:

I shall come with you in order to visit Lord Janārdana. Show me the Lord of Devas residing on Veṅkaṭādri.

On hearing the words of the king the forester took some Śyāmāka grains mixed with honey in a cup made of mango leaves and went to Hari along with the king.

King Toṇḍamān goes near Śrīnivāsa Along with the Niṣāda

76. Watching and observing the rocky surface they went a long way. In a short while they reached the splendid Svāmipuṣkariṇī.

77-82. They, the leader of the Niṣādas (foresters) along with the king, took their holy bath in the prescribed way. To the noble-souled king he pointed out the Lord of Devas stationed on the banks of Svāmipuṣkariṇī at the root of Śrīvṛkṣa (sacred bilva tree?). The Lord shines like Atasī (Linseed) flower. His eyes are large (and longish) like lotus (petals). He has four arms, magnificent limbs, and lotus-like face with a gentle smile. He shines brilliantly with a crown and bracelets. He has worn a divine yellow garment. He is accompanied at his side by Śrī and Bhūmi of very beautiful forms. He is attended upon all round by the conch, discus, sword, iron club, Śārṅga bow and arrow. He is served by other divine weapons too as well as heavenly garlands. He is propitiated by Skanda during the three junctions (i.e. dawn, midday and dusk). The Lord Puruṣottama has his lotus-like feet hidden under an anthill up to the knees. On seeing Lord Puruṣottama thus they joyously bowed down to him.

83. With his eyes beaming like a full-blown (lotus) due to wonder, the king stood with palms joined in reverence. He was in a state of ecstasy and could not see or understand anything else.

84. The forester offered as *Naivedya* the Śyāmāka grains mixed with honey. Half of that he handed to the king and himself ate the other half.

85. Accompanied by the king, he drank the waters of Puṣkariṇī and went back to his sacred cottage in the forest of Śyāmāka plants.

86. The king spent a night there and got up early in the morning. Accompanied by his army, he returned to his city.

Reṇukā Speaks to King Toṇḍamān

87. Again he went to the forest of Devī and got down from his horse. He worshipped Reṇukā on the ninth day in the bright half of the month of Caitra.

88-89. He offered ghee and best cooked rice along with many condiments and articles for seasoning food. Sacrificial offerings of animals were also made to the accompaniment of incense and lights. A hundred pots of liquor flavoured with jasmine and saffron were also offered. The Goddess who was worshipped thus became pleased and granted boons to the king.

90-92. A certain man possessed by the deity spoke to the excellent king: "Listen, O king, to your future. Your kingdom will be rid of all thorns. O king, the capital here will be named after you alone. You will rule for a long time, O great king, in my vicinity. O sinless one, you will get the favour of the Lord of Devas." After granting the boons to him the man possessed by the deity returned to (his) normal state.

The Greatness of Padmasaras as Described by Śuka

93-94. Then the king who received the boons went to sage Śuka once again. He made obeisance to the sage and honoured by him he joyously requested, "O sage, recount to me the greatness of the lake named Kamalā."

***Śrī Śuka said*:**

95. Formerly due to the curse of Durvāsas, O king, Padmā, the beloved of the lotus-eyed Lord, descended from heaven along with Viṣṇu.

96. The great Goddess Ramā reached this lake abounding in golden lotuses. She performed penance for ten thousand years according to divine reckoning.

97-98. Devas looked for Śrī accompanied by Viṣṇu. Devas in the company of Purandara saw the Goddess holding the lotus and sitting in a golden lotus along with the lotus-eyed Lord in this excellent lake, O king.

On seeing her they were delighted. After bowing down to her they stood with palms joined in reverence. Devas along with Indra eulogized the mother of the worlds.

Eulogy of Śrī Lakṣmī by Devas and Others

Devas prayed:

99. Obeisance to Śrī, the mother of the worlds. Obeisance, obeisance to the mother of Brahmā. Hail to you, to the lotus-eyed one. Obeisance, obeisance to the lotus-faced one.

100. Repeated salutes to the Goddess with delighted lotus-like face, having the lustre of lotus. Bow to the deity residing in the forest of Bilvas. Obeisance, obeisance to the consort of Viṣṇu.

101. Obeisance, obeisance to the deity wearing wonderfully variegated silk robes, to the deity with large buttocks. Obeisance, obeisance to the deity with protruding breasts as plump as the ripe Bilva fruit.

102. O splendid deity with hands and soles having the lustre of the petals of deep red lotus, O deity shining with bejewelled armlets, bracelets, waistbands (girdles) and anklets, O lady whose whole body is smeared with the fragrant *Yakṣakardama* ointment, O deity who shines with bangles.

103. O deity adorned with auspicious ornaments and wonderfully variegated pearl-necklaces, O lady whose lotus-like face shines with ear-rings and other ornaments.

104. O goddess with lotus-like hands (or with a lotus in your hands), obeisance to you. Be pleased, O beloved (consort) of Hari. Obeisance, obeisance to you, the (Vedic) lore in the form of Ṛk, Yajus and Sāma.

105. Be pleased, O daughter of the Ocean; look at us with your benign glances. Those who are seen by you shall attain the status of Brahmā, Rudra and Indra.

The Words Addressed to Indra and Others by Lakṣmī Who was Pleased by the Eulogy

Śrī Śuka said:

106. On being eulogized thus by the Devas, the delighted Ramā having the chest of Viṣṇu for her abode, who should be seen only with Viṣṇu spoke to the Suras:

Śrī said:

107-109. You will immediately go back to your own regions after killing the demons. Those who do not have any position (of importance), those men on the earth who have been dislodged from their own positions, shall regain their own positions by eulogizing me with this hymn.

O Devas, those men on the earth who worship me with unbroken Bilva leaves, those who eulogize me with the hymn composed by you, shall become the receptacles of virtue, wealth, love and salvation.

110-111. Those men on the earth, O Devas, who come to this Padmasaras ('Lotus-pond') and take their holy bath (herein) and eulogize me, the beloved of Viṣṇu, shall obtain prosperity, long life, learning, brilliant sons, and all worldly pleasures. After enjoying all pleasures they shall attain salvation in the end.

112. After granting the boons thus the Goddess mounted Garuḍeśāna along with Lord Viṣṇu and went back to the abode in Vaikuṇṭha.

CHAPTER TEN

The Story of Emperor Toṇḍamān

Toṇḍamān Inherits the Kingdom from His Father

Śrī Śuka said:

1. O king, this lake named Padmasaras is destructive of sins. Through glorification, recollection and holy dips it bestows fortune and prosperity on men on the earth. You too take your bath in this and then go to your father.

Śrī Varāha said:

2-5. On hearing these words of Śuka king Toṇḍamān took his bath in the excellent lake Padmasaras, bowed to him, mounted his horse and returned to his city.

The father installed him as a crown-prince for three years. He noted the various good qualities of his son, such as the ability of pleasing and reconciling (turbulent ones), capacity for work, heroism, courage, courteous good conduct and devotion to Brāhmaṇas. So the king consecrated him (by sprinkling water) in accordance with the injunctions and crowned him king in his own place. After consoling his son the king went to the forest along with his wife.

Vasu Sees Śrī Varāha in the Anthill[1]

6-9. After inheriting the empire Toṇḍamān ruled over the kingdom.

In the forest of that Niṣāda the Lord assumed the form of a boar and grazed in the field of Śyāmāka grains every night. During the day time the forester used to see the imprints of the feet of the boar and followed them but failed to see him. One night

1. As stated in the note on pp. 48-49, Toṇḍamān here means the king of Toṇḍamaṇḍala. The disappearance and stay of the divine Boar Viṣṇu into an anthill has its counterpart in the pastoral god Viṭṭhala—Bīradeva (of Maharashtra and Karnatak) who is supposed to have stayed in an anthill. There is a close similarity between catapulting of a primitive god into Viṭṭhala (of Pandharpur) and Veṅkaṭeśa, the veritable Viṣṇu from Vaikuṇṭha —Tr.

with a bow (in his hand) he lay in wait. Then he saw the boar of magnificent features, having the lustre similar to that of a crore of moons. He was grazing in the middle of the Śyāmāka field. On seeing him he took up his bow and roared like a lion.

10. On hearing that roaring sound the boar came out of that Śyāmāka field hurriedly and went away. The king of Niṣādas followed the boar.

11. During the whole of the remaining part of the night the leader of the foresters pursued the boar of lunar lustre. (Ultimately) he saw it entering an anthill.

12. When the boar vanished within the anthill, it appeared as though the full moon had set behind a mountain. He became surprised as well as furious. The leader of the hunters dug up the anthill.

13-14. The boar was seen but the hunter swooned and fell down. On seeing his father fallen unconscious the son who was very devout, eulogized Lord Varāha (Boar). Thereby Hari became pleased. Possessing his father the Slayer of Madhu said:

Śrī Bhagavān said:

15. I am Varāha, the Lord of Devas. I permanently reside here. Tell the king to install me here and worship me.

16-17. The anthill should be washed with the milk of a black cow. The idol of Varāha should be taken out, placed on the ground and then installed on the rocky slab rising from the anthill by Brāhmaṇas and anchorites. Toṇḍamān, the excellent king, should worship me by means of various kinds of food offerings and other articles of enjoyment.

18-19. After saying this the Lord left him (Vasu). He became normal. The son of the hunter bowed down to his father who was comfortably seated. He intimated to his father everything as said by the Lord. On hearing the whole of the splendid statement of his son he became surprised.

Vasu Recounts to King Toṇḍamān the Story of Varāha

20. The hunter hastened (to the city) along with his followers to report this to the king. Vasu, the lord of the hunters, approached the entrance to the royal palace.

21-22. Knowing that the king of hunters had come, the excellent king called him in through the gatekeepers. The king honoured Vasu and his son along with their followers and attendants in the Assembly together with his ministers. The delighted king asked Vasu, the forester, "O forester, what is the purpose of your visit? Tell me."

Vasu said:

23-25. O king, a mysterious thing has been witnessed (by me) in my forest. Listen, O king. A certain white boar grazed the Śyāmāka rice at night. With a bow in my hand I pursued that boar, O king. On being chased that boar ran with the speed of wind and entered an anthill on the banks of Svāmipuṣkariṇī even as I was watching, O king.

26-27. I furiously dug up the anthill, but fell unconscious on the ground. This, my son, came and saw me lying on the ground unconscious. Purifying himself he eulogized the Lord of Devas, the Slayer of Madhu. Thereupon Lord Varāha possessing me spoke to my son:

28-33. "O lord of hunters, immediately intimate to the king all my account. Let the king wash the anthill with the milk of a black cow sprinkled on it. A splendid rocky slab will be seen within the anthill. The king should prepare through a sculptor an idol of mine in sitting posture with the face of a Boar with Goddess Earth seated on my left lap. It shall be installed by prominent sages and anchorites. Toṇḍamān should worship the same along with the excellent sages. He should slowly wash and bathe (the idol of) Śrīnivāsa whose pair of feet are covered by the anthill. He should do so (wash) with the milk of a dark tawny-coloured cow. Everyday it should be bathed as far as the foot-pedestal. He should get built ramparts (walls) on both the northern and southern sides."

After saying this the Lord left me. O king, I became normal. It is to communicate this act of the Lord of Devas to you that I have come.

The King's Journey to Śeṣācala Through the Sub-terranean Path as Per Instructions of the Niṣāda and those Received in His Dream

Śrī Varāha said:

34-37. On hearing it Toṇḍamān became surprised and delighted very much. After consultation with Puṣkara and other ministers he came to a decision on the issue. He became desirous of going to Veṅkaṭādri. He called together all the cowherds and ordered: "Bring all my tawny-coloured and black-coloured cows along with their calves near Veṅkaṭādri."

After commanding the cowherds thus he bade farewell to the Ministers saying, "The journey shall take place tomorrow." After dismissing all the officers of administration the king of perfect self-control entered the inner apartment. After telling that story to his wives at night the king went to sleep.

38-41. In his dream Śrīnivāsa pointed out the path of the cave to the king (who saw that) Hari had strewn sprouts and tender shoots from the city to the entrance to the cave.

After seeing such a dream that king hurriedly got up in the morning. He called together all the Ministers, the officers of the government and the Brāhmaṇas and told them about the dream in the manner it had occurred. He saw the sprouts at the entrance.[1]

At the proper auspicious hour Toṇḍamān mounted his horse and proceeded slowly following the sprouts and shoots with great delight. Then he reached the cave. On seeing it the king was surprised. He built a city there.

The King Performs the Rite of Abhiṣeka and Builds a Rampart Wall at the Instance of the Lord

42-43. After making the cave come within the (precincts of the) city he got a rampart wall built. The king stayed there and conquered the whole of the earth. He performed the rite of washing (the Varāha's anthill) with milk as instructed by the Lord of Devas and then made arrangements to build the rampart wall.

1. The author hereby suggests that "Pallava" is the name of the dynasty that ruled over Toṇḍamaṇḍala (Kāñcī).

44-47. At that time the king was commanded by the Lord of Devas himself: "Guard these two excellent trees of Tintiṇī (Tamarind) and Caṁpaka. The Tamarind tree is my abode while the Caṁpaka is the abode of Lakṣmī. They are always to be bowed to by kings, sages, Devas and human beings. After retaining these two, O excellent king, cut off all the other big trees. Build the rampart wall alone for me with an ornamented gateway and doors. A king of your lineage, Nārāyaṇa by name, a great devotee of mine, will make the *Vimāna* (Temple). He will adorn it with gold."

Śrī Varāha said:

48-50. After saying this to King Toṇḍamān the Lord of Śri became silent.

On hearing the words of the Lord and after building the rampart wall he worshipped the Lord along with the sages born in the families (belonging to the group) of Vaikhānasas (anchorites). Everyday the king came by the sub-terranean path and bowed down to the Lord. The excellent king ruled the kingdom virtuously, enjoying excellent pleasures.

The Story of the Brāhmaṇa Vīraśarman who had Returned from the Pilgrimage to Gaṅgā

51-54. At that very same time an excellent Brāhmaṇa of the southern region was on his way (to Kāśī) for taking a holy bath in Gaṅgā. He had started from his city along with his wife. The Brāhmaṇa lady became pregnant on the way. On seeing that his pregnant wife would not be (physically) capable enough to follow him the Brāhmaṇa wanted to see the king. He came to the entrance to the royal palace. Informed by the gatekeeper, the king called the excellent Brāhmaṇa, honoured him duly and enquired about his health and happiness.

The king asked:

55-58. What is the purpose of your visit, O Brāhmaṇa? What shall I do for you?

The Brāhmaṇa said:

O excellent king, I am Vīraśarman belonging to Vasiṣṭha Gotra. I am a Sāmavedin. Eager to have a holy bath in Gaṅgā, I started from my place along with my wife. On the way this meritorious lady of the family of Kuśika, well-known by the name Lakṣmī, has become pregnant. She is a chaste lady of very good conduct. I wish to keep her here in your abode and proceed with (my pilgrimage and) holy observances. Hence, O king, give her food and regular cash allowance as much as she wishes for. Let Lakṣmī be looked after till my return.

Śrī Varāha said:

59-61. On hearing his words the king sanctioned food grains and cash allowance to her for six months and gave her residence in the inner apartments.

After keeping her there the Brāhmaṇa became pleased and set out for the holy bath in Gaṅgā. He went to Gaṅgā Bhāgīrathī at the excellent holy place Prayāga. After bath he proceeded to Kāśī where he stayed for three days. After that he arrived at Gayā and the excellent Brāhmaṇa performed the Śrāddha ritual unto his (paternal) ancestors.[1]

62. After going to the city of Ayodhyā he went to Badarīvana. From there he went to Śālagrāma[2] and then started back towards his own native place.

63-66. After a lapse of two years on an auspicious day in the month of Caitra the excellent Brāhmaṇa returned. After proceeding ahead slowly he went to the king once again on the eleventh day in the bright half of Mādhava (Vaiśākha) month.

The king had forgotten about the Brāhmaṇa lady. As the king did not remember (to sanction the allowances) the proud Brāhmaṇa lady died in the house. Her dead body became very dry.

Vīraśarman opened his box of sealed pots of Gaṅgā water and handed one of the splendid pots to the king and asked him, "Is my wife happy and well?"

1. This is the proper order in *Tristhalī Yātrā*.

2. A place near the source of Gandak where Bharata and sage Pulaha performed penance (De 174).

67-70. The king now remembered everything. He said to the Brāhmaṇa, "Be pleased to wait." He went into the inner apartment and found her dead.

Without telling the Brāhmaṇa anything he entered the excellent cave. He bowed down to Śrī Nṛsiṁha and then again came back to the excellent cave. He went to visit the great Lord Śrīnivāsa accompanied by Śrī and Bhūmi. On seeing him come suddenly Dharā and Ramā hid themselves. As he was bowing down, the Lord said to him, "O king, why have you come at this odd hour?" After bowing down to the Lord the frightened king told him that the lady had died.

The Greatness of the Excellent Lake Asthisarovara

71-73. On hearing that the Lord of Devas said: "O king, do not be afraid of the excellent Brāhmaṇa. Place the dead lady in a palanquin accompanied by your own womenfolk. To the east of my shrine, O king, there is a lake named Asthisaras which prevents premature death. Bathe the dead body in that lake on the Dvādaśī (twelfth) day. She will be resuscitated. She will become united with the Brāhmaṇa as well as with the other ladies. Go quickly, O excellent king. Carry out the instruction given."

74-80. On hearing these words of the Lord the king went back to his city. He placed that lady and other womenfolk in beautiful palanquins. Keeping the Brāhmaṇa at the head, the king went to visit the Lord. After reaching the Asthikūṭasaras he made the womenfolk take their bath. That (Brāhmaṇa lady) in the form of skin and bones was thrown by them into the excellent lake. She regained her life and all her limbs became fully developed as before. That lady of great auspiciousness rose up from the lake along with the womenfolk and queens after their bath. She rejoined the Brāhmaṇa, her husband, who had returned (from the pilgrimage) and became pleased.

After worshipping Hari the king gave money to the Brāhmaṇa to the tune of a thousand gold coins as well as different kinds of garments. He then bade farewell to him and allowed him to go back to his own land, showing him due respect. The Brāhmaṇa heard about the incidents that had occurred in the life of his wife as well as the power of Veṅkaṭeśa. He showered blessings on the king and went back to his native land.

After the Brāhmaṇa had gone Śrīnivāsa spoke to the king once again:

81-83. "Everyday at midday, O king, after the food offering, come here and worship me with golden lotuses as you please. Then go back to the city, O lord of men, and rule over the kingdom as required by your duty (as a king). Whatever is desired by you, O king, will undoubtedly happen. You should not come at odd time, O king, on any occasion. After regularly performing the timely worship return to your capital and stay there."

The king said:

84-85. O Lord of Devas, I shall do so. I shall perform worship at midday too.

Thus at the behest of the Lord he performed worship everyday with golden lotuses.

The Story of the Devotee Named Bhīma Born in a Potter's Family in the Village Kurvagrāma

Once he saw a Tulasī (Basil) flower made of clay above his golden lotuses.

86-88. On being struck with wonder the excellent king asked the Lord of the Chiefs of Devas:

The king enquired:

By whom are you worshipped with lotuses and leaves of Tulasī made of clay?

On being asked by the king the Lord of Devas recollected and said to the king: "A certain potter, a great devotee of mine, resides in Kurvagrāma.[1] He worships me in his house, O king, and that (worship) is accepted by me."

1. The village of Kurvas, probably a Sanskritization of 'Kurava', a hill-tribe living in and around the Tirupati hill.

On hearing the words of the Lord thus the king went to meet him (the potter).

89. He went to the city of Kurvapura and called at the abode of the potter. On seeing the king come he stood there in front of him bowing down.

90. The excellent king asked (the potter) named Bhīma who stood thus:

Toṇḍamān asked:

O Bhīma of excellent family, how do you worship the Lord? Tell me.

Śrī Varāha said:

91. On being asked the potter said: "I have never known any worship. By whom has this been said, O excellent king, that the potter worships?"

Toṇḍamān said:

92-94. Your worship has been mentioned to me by Lord Śrīnivāsa.

On hearing the words of the king he remembered the boon granted to him formerly by the Lord.

Bhīma said:

"When the worship (that you perform) is revealed, when king Toṇḍamān comes, when you have a conversation with him, you will attain salvation"—formerly Veṅkaṭeśvara, the Lord, had granted this boon.

The Devotee Named Bhīma, Resident of Kurvagrāma Attains Vaikuṇṭha along with His Wife

95-99. After saying thus the potter along with his wife (got ready for their salvation).

On seeing that the heavenly chariot had come they saw Lord Janārdana. Bowing down to the Lord along with his wife the excellent devotee cast off his life.

Even as the king of kings was watching he assumed a divine form and got into the heavenly chariot. He then went to Viṣṇu's region along with (his wife turned into a) goddess.

On seeing this wonderful event the king became delighted. He returned to his own city. He crowned his son named Śrīnivāsa in accordance with the injunctions. He directed his son thus: "Protect the earth and the people virtuously." After giving him directives the intelligent king performed a great penance. As he performed the penance, Lord Hari appeared before him directly.

King Toṇḍamān Attains Sārūpya Through the Grace of Viṣṇu

100-103. Lord Hari became visible to him as seated on Garuḍa in the company of Ramā and Bhūmi.

Śrī Bhagavān asked:

O excellent king, what shall I do for you? I have been propitiated by your penance.

On being told thus by the Lord of Devas Toṇḍamān, the king of kings, became delighted. With palms joined in reverence he said in faltering words:

"I wish to reside in your world that is devoid of death and old age. Grant me this boon alone, O Mādhava. This is what is desired by me."

Śrī Varāha said:

104-106. After saying this he prostrated on the ground before the Lord with eight limbs touching the ground. He cast off the body and climbed into a heavenly chariot. He attained *Sārūpya* ('similarity of form') with the Śārṅga-wielding Lord and was eulogized by Gandharvas. He attained that region of Viṣṇu which is devoid of grief and delusion, which is free from death and old age and from which there is no return (to worldly existence).

The Benefit Accruing from Listening to, Reading and Reciting the Greatness of This (Episode)

107-109. O goddess of Devas of excellent complexion, he

who recounts or listens to this future event recounted by me, goes to the world of Viṣṇu.

Śrī Sūta said:

He who listens to or reads with devotion this narrative of the future events and the sequel, the meritorious traditional story, enjoys all desirable things (in the world) and on death goes to the region of Viṣṇu.

CHAPTER ELEVEN

Kāśyapa Absolved of Sins

Kāśyapa's Absolution of Great Sins Through the Holy Bath in Svāmipuṣkariṇī

Śrī Sūta said:

1. Henceforth, O excellent Brāhmaṇa, I shall tell you in details a great and sacred story concerning the splendid Svāmipuṣkariṇī.

2. Formerly a certain Brāhmaṇa named Kāśyapa had his holy bath in this auspicious and most excellent Tīrtha and he was liberated from a great sin leading to (his fall into) hell.

The sages said:

3-4. O sage, what sin did this Brāhmaṇa named Kāśyapa commit? What was the sin from which he was liberated instantaneously by taking holy bath in the excellent Tīrtha here? O Sūta, kindly narrate this to us who faithfully listen to it. No thirst can remain in the persons who are satisfied by the nectar of your words.

Śrī Sūta said:

5. I shall recount the legendary story illustrating the greatness of Śrī Svāmipuṣkariṇī. It is destructive of the sins of those who read it.

The Anecdote of Parīkṣit[1]

6-7. Formerly there was a king named Parīkṣit. He was the son of Abhimanyu. He lived at Hastināpura protecting the earth righteously. Once while that king was engaged in hunting, he roamed about in the forest. The king who was sixty years old became afflicted with hunger and thirst.

8-9. He was eagerly searching for a deer that had vanished. The excellent king saw a sage engrossed in meditation. He asked, "A certain deer has been hit by me in this forest, O sage, with an arrow just now. O learned one, it was frightened and has fled. Was it seen by you?"

10-12. The sage was engaged in meditation. Further he was observing the vow of silence. Hence he did not say anything. With the tip of his bow the king lifted a dead serpent and placed it on the shoulders of that great sage angrily. Then he returned to the city.

The sage had a son named Śṛṅgin. He had a friend named Kṛśa, an excellent Brāhmaṇa. The friend named Kṛśa said to his companion Śṛṅgin:

13. "Friend, your father wears a dead serpent over his shoulders now. You need not be proud. You need not be angry. It is in vain."

14-15. Śṛṅgin became furious and desired to curse the king: "The foolish and ignorant person who placed the dead serpent on my father will die within seven days on being bitten by the serpent Takṣaka."

The son of the sage cursed Parīkṣit, the descendant of Subhadrā, thus.

16. On hearing that the king had been cursed by his son, his father, the eminent sage named Śamīka, said to his son Śṛṅgin:

1. This story is adopted from Mbh, Ādi Chs. 40-43. The Mbh story is a Purāṇic way of telling how Takṣaka tried to take political revenge on Arjuna's grandson for his (Arjuna's) driving out the Nāgas from their Fatherland, the Khāṇḍava forest.

17. "Why have you cursed the king, the protector of all the people? How can we live peacefully in the world full of anarchy?

18-19. Anger gives rise to sin. Happiness is attained through kindness and mercy. He who by means of patience and forbearance dispels surging anger, obtains supreme happiness in this as well as the other world. Indeed, only those persons who are endowed with forgiveness obtain the highest good."

20-21. Then Śamīka told his disciple named Gauramukha: "O Gauramukha, go to king Parīkṣit and report to him about this curse uttered by my son, namely the biting by Takṣaka, the king (of serpents). O highly intelligent one, return to my presence quickly."

22. On being told thus by Śamīka Gauramukha went to the king. After approaching him he said to king Parīkṣit, the descendant of Subhadrā:

23-25. "On seeing the dead serpent placed on his father's shoulders by you, Śṛṅgin, the son of Śamīka, has angrily cursed you: 'On the seventh day from today the son of Abhimanyu shall be bitten by Takṣaka, the great serpent, and shall immediately be burned by the fire of his poison.' O king, Śṛṅgin, the son of that sage, has cursed you thus. It is to tell you this that his father has deputed me to you."

26-27. After saying this to the king Gauramukha returned in a hurry. After the departure of Gauramukha the king who was grief-stricken, got a *Maṇḍapa* (hall) built in the middle of Gaṅgā. It was so high that it touched the clouds. It was supported by a single pillar.

28-29. With great concentration he prepared himself to quell the poison of Takṣaka through physicians conversant with medicinal herbs and the knowers of *Mahāgāruḍa Mantra*. The king endowed with great devotion to Viṣṇu sat within the lofty Maṇḍapa accompanied by the most excellent ones among many celestial sages, Brāhmaṇas, sages and saintly kings.

30. At that time, a certain Brāhmaṇa named Kāśyapa, the most excellent one among those who were experts in the use of spells (Mantras), proceeded (towards the royal abode) in order to save the king from the greatly virulent poison of Takṣaka.

31-34. The leading Brāhmaṇa who was very poor and was desirous of wealth (came to that place) on the seventh day. In the meantime Takṣaka also came there in the guise of a Brāhmaṇa. On the way he saw Kāśyapa and spoke to him, "O Brāhmaṇa, O great sage, where are you going now? Tell me."

On being asked thus, the Brāhmaṇa Kāśyapa told Takṣaka:

"Today Takṣaka will be burning the great king Parīkṣit with the fire of his poison. I am now going to him in order to quell it."

On being told thus Takṣaka spoke to that Brāhmaṇa once again:

35-37. "I am Takṣaka, O excellent Brāhmaṇa. One who is bitten by me cannot be cured even in a hundred years, even by means of ten thousand *Mahā Mantras*. If you are now competent to treat one who is bitten by me, I shall bite a tree several Yojanas high. You revive it. Then I shall conclude that you are adequately competent (to quell my poison), O Brāhmaṇa."

After saying thus Takṣaka bit that tree.

38-42. That exceedingly lofty tree was reduced to ash. Before this incident a certain man had climbed that tree. He too was burnt by the fire of Takṣaka's poison. Both of them, Kāśyapa and Takṣaka, were not aware of that man.

Kāśyapa vowed within the hearing of Takṣaka, "Let all the Brāhmaṇas and others witness the power of my Mantra now."

After saying this Kāśyapa, the most excellent one among those conversant with spells, resuscitated that tree which had been reduced to ash by the fire of poison. He brought it back to life by means of the power of his spell. That man also was revived along with the tree. Thereupon, Takṣaka spoke to Kāśyapa, that expert in the use of spells:

43-46. "O Brāhmaṇa, whatever you do, see that the words of the sage do not turn out to be false. I shall give you twice the amount that the king is likely to give you. O excellent Brāhmaṇa, return immediately." After saying thus Takṣaka gave him the most valuable gems and made the Brāhmaṇa Kāśyapa who was well-versed in spells, return (to his own place).

With the vision born of knowledge Kāśyapa found out that the king was destined to live only for a short period. Having obtained the gems from Takṣaka Kaśyapa quietly went back to his hermitage.

Takṣaka called together all the serpents at that very moment and told them:

47. "Ye all assume the guise of sages and go to that king immediately. Give fruits as presents to Parīkṣit."

48-51. Saying "So be it", all the serpents offered fruits unto the king. Takṣaka assumed the form of a worm and hid himself in a certain jujube fruit ready to bite the king.

King Parīkṣit distributed all the fruits given by the serpents in the guise of Brāhmaṇas to the ministers and elderly gentlemen. But out of curiosity he took a big fruit in his hand. At that time the sun was about to set.

52-55. The men present there, all the Brāhmaṇas and the kings, said to one another, "May the words of the sage not be false"(?). Even as they were saying thus, a red worm was clearly seen by king Parīkṣit and by all the others. The king said, "Will this worm bite me now, O excellent Brāhmaṇas?" Saying thus he placed that fruit upon his neck along with the worm. Takṣaka who was residing in the fruit placed upon his neck suddenly came out of that fruit and coiled round the body of the king.

56-59. When the king was encircled by Takṣaka, all those who were at the sides fled out of fear. Afterwards, O Brāhmaṇas, the king was immediately burned and reduced to ash along with the palatial building by the powerful fire of the poison of Takṣaka.

Along with the priests the ministers of that king performed the obsequies of the king and crowned his son named Janamejaya in the kingdom with a desire to protect the whole world.

The Brāhmaṇa, the excellent sage named Kāśyapa who had come to save the king from Takṣaka, was censured by all the people.

60-62. He wandered over all the territories. He was rebuked and reviled by all good people. He did not get any place to stay in any village or in a hermitage. To whichever land he went he was driven out from those places by the general public. Then he sought refuge in (Sage) Śākalya. Kāśyapa who was censured by good people, bowed down to sage Śākalya. He intimated this to the noble-souled Śākalya:

Kāśyapa said:

63-67. O Śākalya, O favourite of Hari, O holy lord conversant with all types of pious activities, the sages, Brāhmaṇas, friends and others censure me. I do not know the reason why men censure me. Neither Brāhmaṇa-slaughter, nor drinking of liquor, neither defiling the bed of the preceptor, nor stealing, nor the sin of associating with these (sinful) people have been committed by me. O sage, none of the other types of sins too has been committed by me. Yet, people, kinsmen and others censure me for nothing. If you know the fault committed by me, O Śākalya, tell that to me.

When this was said by Kāśyapa, the great sage named Śākalya meditated for a short while and spoke thus to Kāśyapa, O excellent Brāhmaṇas:

Pious and Virtuous Acts Enunciated by Śākalya

Śākalya said:

68-73. You went to save the great king Parīkṣit from Takṣaka. But on your way you were prevented by Takṣaka.

They call that person a *Brahmaghātaka* (i.e. slayer of a Brāhmaṇa) who is competent to treat a person afflicted by poison or sickness but does not save such a person in this world. Whether it is due to anger, lust, fear, covetousness, jealousy or delusion, O leading Brāhmaṇa, if a person does not save a man afflicted due to poison or other ailments (he has no way of atonement). A Brāhmaṇa-slayer, a drink-addict, a thief, a defiler of preceptor's bed and one who is defiled by associating with these—none of these has any way of expiation.

There is some kind of atonement (from sin) for a person who sells his daughter, who sells horses as well as one who is ungrateful. Such expiation is found in scriptures. But the person who, though competent, does not save one who is afflicted by poison or ailments, has no mode of atonement. Even by means of ten thousand kinds of expiations he cannot be saved from his sins.

74-78. No righteous person should take food with him in the same row. He should not converse with him. He should not look at that man at any place. Merely by talking to him one will incur great sins.

That great king Parīkṣit was very virtuous and had spotless reputation. He was a devotee of Viṣṇu. He was a great Yogin and protector of the four castes. He had heard devoutly the story of Hari from the son of Vyāsa (i.e. Śuka). You did not protect him. At the words (i.e. request) of Takṣaka you returned. Therefore, you are blamed by leading Brāhmaṇas and kinsmen.

Although the end of the life of the great king Parīkṣit was imminent, treatment must have been administered by learned men till the death (of the patient).

79-81. "As long as the vital airs cling to the throat of a man about to die, it is necessary that treatment should be continued. The way of Kāla (Death)is crooked." This verse has been quoted by persons who have mastered the science of medicine. Therefore, though you were capable of treating, you did not administer medicine. You returned from half the way. Hence you are despised.

On being told by Śākalya thus Kāśyapa said:

Kāśyapa said:

82-84. O sage of holy rites, tell the means of quelling this sin of mine, so that my kinsmen and friends will accept me once again. O Śākalya, O favourite of Hari, have pity on me.

On being requested by Kāśyapa thus, Śākalya the eminent sage meditated for a short while and spoke thus to Kāśyapa out of sympathy:

Śākalya said:

85. I shall tell you the means for quelling this sin. That should be carried out by you immediately. Do not delay, O Brāhmaṇa.

86. On the banks of Suvarṇamukharī there is (a mountain) well-known as Veṅkaṭādri. It is the place of residence of the Lord of Lakṣmī. It is honoured in all the worlds.

87-88. On that meritorious holy mountain Śeṣagiri which is bowed to by Suras and Asuras and which destroys the sins of Brāhmaṇa-slaughter, drinking of liquor and stealing of gold, there is (a lake named) Svāmipuṣkariṇī, the dispeller of all sins. It is to the north of Śrīnivāsa. It yields auspiciousness.

89-92a. Go to the mountain Veṅkaṭādri. Take your holy bath in the auspicious Svāmipuṣkariṇī with due *Saṅkalpa* (i.e. ceremonious pronouncement of one's resolve). Visit Hari, Lord Varāha, go along the western bank, go to Hari's temple and there, in accordance with the injunctions, visit Śrīnivāsa residing on Svarṇācala. Worship the Lord Supreme, the bestower of immunity from fear, the Lord holding the conch and the discus, the Lord adorned with the garland of sylvan flowers. On visiting him you will be rid of your sins. Do not be in any doubt, O Brāhmaṇa.

92b-94a. On being told thus by Śākalya, Kāśyapa, the eminent sage, went to the prominent mountain Veṅkaṭa Śaila bowed down to by Suras and Asuras. He took his holy bath in the auspicious Puṣkariṇī with all requisite observances. The Brāhmaṇa Kāśyapa who was a master of medicine and medical science, regained normalcy (i.e. his previous status).

94b-96. All the kinsmen, O Brāhmaṇas, honoured Kāśyapa, the excellent Brāhmaṇa, in the way proper to him (saying) "There is no doubt. You are worthy of being honoured."

Thus, O Brāhmaṇas, the greatness of Veṅkaṭācala has been recounted to you. One who listens to this with devotion is honoured in the world of Viṣṇu.

CHAPTER TWELVE

The Greatness of Svāmipuṣkariṇī

Redemption from Tāmisra and other Hells Through Holy Bath in Svāmipuṣkariṇī

The sages said:

1-2. O Sūta conversant with the essence of all things, O master of Vedas and Vedāṅgas, O holy lord, describe to us the greatness of Śrī Svāmipuṣkariṇī, merely by remembering which a man on the earth shall become liberated.

Śrī Sūta said:

3-8. Those who praise, those who take their holy bath in and those who speak about Svāmitīrtha never experience the tortures of the hells of twenty-eight types,[1] viz. Tāmisra, Andhatāmisra, Raurava, Mahāraurava, Kuṁbhīpāka, Kālasūtra, Asipatravana, Kṛmibhakṣa, Andhakūpa, Sandaṁśa, Śālmalī, Lālābhakṣa, Avīci, Sārameyādana, Vajrakaṇaka, Kṣārakardamapātana, Rakṣogaṇāśana, Śūlaprotanirodhana, Tirodhāna, Sūcīmukha, Pūyaśoṇitabhakṣa, Viṣāgniparipīḍana etc. (a few missing). O Brāhmaṇas, by taking holy dip in Svāmitīrtha a man does not fall into any of the hells numbering twenty-eight.

9-10. If anyone steals wealth, children or wives of others, he is bound with Kālapāśa (Noose of the god of Death) by the terrible messengers of Yama and he is dropped into the terrible hell Tāmisra. He is kept there for a number of years. If the person takes his holy bath in Svāmitīrtha, he is not thrown into that (hell).

11-13a. A base man who is antagonistic to his mother, father or Brāhmaṇas is thrown into the hell Kālasūtra which extends over ten thousand Yojanas. He is cast into a copper-threshing mill which is heated by fire from below and by the Sun's rays from above while the victim is afflicted with hunger. If he takes his holy bath in Puṣkariṇī, he is not thrown into that (hell).

13b-14. A man who transgresses the path laid down in the Vedas and clings to evil ways is thrown into the terrible hell Asipatravana by the servants of Yama. If he takes his bath in Svāmitīrtha, he is not cast into that (hell).

15-17. A man who (exclusively) eats sauce of ground peas etc. in a different row, a man who, due to delusion, takes food without performing the five Yajñas, O Brāhmaṇas, is thrown into the hell Kṛmibhojana by the soldiers of Yama. He will be eaten by hundreds of worms. He will be compelled to eat the worms.

1. The different types of hells, the tortures therein and sins for which they are meant are detailed in different Purāṇas like MkP, PdP and others. They differ in some details from this chapter. These deterrent punishments are procalimed in order to dissuade people from committing immoral acts.

He himself will be turned into a worm and will stay there till the sins are exhausted. If he takes his holy bath in Svāmitīrtha, he is not thrown into that (hell).

18-20a. If any person takes away the wealth of a Brāhmaṇa with (showy) friendliness or through force, if a king or his officer takes away the wealth of others (illegally), he is tortured by means of tongs heated in fire pits full of red hot iron balls in the terrible hell Sandaṁśa by Yama's men. If he takes his holy bath in Svāmitīrtha, he is not thrown into that (hell).

20b-23a. If a base man carnally approaches a forbidden woman or if a woman carnally approaches a forbidden man, O Brāhmaṇa, they are compelled to embrace red hot iron (dummy of a) woman or man as the case may be. They will stand like this as long as the moon and the sun last. They are thrown into the terrible hell named Sūcī by the servants of Yama. If he or she takes the holy bath in Svāmitīrtha, they are not thrown into that (hell).

23b-24. A person who harasses or torments any creature in diverse ways and modes of affliction, is thrown into the terrible hell Śālmalī full of thorns. If he takes his holy bath in Svāmitīrtha, he is not thrown into that (hell).

25-26a. If a king or his servant closely follows a heretic, if anyone breaks the boundaries of piety and virtue, he is thrown into Vaitaraṇī. If he takes his holy bath in Svāmitīrtha, he is not thrown into that (hell).

26b-28. A person defiled by the contact of a Śūdra woman, a person devoid of cleanliness and good conduct, a person bereft of shame, a person who has abandoned (i.e. flouted the authority of) the Vedas, a person of perpetual brutish activities is thrown into Atibībhatsa ('extremely hideous') hell filled with putrid matter, faeces, urine, blood, phlegm, bile etc. by the servants of Yama. If he takes his holy bath in Svāmitīrtha, he is not thrown into that (hell).

29-30. If a person going on a hunt torments deer and wild animals through hounds and arrows, he will be pierced through by volleys of arrows in the other world by the servants of Yama. He is thrown into the hell named Prāṇarodha by the servants of Yama. If he takes his holy bath in Svāmitīrtha he is not thrown into that (hell).

31-32. If a hypocrite kills animals in a Yajña without the rites performed in accordance with the injunctions, O Brāhmaṇas, he is cast into the hell Vaiśasa in the other world by the servants of Yama. He is cut, shorn and chipped by the soldiers of Yama. If he takes bath in Puṣkariṇī, he is not thrown into that (hell).

33-34a. If a person compels his own wife of the same caste to drink semen virile, in the other world he is thrown into a pit of semen virile and compelled to drink it. If he takes his holy bath in Puṣkariṇī, he is not thrown into that (hell).

34b-36a. If a person waylays men and robs them, if a person administers poison, if a person burns down a whole village, or if a person steals the merchandise of a trader, O excellent Brāhmaṇas, in the other world he is thrown into the terrible hell named Vajradaṁṣṭra and kept there for a long time. If he takes his holy bath in Svāmitīrtha, he is not thrown into that (hell).

36b-37. There are many other hells in the other world, but by taking a bath into Svāmitīrtha a man does not fall into them.

By taking bath once in Puṣkariṇī one derives the benefit of a horse-sacrifice.

38. (By him) knowledge of the soul shall be attained directly as well as the four types of salvation. (His) intellect does not revel in sin nor shall there be any misery.

39. The benefit that is obtained by men through *Tulāpuruṣa-dāna* (i.e. making a gift of some stipulated articles weighed against the donor) is obtained by persons by taking holy plunge in Svāmitīrtha.

40. The benefit that is obtained by men by means of a gift of a thousand cows is obtained by men by taking holy bath in Svāmitīrtha.

41. By taking a holy dip in Svāmitīrtha a person immediately attains whatever he desires among (the objectives in life such as) virtue, wealth, pleasure and salvation.

42. Whether one has committed great sins or even has committed all sins, O Brāhmaṇas, one becomes purified immediately by taking bath in Svāmitīrtha.

43. By taking holy bath in Svāmitīrtha men shall obtain intellect, fortune, fame, wealth, knowledge, virtue, detachment and purity of mind.

44-45. Ten thousand sins of Brāhmaṇa-slaughter, ten thousand sins of imbibing liquor, ten thousand sins of carnally approaching the preceptor's wife committed by habitual sinners, ten thousand sins of theft of gold and crores of the sins of associating with these sinners—all these are quickly dissolved by taking holy plunge in Svāmitīrtha.

46-47. All the sins on a par with the sin of Brāhmaṇa-slaughter, the sin of drinking liquor, the sin of carnally approaching the wife of the preceptor, the sin of stealing gold and the sin of associating with these sinners—O believers in Veda, all these perish by taking holy bath in Svāmitīrtha.

If Persons have no Faith in the Greatness of Svāmitīrtha, They will Fall into Great Hells

48-49. No doubt should be entertained in the matter mentioned above. Otherwise the servants (of Yama) will place heated axe at the tip of his tongue. If anyone says that this is exaggerated praise, he shall fall into a hell. He should be known as a pig excluded from all holy rites.

50-52. Alas, the folly, alas, the silliness, the stupidity of (ordinary) people, O excellent Brāhmaṇas, who try to revel in other places and avoid this holy spot even while there is the Tīrtha named Svāmitīrtha which is destructive of all sins, which bestows the knowledge of non-duality on men, which yields worldly pleasures and salvation, which grants all desired objects always and is destructive of ignorance! Alas, the extent of (their) delusion which cannot be adequately expressed by me!

53-54. One who has taken his bath in Svāmitīrtha need not be afraid of the god of Death. Those men who visit Svāmitīrtha and take bath therein, eulogize it, praise it, touch it or bow down to it, do not drink the breast-milk of mothers (again) (i.e. get *Mokṣa*), O Brāhmaṇas.

55. Thus, O Brāhmaṇas, the greatness of Svāmitīrtha has been narrated to you. It yields worldly pleasures and salvation to men. It dispels all sins.

CHAPTER THIRTEEN

The Greatness of Svāmipuṣkariṇī

THE STORY OF DHARMAGUPTA

Śrī Sūta said:

1. I shall recount the greatness of Svāmitīrtha once again out of respect for you all, O residents of Naimiṣa forest.

2. There was a great king named Nanda. He was born of the Lunar race. He ruled righteously over this oceangirt earth.

3-4a. He had a son who is remembered by the name Dharmagupta. Nanda entrusted the burden of protection of the kingdom to his son. The old king who had controlled his sense-organs and mastered (craving for) food entered a penance grove.

4b-5. When the father had gone to the penance grove, the king named Dharmagupta protected the earth. He was conversant with virtue (*Dharma*). He was skilled in statesmanship. He worshipped Devas, the chief of whom is Indra, by means of many kinds of Yajñas.

6-7a. To Brāhmaṇas he gave monetary gifts and land grants. When that king was ruling, all the people were devoted to their duties. There were no depredations of thieves etc. in that kingdom.

7b-10. Once Dharmagupta mounted his excellent horse, O eminent Brāhmaṇas, eager to go ahunting. He roamed about in the forest very terrible due to lions and tigers. The quarters in the forest were covered with Tamāla (Indian Cinnamon), Tāla (palm tree), Hintāla (marshy date tree) and Kurabaka (red amaranth). The spaces in between the cardinal points echoed with the humming sound of the swarms of inebriated bees. All the lakes in the forest were full of water and abounded in golden lotuses, white lotuses, blue lotuses and water lilies. There were many ascetics who graced the forest.

11. While king Dharmagupta roamed about in the forest, O Brāhmaṇas, night befell him enveloping all the surrounding quarters with darkness.

12. The king endowed with humility performed the evening

prayer (Sandhyā) in the forest and repeated the Gāyatrī Mantra, the mother of the Vedas.

13-14. Afraid of lions, tigers and other (wild animals) the prince resorted to a tree. A certain bear that was frightened of a lion came near the prince. A certain lion roaming in the forest chased the bear. The bear chased by the lion came to the tree and climbed it.

15. On climbing the tree the bear saw the king of noble soul and great strength and exploit perched on the tree.

16-18. On seeing him the wild bear said to the king: "O eminent king, do not be afraid. Let us both stay here the whole of the night. A lion of very huge body with great strength and large curved teeth has come to the foot of the tree. He is excessively terrible. During the first half of the night you may go to sleep being protected by me. I will remain awake. Thereafter, O king of great intellect, protect me as I sleep during the later half of the night."

19. On hearing his words the son of Nanda went to sleep. Then the lion told the bear, "Let this king who is asleep be given away to me."

20. The bear who was conversant with virtue said to the lion, O excellent Brāhmaṇas: "You do not know righteousness, O king of beasts roaming in the forest.

21. Those who are guilty of breach of trust will face great difficulties in the world. The sins of those who are treacherous to friends cannot be destroyed even by means of ten thousand Yajñas.

22. One can somehow expiate for all the sins such as that of Brāhmaṇa-slaughter etc., but the sin of the treacherous ones will not perish even after crores of rebirths.

23. O lion, I do not consider Meru too heavy to the surface of the earth. I consider a treacherous fellow burdensome and very heavy (to the earth)."

24-27. On being told thus by the bear the lion kept quiet. When Dharmagupta woke up, the bear went to sleep on the tree. Thereupon, the lion spoke to the king, "Give away this bear to me." On being told thus by the lion the king unhesitatingly dropped to the ground that bear that had gone to sleep placing its head on his lap! While being dropped down by the king, the bear supported himself by holding on to the tree. Fortunately he did not fall on the ground from the tree. Then the bear approached the king and angrily spoke these words:

28. "O king, I am a scion of the family of Bhṛgu. My name is Dhyānakāṣṭha. I can assume any form I wish. I have assumed this form of a bear.

29. Why did you let me down while I was asleep though I am devoid of any sin, O king? By my curse you shall instantly become insane. You will be roaming about over the earth."

30. After cursing the king thus the sage spoke to the lion: "You are not (really) a lion. You are a great Yakṣa, a minister of Kubera.

31. Out of your ignorance once you joyously sported about in the company of women in the presence of Gautama on the mountain Himavān.

32. By chance Gautama came out of his hut to fetch sacrificial twigs. On seeing you naked he pronounced a curse:

33. 'Since you remained in my hermitage today without any clothes on, you will undoubtedly be turned into a lion today.'

34. Formerly you were a Yakṣa and a minister of Kubera named Bhadra. It was through the curse of Gautama that you obtained the form of a lion.

35. Indeed Kubera is by nature righteous. His servants too are like him. Hence why do you kill me, a sage and resident of the forest?

36-37. O lord of beasts, I know all this through the power of meditation."

On being told thus by Dhyānakāṣṭha he immediately abandoned the form of lion and resumed the form of Yakṣa, the minister of Kubera. With palms joined in reverence he bowed down to sage Dhyānakāṣṭha and said:

38-42a. "O great sage, today all those previous events have been recollected by me. At the time of cursing me Gautama had mentioned about the end of the curse as well. Gautama, the eminent sage, had said to me thus, O Brāhmaṇa: 'When you carry on a conversation with Dhyānakāṣṭha in the form of a bear, you will get rid of this form of lion and will regain the form of Yakṣa.' Since my form of lion has been destroyed now, I know you, O great sage, as the pure ascetic named Dhyānakāṣṭha who can always assume any form he likes."

After saying this, the eminent Yakṣa bowed down to Dhyānakāṣṭha, got into an excellent aerial chariot and went to Alakāpurī.

42b-43. On seeing the excellent king in the form of a mad man the ministers took him to his father's presence on the banks of Revā. To him they intimated the mental derangement of his son.

At the Instance of Jaimini Dharmagupta Takes His Holy Bath in Svāmitīrtha whereby His Madness Disappears

44-46. After knowing the account of his son, Nanda, the father, took the son immediately to the presence of Jaimini. To him he reported the story of the son from the beginning:

"O Holy Lord Jaimini, my son has become insane now. O great sage, tell me the means of curing his madness."

47. On being requested thus, Jaimini, the eminent sage, meditated for a long time. After meditating long he said to king Nanda:

48. "It was on account of the curse of Dhyānakāṣṭha that your son became mad. I shall tell you the means of getting liberated from his curse.

49-53a. On the sacred mountain Veṅkaṭādri which is destructive of all sins and consists of many kinds of minerals, on the banks of Suvarṇamukharī there is a very great Tīrtha named Svāmipuṣkariṇī. It is the holiest of holy Tīrthas; it is the most auspicious of all auspicious places. It is mentioned in the Vedas; it is highly meritorious; it dispels the (great) sins like Brāhmaṇa-slaughter etc. O highly intelligent one, take your son there and make him bathe therein. Immediately his madness will disappear. There is no doubt about that."

On being told thus Nanda bowed down to Jaimini, the eminent sage, took his son and went to Svāmipuṣkariṇī.

53b-57. There he made his son take his bath with the requisite holy observances. Merely by taking his bath the son got rid of his madness instantaneously. King Nanda too took his holy bath in the waters of Svāmipuṣkariṇī.

Along with his son, the father stayed there for a day, worshipping Veṅkaṭeśa, Śrīnivāsa, the storehouse of mercy. Nanda took leave of his son and went to the forest for penance.

After the father had departed the son, king Dharmagupta, offered much wealth devoutly to Veṅkaṭeśa, O Brāhmaṇas. He gave money, foodgrains and land to Brāhmaṇas.

58-60. Thereafter, he went to his city along with his ministers. He righteously protected the kingdom inherited from his father and grandfather and rendered it devoid of thorns (i.e. enemies and troubles). O Brāhmaṇas, Dharmagupta was highly virtuous.

Those man who are afflicted with madness, epileptic fits, evil spirits etc., O eminent Brāhmaṇas, shall be liberated from them by taking the holy bath here in Puṣkariṇī. It is the truth, truth alone that I speak.

61. He who goes to another Tīrtha abandoning Svāmipuṣkariṇī, leaves off the tasty cow's milk and requests for the juice of spurge (i.e. a kind of plant having milky juice).

62-64. All those men who take their bath in any water anywhere repeating (the name) 'Svāmitīrtha' three times, O Brāhmaṇas, will go to Brahmā's region.

Thus, O Brāhmaṇas, the auspicious story of Dharmagupta has been related to you. Merely by listening to this the sin of Brāhmaṇa-slaughter perishes.

CHAPTER FOURTEEN

The Greatness of Svāmipuṣkariṇī (continued)

The Story of a Brāhmaṇa Named Sumati

Śrī Sūta said:

1-2. O ascetics, O ye all residents of Naimiṣa forest, I shall recount once more the greatness of Svāmitīrtha. Formerly, on account of his association with a Kirātī ('huntress') Sumati, a Brāhmaṇa, drank liquor. He took his bath in Puṣkariṇī and was liberated from the sin.

The sages asked:

3-4. Whose son was Sumati? How did he come (i.e. become addicted) to drink liquor? How was he enamoured of a Kirāta woman? O Sūta, the most excellent one among those conversant with the Purāṇas, kindly narrate this now in detail to us all.

Śrī Sūta said:

5-6. In the land named Mahārāṣṭra there was an orthodox Brāhmaṇa well-known as Yajñadeva. He was a master of the Vedas and Vedāṅgas. He was very compassionate, hospitable to guests and a regular worshipper of Śiva and Nārāyaṇa. That Yajñadeva had a son named Sumati.

7. He left his father and deserted his chaste wife. Devoted to an assembly of lecherous persons, he went to the Utkala land (Orissa).

8. In that land there lived a Kirāta woman (a Kirātī) who was young and of enchanting beauty. For a long time she tempted young men and took away all their wealth.

9. Sumati, the base Brāhmaṇa, went to her house. That huntress (Kirātī) caught hold of Sumati, (though) he was a Brāhmaṇa without wealth.

Due to His Association with the Kirātī the Brāhmaṇa Named Sumati Incurs a Great Sin

10-12. Sumati associated with her. He was solely interested in sexual union with her. From here and there he stole many things and much wealth and always handed them over to her. He sported with her for a long time. He took food in her house. He drank liquor along with her from the same goblet. Sporting about thus with her for a long time, eagerly engaged in sensual pleasures, he never remembered his parents or wife.

13. Once he went to the house of a certain Brāhmaṇa to commit theft along with the Kirātas. He too assumed the guise of a Kirāta.

14-15. He was rash and ferocious. With a sword in his hand he went to steal his wealth. With his sword he killed the master of that house, took away plenty of wealth and went to the house of the Kirātī.

The terrible, hideous, evil spirit of the sin of Brāhmaṇa-slaughter followed him as he proceeded ahead.

16. Clad in dark-blue clothes, the terrible spirit with extremely red hair roared boisterously shaking heaven and earth.

17-18. Chased by the ogress, he wandered over the whole of the earth. Thus roaming over the entire earth once Sumati went to his own village. The evil Brāhmaṇa of vicious soul was frightened on being chased by that evil spirit. He went into his own house.

19. The devil of the sin of Brāhmaṇa-slaughter pursued him and went to the house along with him. Saying "Save me, save me", Sumati sought refuge in his father.

20. Saying to him, "Do not be afraid", the father exerted himself to protect him. At that time Brahmahatyā spoke to his father:

Brahmahatyā said:

21-22. O Yajñadeva, O excellent Brāhmaṇa, do not accept him. He is a drink-addict. He is a thief. He is murderer of a Brāhmaṇa. He is a great sinner. He is antagonistic to his mother and father, a deserter of his wife. He is a sinner. He is defiled due to his association with a Kirātī. Leave him off. He is vicious.

23-24. If you agree to protect, O Brāhmaṇa, this son who is a great sinner, I will devour your wife, his wife, you as well as this son, O Brāhmaṇa. I will devour the whole family. Hence leave this son off. If you leave this son off, I will release all of you now.

25. It does not behove you, O highly intelligent one, to get the whole family destroyed for the sake of one member.

On being told thus by her, Yajñadeva spoke to her:

Yajñadeva said:

26. Affection for my son afflicts me. How can I forsake him?

On hearing that utterance of the Brāhmaṇa Brahmahatyā spoke to him:

Brahmahatyā said:

27-29. He has become fallen. He has been banished from the social system of castes and stages of life. Do not show any affection to this son. Even his sight is censurable.

After saying this, even as Yajñadeva was looking, that Brahmahatyā struck his son named Sumati with her palm. Crying out "O father, O father" he lamented much.

Means of Getting Free from Brahmahatyā Suggested to Sumati by Durvāsas

30-31. The father, mother and wife of Sumati lamented then.

In the meantime the great Yogī Durvāsas, the virtuous and excellent sage, a part of Śaṅkara himself, fortunately came there. On seeing that sage, the incarnation of Rudra, Yajñadeva eulogized and bowed to him. On behalf of his son he begged of him an asylum:

32-37. "O great Yogin, O Durvāsas, you are a part of Śaṅkara himself. Persons devoid of merit will never have a vision of yours. My son is slayer of a Brāhmaṇa, a drink-addict and a thief. Even the ogress of the sin of Brāhmaṇa-slaughter has come to strike him down. Tell me the means whereby this son of mine shall be rid of the great sins and this terrible Brahmahatyā shall cease to be (i.e. to torment him) quickly. Take pity on my son. He is the only son of mine, O sage. I have no other son. If he dies, my family will become extinct and uprooted. There will not be anyone to offer riceballs to the Manes. So, O holy lord, O sage, take pity on us."

38. On being told thus, Durvāsas, a part of Śaṅkara, meditated for a long time and said to Yajñadeva, the most excellent Brāhmaṇa:

Durvāsas said:

39. O Yajñadeva, an extremely terrible sin has been committed by your son. His sin cannot be expiated even by ten thousand modes of expiation.

40. Still I shall suggest an atonement for the suppression of that sin of your son. O Brāhmaṇa, listen (carefully) with your mind not distracted by anything else.

41. On the highly meritorious mountain Veṅkaṭādri which is destructive of all sins, there is a lake named Svāmipuṣkariṇī that bestows auspiciousness.

42-43. If your son takes his bath there he shall be rid of sins instantaneously.

Sumati Liberated from Brahmahatyā Through Holy Bath in Svāmipuṣkariṇī

On hearing these words of the sage Yajñadeva of great intellect took his son and went to Svāmipuṣkariṇī. He made his son bathe there—his son Sumati who was tormented by the evil spirit of the sin of Brāhmaṇa-slaughter.

44-45. A sweet-toned ethereal voice said to the Brāhmaṇa:

"O Yajñadeva of good holy rites, O Brāhmaṇa of exalted magnificence, your son has become purified by means of this holy bath. O Brāhmaṇa, do not entertain any doubt. That Tīrtha has a power of this sort. It is an axe unto the tree of sins."

46. Thus, O Brāhmaṇas, the ancient legend has been recounted to you all. It yields the benefit of a Vājapeya sacrifice to those who listen and read.

CHAPTER FIFTEEN

The Greatness of Rāmakṛṣṇa Tīrtha

Śrī Sūta said:

1-3. Listen with great concentration (of mind) to the greatness of Kṛṣṇa Tīrtha located on the mountain named Veṅkaṭa that is highly meritorious and destructive of all sins.

By merely taking the bath here even an ungrateful person will be liberated (from sins). All those persons who insult and dishonour fathers, mothers, preceptors and elders, those who are deluded, those who are wicked in their minds, and others who are ungrateful and shameless, become purified merely by bathing in this Kṛṣṇa Tīrtha.

4-5. Formerly there lived a sage named Kṛṣṇa on the mountain named Veṅkaṭa. He was engaged in penance. He meditated on Viṣṇu with great concentration. It was he who made a Tīrtha for the purpose of bathing. It is an excellent Tīrtha. By taking bath there even once even an ungrateful man becomes liberated.

6. In this connection I shall recount the ancient legend that is destructive of sins. Merely by listening to it a man attains salvation.

7-8. Formerly there was a prominent Brāhmaṇa named Rāmakṛṣṇa. He was a great sage. He was of good conduct and habits. He was truthful and eloquent. He was endowed with kindness for all living beings. He behaved impartially towards enemies as well as friends. He had perfect control over his sense-organs. He was an ascetic who had conquered his senses. He was an expert in the knowledge of the Supreme Brahman. He resorted solely to Brahman.

9-12a. That sage of such a magnanimity performed a very severe penance. He was motionless in every limb wherever he stood on the surface of the earth. He did not move even to the extent of an atom from his position.

He stood there and performed penance for many hundreds of years. An anthill was formed over him and it covered all his body. Though the whole of his body was thus covered by the anthill, Rāmakṛṣṇa, the great sage, went on with his penance and was not aware of the anthill.

12b-15. While he was performing the penance, Vāsava (the Rain-god) let loose groups of clouds and showered heavily on the great sage. Thus he continuously showered for seven days. Though he was showered with great torrential downpour, the sage received that shower (quietly) with closed eyes. Deafening the ears with loud rattling and rumbling of the clouds, a great thunderbolt fell upon the anthill.

The Lord Delighted by the Penance of the Great Sage Rāmakṛṣṇa Appears Before Him

16-18. While the Lord of Clouds showered rain unbearable due to cool winds etc., the top of the anthill crumbled on being struck by the thunderbolt. Then the Lord holding the conch, the discus and the iron club manifested himself. He was seated on Garuḍa and was adorned with garlands of sylvan flowers. Being pleased with the penance of Rāmakṛṣṇa, he spoke these words:

19-21a. "O Rāmakṛṣṇa, O storehouse of penance, O master of the contents of the Vedas and Śāstras (scriptural texts), an excellent man who takes bath (in the Tīrtha) on the day of my manifestation (attains great merit). The benefit and merit that he gets cannot be recounted even by Śeṣa. It is laid down that the time for the holy bath, O Brāhmaṇa, is when the Sun is in the Zodiac Capricorn, on the great lunar day of Full Moon in conjunction with the constellation Puṣya.

21b-24. A man of great intellect who bathes in Kṛṣṇatīrtha on that day shall get rid of all sins. He shall obtain all desires. Devas, human beings and all the Guardians of the Quarters with great prowess arrive there in order to take their holy bath in the auspicious waters of Kṛṣṇatīrtha and for the sake of washing off their sins.

All these noble souls gain lustre similar to that of crores of suns. Indeed they all become purified through the bath in this Tīrtha.

25. This great Tīrtha shall be named after you. It will become very famous in the world."

After saying this Śrīnivāsa vanished there itself.

26-27. Of such power is that Tīrtha. It dispels great sins. It bestows purity of intellect on men. It grants all prosperity and magnificence.

Thus, O Brāhmaṇas, the greatness of Kṛṣṇatīrtha has been recounted to you. It enables those who listen to and read this (account) to attain the world of Viṣṇu.

CHAPTER SIXTEEN

The Merit of Making a Gift of Water

Praise of the Gift of Water on Śrīveṅkaṭādri

Śrī Sūta said:

1. One who does not offer water particularly to the thirsty on the highly meritorious mountain named Veṅkaṭa shall be born amongst lower animals.

2. Hence on the prominent mountain Veṅkaṭa a gift of water should be made in accordance with one's capacity. It is a great thing that instils life in all.

3. In this connection they cite this ancient legendary story of an exceedingly wonderful conversation between a Brāhmaṇa and a house-lizard.

Hemāṅga Becomes a House-Lizard for not Offering Water

4. Formerly there was a king named Hemāṅga in the family of Ikṣvāku. He was hospitable to Brāhmaṇas and deeply engrossed in meditation on Brahman. He had conquered enemies and had perfect control over his sense-organs.

5. He had gifted away as many cows as there are particles of earth, drops of water or stars in the sky.

6. The earth is known as *Barhiṣmatī* ('abounding in Darbha grass') on account of the Darbha grass used (and strewn in) the Yajñas performed by him. Many Brāhmaṇas had been satisfied by him through the gift of cows, lands, gingelly seeds, gold etc.

7. It is heard (i.e. reported) that there are no (kinds of) gift not distributed by him. But, O Brāhmaṇas, water was not given by him because he thought that it was easily available.

8-9. When urged by Vasiṣṭha, the noble-souled son of Brahmā, he viciously argued, "It is worthless. It is available everywhere. What benefit can accrue to the donor who gifts it?"

The lord of dull understanding still did not offer water. He reasoned thus, 'There shall be merit in gifting away what is rare to get.'

10. He adored and worshipped Brāhmaṇas who were mutilated or physically handicapped in one or more limbs and who were poor and unable to sustain themselves for want of means of livelihood. He did not honour Brāhmaṇas well-versed in the Vedas, who were knowers and expounders of Brahman:

11-12. 'All people will worship renowned persons with due veneration and honour. But what about helpless persons, persons devoid of learning, persons with defective limbs and poor householders? So they are the objects of my mercy.'[1] Thus he gave whatever he possessed to (physically) defective recipients.

13-15. On account of that great sin he was born as a *Cātaka* bird in three births, as a vulture in one birth and as a dog in seven births. Afterwards this king became a house-lizard, O Brāhmaṇa, in the abode of Śrutakīrti, a king of Mithilā.

He lived in the street near the threshold of that king feeding himself on insects and worms. That wicked soul thus lived for eighty-eight years.

Hemāṅga Recollects the Previous Birth as a Result of Being Sprinkled with Water with which the Feet of Śrutadeva were Washed

16. Once an excellent sage well-known as Śrutadeva came to the abode of the king of Videha at midday. He was utterly tired then.

1. The Purāṇa is advocating a strange doctrine. Instead of appreciating the humanitarian attitude of the king in helping the helpless and physically handicapped people, he is made a house-lizard. Probably scarcity of water on the Veṅkaṭa hill in summer may be the reason for inventing the story to persuade people to make arrangement of potable water on the Tirupati hill.

17-18. On seeing him the king was much delighted. He got up instantaneously with *Madhuparka* (i.e. respectable offerings to an honoured guest); he received him respectfully. The water with which his feet were washed, was sprinkled by the king over his own head. As fate had destined its timing, some of the drops of that water thus sprinkled fell on that house-lizard.

19. Immediately the lizard remembered the previous births. It was dejected on account of what had been committed. "Save me, save me", cried it aloud to the Brāhmaṇa who had come to the house.

20-21. On hearing the sound of a lowly creature the Brāhmaṇa became surprised. (He said,) "Whence do you cry, O lizard? What was that action that has resulted in this plight of yours? Are you a god or a demi-god, or a king, or an excellent Brāhmaṇa? O highly fortunate one, who are you? Tell me. I shall redeem you today."

22-27. On being told thus the king told Śrutadeva: "I was a great king born of the family of Ikṣvāku. I was an expert in the art of wielding weapons. I had gifted away as many cows as there are dust particles on the earth, drops of water in the ocean and stars in the sky.

I had performed all sorts of Yajñas. I had arranged for *Pūrtas* (i.e. works of public welfare, viz. building of rest-houses, tanks etc.) as well. Many gifts were offered by me. Pious rites were well-performed. Despite that I have fallen in a hellish condition, O holy lord; I have not attained heavenly worlds.

Three times I was born as a *Cātaka* bird, once as a vulture and as a dog in seven births. While this king was sprinkling the water with which your feet were washed over his head, a few drops were scattered away. I was sprinkled somehow with them. Thereby my sins were destroyed and I recollected previous births.

28-29. O Brāhmaṇa, I have yet to take twenty-eight births as a house-lizard. They are ordained by fate. I am much afraid of those (too) many births. I do not see the reason thereof. Explain to me that in detail."

On being requested thus the Brāhmaṇa told him what was seen by him through the eye of perfect knowledge.

Hemāṅga is Liberated from the State of House-Lizard Through the Merit Offered by Śrutadeva

30-31. "Listen, O king, I shall tell the reason for your miserable plight. Water was not offered by you on the mountain named Veṅkaṭa. Thinking that water is easily available, you came to the conclusion that it had no value. Ignorant that you were, you did not give water to Brāhmaṇas and other wayfarers even during the summer season.

32-35. You left out deserving persons and showered gifts on the undeserving. *Homa* is not performed on the ash after setting aside the blazing fire. Is the holy basil plant abandoned and the eggplant worshipped? The state of being helpless, mutilated or completely devoid of limbs cannot be the ground (of charitable gifts). The lame one and others who are helpless are only objects of compassion.

Those who are engaged in penance, those who possess knowledge (of the Supreme Being) and those who are devoted to Śrutis and Śāstras are persons in the form of Viṣṇu. They are always to be worshipped and never the others. There too the *Jñānins* (i.e. persons with spiritual knowledge) are extremely dear to and favourites of Viṣṇu always.

36. O king, even to the persons with knowledge it is Viṣṇu alone who is the most favourite. Hence a person with knowledge is always worthy of being worshipped. It is laid down in Smṛtis that he is more venerable than the most venerable ones.

37. Water was not offered nor good men were served by you. Therefore, you attained this miserable plight, O scion of the family of Ikṣvākus.

38. I shall give you the merit acquired on the Veṅkaṭa mountain for the quelling of your (sinful) Karmas, past, present and future by means of that."

39-40. After saying this, he touched water and bequeathed his excellent merit of the holy bath performed (by him) on one day. With what was given by the Brāhmaṇa all its (house-lizard's) sins were destroyed. Hence the house-lizard abandoned the terrible form befitting its action. Immediately a man was seen (there).

41-42. He was seated in a divine aerial chariot. He wore

divine garlands and garments as well as ornaments. Even as good men were watching within the abode of the king of Mithilā, he joined his palms in reverence, circumambulated and bowed down (to the Brāhmaṇa). On being permitted the king (started from there) and went to heaven, eulogized by the immortal ones.

43-47. There he enjoyed great pleasures for ten thousand years without any weariness. He himself was reborn as the mighty warrior Kakutstha[1] in the family of Ikṣvāku. That great king was the protector of the seven continents. He was hospitable to Brāhmaṇas and honoured by good men. He was on a par with Devendra and was a part of Viṣṇu.

Enlightened by Vasiṣṭha he performed all the good holy rites and thereby destroyed all inauspiciousness etc. He acquired divine knowledge and attained *Sāyujya* (identity) with Viṣṇu.

Hence Veṅkaṭa mountain is meritorious and destructive of sins. Offering water therein bestows the world of Viṣṇu.

Thus, O Brāhmaṇa, the importance of the gift of water on the highly meritorious Veṅkaṭādri which is destructive of all sins, has been recounted by me.

CHAPTER SEVENTEEN

The Greatness of Veṅkaṭācala

A Description of the Holy Place Śrī Veṅkaṭācala

Śrī Sūta said:

1. I shall once again relate the greatness of Veṅkaṭādri to you all. Listen with great concentration and mental purity.

2. All the Tīrthas on the earth as well as within the universe are present on the mountain named Veṅkaṭa.

1. A famous king of the Solar race. His real name was Purañjaya. He promised to help Indra against Asuras provided he carried him on his shoulders. Indra assumed the form of a bull. Purañjaya occupied the bull (Indra) and defeated the demons. Hence he became known as *Kakutstha*, 'the occupant of the hump' (*Vide Raghuvaṁśa* 6.71).

3-6. Devas, Sages, Siddhas, Sanaka and other Yogins, the people of the regions Aṅga, Kosala, Karṇāṭa, Kāśī, Gurjara, Cola, Kerala, Pāṇḍya and all other lands visit this place along with their families to serve every year Lord Puruṣottama living on that excellent mountain. The Lord holds the conch and discus. He wears the splendid yellow robe. His chest is adorned with Kaustubha jewel. He gives immunity from fear to the devotees. The Lord of Devas has large eyes. He is the eternal Lord who can be known only through the Vedas.

7. Those who visit the shrine in the month of Bhādrapada at the time of the great festival of Veṅkaṭeśa shall be free from sins. They will be the most excellent among excellent ones.

8-10a. Brahmā, the grandfather of the world, celebrated the great festival of hoisting the flag of Śrī Veṅkaṭeśa in the month (when the Sun was in the Zodiac) of Kanyā (Virgo). Every year for the sake of visiting the Lord at the time of Brahmotsava[1] of the Lord, all human beings, all Devas, Gandharvas, Siddhas and Sādhyas of great prowess gather there, O excellent Brāhmaṇas.

10b-11. Just as the Vedic lore is the best among all lores, Praṇava (*Oṁ*) among all Mantras, life (vital air) among all the dearest objects and the Wish-yielding Cow among all the cows, so the great mountain of Veṅkaṭa is the most excellent one among all sacred places.

12. The great mountain of Veṅkaṭa is the most excellent one among holy spots like Śeṣa among all serpents, Garuḍa among all birds, like Viṣṇu among Devas and Brāhmaṇa among all castes.

13-16. The prominent mountain of Veṅkaṭa is the most excellent one among holy spots. Like the divine tree among trees, like wife among intimate associates, like Gaṅgā among Tīrthas and like Ravi (Sun) among luminaries, the great mountain Veṅkaṭa is the most excellent one among holy spots.

---

1. This is the most important festival of god Veṅkaṭeśvara. It is celebrated in the month of Śrāvaṇa (August-September). For its description cf. VrP II. 50-53. It is called Brahmotsava as it is believed to have been started by god Brahmā. Historically it started in CE 966 through the donation of the Pallava Queen Samavāi. Royal dynasties of the South generously supported this celebration.

Like Vajra (thunderbolt) among weapons, like gold among metals, like Rudra among the followers of Viṣṇu and like Kaustubha among jewels, the great mountain Veṅkaṭa is the most excellent among holy spots. There is nothing else like this which increases the pleasure of Viṣṇu.

17-20. There is no other month like the month of Mādhava. There is no other Yuga equal to Kṛta. There is no scripture like the Vedas. There is no Tīrtha equal to Gaṅgā. There is no other gift equal to that of water. There is no pleasure equal to that of wife. There is no wealth on a par with agriculture. There is no other profit greater than life. There is no penance greater than fasting. There is no happiness greater than charitable gift. There is no other virtue on a par with mercifulness. There is no other luminary equal to the eye. There is no satisfaction on a par with eating food. There is no trade on a par with agriculture. There is no friend equal to Dharma. There is no fame equal to *Satya* (truthfulness).

21. Just like all these cited above, there is nothing equal to the abode of the Lord (Veṅkaṭeśa).

22. The chief of mountains named Veṅkaṭa is such a great holy spot, O eminent sages, the glorification (of which) dispels all sins. Salutation to it bestows all types of happiness in the world. The pilgrimage to it is worthy of being worshipped by Suras.

23-25. I again emphatically tell its greatness: All the Tīrthas reside there. Thus among all of them the chief Tīrtha is the lake named Śrīsvāmi (i.e. Svāmipuṣkariṇī).

How is its greatness to be described by me? On its western bank shines Bhūvarāha (Boar idol), the gentle idol in the act of embracing his beloved. He helps all the people of the world.

On the southern bank of Śrīsvāmipuṣkariṇī perpetually resides Veṅkaṭeśvara, the bestower of boons, with his body embraced by Lakṣmī.

26. Thus, O Brāhmaṇas, the excellent greatness of the holy spot has been narrated to you. He who listens to this always is honoured in the world of Viṣṇu.

CHAPTER EIGHTEEN

The Glory of Śrī Veṅkaṭeśvara

Śrī Sūta said:

1. Now I shall recount the greatness of Veṅkaṭeśvara, on hearing which one becomes liberated from all sins. There is no doubt about it.

2. One who visits even once Lord Śrī Veṅkaṭeśvara attains salvation. He shall attain *Sāyujya* with Viṣṇu.

3-4. The merit that is acquired in the course of ten years in Kṛtayuga, is achieved by men in Tretā in a single year, in Dvāpara in five months and in Kaliyuga in a single day. The benefit thereof to men is increased by crores moment after moment.

5. Undoubtedly this shall happen in the case of those who visit Śrīnivāsa. All the Tīrthas are present in Lord Śrī Veṅkaṭeśvara.

6-7. All Devas, sages and Manes are present there.

Those who remember the great Lord, the bestower of liberation, Lord Śrīnivāsa, once, twice or thrice a day or always, or those who glorify him, O Brāhmaṇas, are liberated from the cage of sins.

8. They go to Nārāyaṇa, the great Lord, Veṅkaṭeśa whose body consists of existence, knowledge and bliss and who was worshipped by Śaṅkharāja.

9-11. Merely by remembering him no torture by Yama will take place.

If men worship, even once, the great Lord Śrīnivāsa, of what avail are charitable gifts, holy rites, penances and sacrifices.

If a person does not contemplate upon the great Lord Veṅkaṭeśa even for a moment, he is ignorant; he is a sinner; he is dumb and deaf; he should be known as sluggish and blind. He will always have vulnerable points.

12. O eminent sages, if Śrīnivāsa, the great Lord, is visited once (only), of what avail is going on (the pilgrimage of) Kāśī, Gayā and Prayāga?

13-16. After obtaining the rare humanbirth, if men on the earth visit or worship the great Lord Veṅkaṭeśa, their birth has become fruitful; they alone are blessed and not others. If Veṅkaṭeśa, the great Lord, is visited or worshipped, of what avail are Śaṁbhu, Brahmā, Śakra or all the Immortal Ones? Those men who are endowed with devotion to Veṅkaṭeśa, the great Lord, although they bow down, remember or worship those mentioned previously, do not experience miseries; they do not go to the abode of Yama.

17. Thousands of the sins of Brāhmaṇa-slaughter and ten thousands of the sins of drinking liquor dissolve entirely, if Lord Nārāyaṇa is seen.

18. If people wish for perpetual happiness and kingdom in heaven, let them joyously bow down at least once to the Lord residing on Veṅkaṭādri.

19. Whatever may be the sins committed in the course of crores of births, all of them perish by visiting Veṅkaṭeśvara.

20. If anyone remembers Veṅkaṭeśa, the great Lord, on account of his association with other people, or out of curiosity, or due to covetousness or on account of fear, he shall not be miserable here or hereafter.

21. One who glorifies and worships the Lord of Devas on Veṅkaṭācala shall certainly attain *Sārūpya* with Viṣṇu. There is no doubt about it.

22. Just as a well-kindled fire reduces firewood to ash in a moment, so also a visit to Veṅkaṭeśa destroys all sins.

23-27a. Devotion to Lord Veṅkaṭeśvara is said to be of eight types:[1] (1) Tenderness towards those people who are devotees of Veṅkaṭeśvara; (2) Complete satisfaction (on witnessing) the worship of Veṅkaṭeśvara; (3) Devoutly worshipping the Lord oneself; (4) Physical activity for the sake of the Lord; (5) Desire and respectful eagerness to listen to stories of the greatness of the Lord; (6) Excessive emotional excitement manifested in tone, eyes and all parts of the body; (7) Continuous recollection of Lord Śrīnivāsa; and (8) Maintenance of oneself solely depending upon that Lord, the resident of Veṅkaṭādri.

---

1. This list is different from the standard nine types of devotion like *Śravaṇa* (Listening). *Kīrtana* (Glorification), *Smaraṇa* (Remembrance) and others. There is a some overlapping here.

O Śaunaka and other sages of great prowess, if this eight-fold devotion is present in any one, he alone will attain salvation even if he be a Mleccha (Barbarian).

27b-29. Salvation is certain through the knowledge of Brahman acquired by means of single-minded devotion and listening to the Vedānta in regard to ascetics who have sublimated their sexual urge.

O Brāhmaṇas, that very salvation can be acquired solely through visiting Lord Veṅkaṭeśvara by the people of all castes and stages in life without the knowledge arising through listening to the Upaniṣads, without being in the stage of anchorite and without even detachment (from worldly life).

30-34. Ere long one will have the salvation that bestows exemption from rebirth.

By the favour of Śrīnivāsa worms, insects, Devas, sages and ascetics are all equal (of the same status) on the prominent mountain of Veṅkaṭa.

Do not be afraid, thinking 'Many sins have been committed by me.' Let no one be proud, saying 'Meritorious deeds have been performed by me.'

When Veṅkaṭeśa, Śrīṇivāsa, the great Lord, is visited, no one shall be inferior or superior. All of them are great people.

If a person devoutly visits Śrīnivāsa, the great Lord, on the exceedingly meritorious (mountain) named Veṅkaṭa which is destructive of all sins, no one will be on a par with him in the world, even if a person has mastered all the four Vedas.

35. He who devoutly worships Veṅkaṭeśvara, the Lord of Devas, goes to Hari's abode along with a crore of the members of his family.

36-37. Nothing is equal or superior to Śrīnivāsa in meritoriousness.

If anyone out of delusion hates the Lord residing on Veṅkaṭādri, it means that ten thousand sins of Brahmin-slaughter have been committed by him causing fall into hell. Even by merely talking to him a man will fall into hell.

38. The Vedas are devoted to Śrīnivāsa. Sacrifices pertain to Śrīnivāsa. Everything is solely devoted to Śrīnivāsa. There is nothing other than Śrīnivāsa.

39-42a. One should forsake everything else and resort to Śrīnivāsa.

By rendering service to Śrīnivāsa one attains crores of times of the benefit accruing from performing all the Yajñas, penances, charitable gifts and holy baths in all the Tīrthas.

One who meditates on Veṅkaṭādrinivāsa for two *Ghaṭikās* (i.e. 48 minutes) shall sustain twenty-one generations of his family and is honoured in the world of Viṣṇu.

If holy bath in Svāmipuṣkariṇī Tīrtha and visit unto the Lord is performed by people, why should they resort to the waters of Gaṅgā?

42b-44a. If a person never visits Veṅkaṭeśa, the great Lord, he should be known as a person of mixed caste and not a person born of the seed of (his legal) father.

Hence, O Brāhmaṇas, by all efforts Veṅkaṭeśa, the storehouse of mercy, should be seen (visited) with a desire for the other world.

44b-45. Thus, O Brāhmaṇas, the greatness of Veṅkaṭeśa has been narrated to you.

He who devoutly listens to this always and reads it, shall obtain the benefit of the service unto Veṅkaṭanātha.

CHAPTER NINETEEN

The Greatness of Pāpavināśana Tīrtha[1]

PERMANENT RESIDENCE OF BRAHMĀ AND OTHERS ON ŚRĪ VEṄKAṬĀCALA

Śrī Sūta said:

1. Henceforth I shall recount the greatness of Veṅkaṭācala to you all. Listen with attention and a pure mind.

2. There are thousands, lakhs and crores of lakes and rivers, oceans of great merit, forests and hermitages.

1. This chapter states the procedure of the Yātrā of Veṅkaṭādri.

3. There are meritorious holy places like Vedāraṇya, Vasiṣṭha and other sages, Siddhas, Cāraṇas and Kinnaras.

4. Lord Madhusūdana (Viṣṇu) is present there along with Lakṣmī and Dharaṇī. The Four-faced Lord (Brahmā) (resides there) with Sāvitrī and Sarasvatī.

5. The Three-eyed Lord of Devas, the destroyer of Tripura (lives there) with Pārvatī. Heramba, Ṣaṇmukha and others, Devas with Indra as their leader (all these live there).

6. O Brāhmaṇas, Planets beginning with the Sun, the eight Vasus, Pitṛs and Guardians of the Worlds and other groups of Devas (reside there).

7. (All these) live day and night within Veṅkaṭācala and on its top, which is destructive of multitudes of great sins and a sanctifier of the worlds.

8-10. Merely by looking at it men can attain intelligence and happiness. The women-folk of Siddhas and Cāraṇas who have taken up residence on its top, always worship Veṅkaṭeśa, the storehouse of mercy. Crores of the sins of Brāhmaṇa-slaughter and crores of the sins of cohabiting with forbidden women perish when the winds from Veṅkaṭācala touch their limbs.

Time for Climbing Śrī Veṅkaṭācala and the Procedure of Meditating on it

11-13. A devotee should request the mountain Veṅkaṭādri which enhances merit: "O golden mountain of great merits, resorted to by all the Devas, even Brahmā and other Devas attend upon you with great faith. O excellent one among mountains! I am treading upon you (of such good qualities). Forgive me this one sin kindly, though I am evil-minded. Show me Mādhava who has taken up his residence on your top."

14. After praying thus the man (the devotee) should gently set his foot on Veṅkaṭādri, the most excellent one among mountains. He shall then gently walk over the sacred Veṅkaṭācala.

15-17. With the specific holy observances he should take bath in Svāmipuṣkariṇī Tīrtha on (mountain) Vaṅkaṭādri of great merits, which destroys all sins. Thereafter, he should offer rice-balls even if they be of the size of a mustard seed. Or he should offer rice-balls equal to the leaves of Śamī tree unto the Manes. Those who are stationed in heaven will attain salvation and those who are in hells will go to heaven.

Greatness of the Tīrtha Named Pāpavināśana

18-20. On the top of the extremely sacred and pure Veṅkaṭācala there is a great and sacred Tīrtha named Pāpavināśana. It is well-known in all the worlds. It is the most excellent of all the Tīrthas, O Brāhmaṇas. Merely by remembering it one will no longer have to enter a womb (i.e. one gets salvation). One (i.e. pilgrim) should go to it which is towards the north of Svāmitīrtha, and take his holy bath. By taking the holy bath there men go to Vaikuṇṭha. There is no doubt about it.

The sages requested:

21. O Sūta, recount the greatness of the Tīrtha called Pāpavināśa. O great sage, you have been enlightened by Vyāsa. Indeed you know everything.

Śrī Sūta said:

22. I shall recount to you all, O excellent Brāhmaṇas, the auspicious story of what happened in the penance-grove of Brahmā on the auspicious ridge of Himavān.

23. That penance-grove is sacred. Brahmā's penance-grove is very auspicious. It is full of trees of various kinds. It is situated on a beautiful side of Himavān.

24. It abounds in hedges and creepers. It is frequented by deer and elephants. It is resonant with the voices (talk, conversation etc.) of Siddhas and Cāraṇas. It is made beautiful due to the whole forest being in full bloom.

25-28. Many ascetics live sparsely in it. It is rendered splendid by sages. It is full of Brāhmaṇas of exalted magnificence, as resplendent as the sun and the fire. There are many anchorites staying there and they are richly endowed with holy rites and regular observances. There are many persons there regularly performing Yāgas with requisite initiation, who practised control over their diet and were self-possessed. It is surrounded by persons conversant with the Vedas and endowed with rich experience by the study of the Vedas. There are persons of all stages of life there, viz. religious students, householders, anchorites and mendicants, all of them strictly adhering to the duties of their stages and performing (all the rites) ordained for their respective castes. It is surrounded by Vālakhilyas and other sages.

The Episode of a Śūdra Named Dṛḍhamati

29-32. Once, O Brāhmaṇas, a certain Śūdra named Dṛḍhamati, a venturesome fellow, joyously came near the Brāhmaṇas in that hermitage.

On coming to the penance-grove he was duly honoured by the ascetics. (After announcing his) name Dṛḍhamati the Śūdra prostrated (before them) with the eight limbs touching (the ground).

On seeing those groups of sages who were on a par with Devas, who had great prowess and were performing different kinds of Yajñas, the Śūdra was much delighted.

He had an inclination to perform an excellent penance. He approached the sage and ascetic, the head of the penance-grove and said:

Dṛḍhamati said:

33. O ascetic, obeisance to you. Save me, O storehouse of sympathy. With your grace I wish to perform a Yāga (sacrifice). Be pleased with me.

The Duties of a Śūdra as Taught to Dṛḍhamati by the Sage Named Kulapati[1]

(*Kulapati said*:)

34-40. A Śūdra is of inferior birth. He cannot be initiated for the performance of a Yāga. So it is heard (i.e. mentioned in the Vedas). If you have the inclination, be engaged in rendering service.

Instructions cannot be imparted at any cost to one devoid of (high) caste. In case he is instructed, the teacher-priest incurs a great sin.

1. VV 34-44 describe the inhuman constraints on Śūdras. Even the knowledge of non-Vedic subjects like poetry, drama, rhetorics is denied to them. For more disabilities vide Kane, HD II. i. pp. 154-64.

No learned man should teach a Śūdra nor shall he preside over his Yāga. He should not teach a Śūdra any (sacred) science such as grammar etc. He should not directly teach a Śūdra poetry, drama, rhetorics, Purāṇa or Itihāsa. If any Brāhmaṇa instructs any Śūdra these subjects at any time, the other Brāhmaṇas must banish that Brāhmaṇa from the village full of Brāhmaṇas. One should abandon a Brāhmaṇa like a Cāṇḍāla if he teaches any Śūdra.

41-44. Therefore, welfare unto you. Render service to Brāhmaṇas with great faith. Rendering service to the Twice-born has been mentioned by Manu and others (as the duty) of a Śūdra. It does not behove you to forsake your natural duty.

On being told thus by the sage the Śūdra thought, 'What should be done by me now? My faith in the holy rites is very intense. I shall endeavour in such a way as to have perfect knowledge.'

After deciding thus mentally Dṛḍhamati, the Śūdra, went far away from the penance-grove and erected a splendid hut.

45-49. There he made a temple and many holy shrines, flower-garden etc. He got a big lake dug up. All these he set up for the sake of the performance of penance by himself.

He performed the rites of ablution and worshipped deities. He practised all holy observances such as fast etc.

He offered oblations and performed *Homas.* Regular in habits and mental resolve he sustained himself on a fruit diet. He conquered his sense organs. Everyday he honoured duly guests that approached him by means of bulbous roots, roots, flowers and fruits. Thus a great deal of time passed by.

Procedure for the Performance of Holy Rites as Revealed (Explained) to Dṛḍhamati by the Brāhmaṇa Named Sumati

50. Once a Brāhmaṇa named Sumati, born in the family of Garga, arrived at his hermitage. He (the Brāhmaṇa) was truthful in speech and had his sense-organs under control.

51. (Dṛḍhamati) propitiated the sage with words of welcome, made him delighted through (offer of) fruits and other things and enquired about his health in the course of narration of holy tales.

52-54. The Brāhmaṇa who was honoured by various services thus, such as offering water for washing and the like, accepted the same and felicitated him with blessings. Delighted in his mind, he took leave of him and went back to his own hermitage. Thus day by day the Brāhmaṇa became more and more favourably disposed to the Śūdra. He paid a visit to his hermitage in order to meet the Śūdra-born (sage). This association of the Brāhmaṇa with the Śūdra-born (sage) lasted for a long-time.

55. Being won over by affection, the Brāhmaṇa could not refuse what had been requested by the Śūdra. Once that Śūdra spoke to the Brāhmaṇa whom he had won over by means of affection. He said to him thus, when the Brāhmaṇa came to him:

56. "Tell me the injunctions regarding the offer of *Havyas* and *Kavyas.* You are considered to be my preceptor." On being requested thus by the Śūdra, he taught him everything.

57. He made the Śūdra perform the holy rites etc. unto the Manes. After the holy rites of Pitṛs (Manes) had been performed, that excellent Brāhmaṇa was sent away by him (with a farewell).

Miseries Undergone by Sumati due to His Imparting of Instructions in Vedic Rites to a Śūdra

58. The Brāhmaṇa was fed and nourished thus for a long time by the Śūdra-born sage. He was therefore excommunicated by Brāhmaṇas. Later he died.

59. He was carried away by the soldiers of Yama and cast into the hells (where he had to remain) for thousands of crores of Kalpas and hundreds of crores of Kalpas.

60. After undergoing the tortures of the hells one by one he became an immobile being. Afterwards he was born as a donkey and thereafter a pig feeding on faeces.

61. He was then born as a dog and he became a crow subsequently. Then he was born as a Cāṇḍāla and thereafter as a Śūdra.

62. Then he was born as a Vaiśya and thereafter as a Kṣatriya. Though obstructed by powerful agencies, he became a Brāhmaṇa thereafter.

63. He was invested with the sacred thread in the eighth year reckoned from the day of conception. Thus the Brāhmaṇa remained in his father's house engaged in the regular practice of rules of his caste.

64-65. Once while he was going through a forest, he was haunted by a Brahmarākṣasa (i.e. a Brāhmaṇa turned into a demon). He cried, whirled, faltered in his steps, prattled foolishly and laughed. Frequently he cried out "Alas! Alas!". He forsook all Vedic rites. On seeing his son in such a plight the father was distressed with agony.

66-67. He affectionately took his son and sought refuge in Agastya who was engaged in a penance in front of Śiva on the banks of Suvarṇamukharī. He devoutly bowed down to the sage. The father of that son reported to him all the actions of the son.

Sumati Goes to Veṅkaṭādri as per Advice of Agastya in Order to Dispel His Misery

68-71. Then the Brāhmaṇa told the great Pot-born Sage (Agastya): "O Brāhmaṇa, this my son has been possessed by a Brahmarākṣasa. He is not at all happy, O Brāhmaṇa. Protect him with your benign glance. I have no other son who could relieve me of my indebtedness to the Pitṛs. O Pot-born Sage, tell me the means whereby his pain and agony will be destroyed. There is no other person in the three worlds habitually engaged in penance like you. Excepting you there is no other person to protect my son. O Sire, take pity on my son. Indeed good people are by nature compassionate."

Śrī Sūta said:

72. On being told thus by him the Pot-born Sage began to meditate. After meditating for a long time he told the Brāhmaṇa:

Agastya said:

73. In his former birth, O highly intelligent one, this son of yours was a Brāhmaṇa named Sumati. That Brāhmaṇa imparted (sacred) knowledge to a Śūdra.

74-75. He instructed him in all the Vedic rites. So he had to undergo the tortures of hells for a period of one thousand crores of Kalpas. At the end of it he was born in various species beginning with immobile things. Now your son is born as a Brāhmaṇa on account of the balance of his (good) Karmas.

76. He has been possessed by a Brahmarākṣasa sent by Yama on account of the cruel sin committed by him in the previous birth.

77. I shall tell you the means of destroying the Brahmarākṣasa. Listen with an attentive mind and great faith.

78. On the banks of Suvarṇamukharī which is resorted to by multitudes of sages, there is the sacred Veṅkaṭācala worthy of being resorted to by Devas.

79. On it there is a great Tīrtha named Pāpavināśana. It is meritorious, famous and destructive of great sins.

80. That Tīrtha is known as the destroyer of evil spirits, ghosts and vampires, goblins and Brahmarākṣasas as well as of great ailments.

81. Take your son and go to that Tīrtha in the middle of the mountain. With great mental purity make your son take his bath in that Tīrtha which is destructive of sins.

82. By means of the holy bath taken on three (consecutive) days that Brahmarākṣasa will perish. There is no other means on the earth to destroy him.

83. Hence go quickly to that mountain named Veṅkaṭa. There make your son bathe in the Tīrtha named Pāpavināśa.

84-85. Do not delay here, O Brāhmaṇa, go there quickly.

On being told thus that Brāhmaṇa bowed down to Agastya and prostrated before him like a log of wood. Permitted by him the Brāhmaṇa went to Veṅkaṭācala along with his son and reached Pāpavināśana.

All the Miseries of Sumati Dispelled Through Holy Bath Taken in Pāpanāśana

86-89. With the rite of *Saṁkalpa* (i.e. ceremonial pronouncement of the decision to perform a religious act) he made the son take bath on three days. The eminent Brāhmaṇa, the father himself, took his bath in Pāpavināśana. After returning he drank water at the conclusion of the daily routine of holy rites. Thereupon his son was released by the Brahmarākṣasa.

He became free from ailments. He became normal with handsome form and features. Endowed with all flourishing riches, he enjoyed many kinds of pleasures. At the end of his life he attained salvation by virtue of his holy bath in Pāpavināśana. His father too, on account of his holy bath there, attained salvation after death.

Misery of Dṛḍhamati who Performed Vedic Rites is Dispelled

90-93. The Śūdra who had been instructed by him underwent the tortures of the hells one by one. Then he was born in many despicable low species. Afterwards he became a vulture on the mountain Veṅkaṭācala. Once he came to the Tīrtha Pāpavināśana in order to drink water. He drank water and sprinkled his own body (with it). At that very time he obtained a divine personality adorned with all ornaments. He got into a celestial aerial chariot and went to heaven.

Śrī Sūta said:

94-95. This Tīrtha, Pāpavināśana, has such power. O Brāhmaṇas, it has got the name Pāpanāśana because it is destructive of sins.

Thus the secret has been told, O eminent sages, of the greatness of Pāpavināśana. It is by means of their holy bath therein that (both) the Brāhmaṇa and the Śūdra of despicable actions became liberated instantaneously.

CHAPTER TWENTY

Merit from Gift of Lands

GREATNESS OF PĀPAVINĀŚANA TĪRTHA

Śrī Sūta said:

1. I shall recount again the greatness of Pāpanāśana. Listen with great concentration and feelings of devotion to the Lord.

2. I shall narrate a legendary story that is destructive of all sins, on hearing which one is absolved of all sins. There is no doubt about it.

THE EPISODE OF A POOR BRĀHMAṆA CALLED BHADRAMATI

3. Formerly there was an excellent Brāhmaṇa named Bhadramati. He was a master of the Vedas and Vedāṅgas, (but) he had no means of livelihood and was very poor.

4. All scriptures were learnt by that intelligent Brāhmaṇa. The Purāṇas and treatises on Dharma had been learnt by him in full.

5. He had six wives named Kṛtā, Sindhu, Yaśovatī, Kāminī, Mālinī and Śobhā.

6. Of those wives he had two hundred sons. All of them—his sons and others—were afflicted with hunger.

7. On seeing his dear sons tormented with hunger and his beloved wives in great distress due to hunger the penniless Bhadramati being greatly agitated in all his sense-organs, cried aloud:

8. "Fie upon a life devoid of fortune!
Fie upon a life bereft of wealth!
Fie upon a life wanting in fame!
Fie upon a life without hospitality!

9. Fie upon a life devoid of moral conduct!
Fie upon a life devoid of knowledge!
Fie upon a life without exertion and industry!
Fie upon a life devoid of happiness!

10. Fie upon a life bereft of kinsmen!
Fie upon a life wanting in renown!
Fie upon the life of a man without any wealth but with many children!

11. Alas! The good qualities such as gentleness,[1] scholarship and nobility of birth—all these do not shine in the case of one sinking in the ocean of poverty.

12. Brāhmaṇa's sons, grandsons, kinsmen, brothers, disciples—all men forsake the man who is without wealth and glory."

13-17. The Brāhmaṇa Bhadramati who was intelligent and self-possessed came to this conclusion: "Irrespective of one's being a Brāhmaṇa or a Cāṇḍāla, it is the fortunate alone who is honoured. In this world a poor man is condemned by all people as though he is a corpse. Alas! A person endowed with riches may be hard-hearted but he is considered to be kind. He may not have any good qualities, but he is considered to be endowed with good qualities. Even if he is a fool, he is considered to be a scholar.

A man may be hard-hearted and be devoid of good qualities and virtue but if he is endowed with the quality of possessing wealth and glory, he is undoubtedly worthy of being honoured.

Alas! Poverty is itself misery but therein false hope or expectation causes greater misery. Persons dominated by (false) hope meet with misery (despair) instantaneously.

18. Those who are slaves unto hopes and desires are slaves of the whole world. The whole world becomes the slave of those who have made hope and desire their slave.

19. Even if a person is conversant with all the contents of all the scriptures, he may still appear to be a fool if he is poor. There is no one to liberate those who have been seized by the great crocodile of poverty.

20. Alas! What a misery! Alas! What a despair! Alas! Poverty (itself) is a misery! There too if one has too many sons and wives, it inflicts more misery."

21. Bhadramati, the master of all the contents of all the scriptures, (ceased to talk) after saying this much. He began to think about some holy rite that would yield plenty of wealth and glory. Bhadramati who was afflicted with deep pain and sorrow remained silent.

---

1. VV 11-20 are a part of floating traditional subhāṣitas censuring poverty (*vide Subhāṣita-Ratna-Bhāṇḍāgāra* on poverty).

Bhadramati is Encouraged to go to Veṅkaṭādri by Kāminī

22-23. At that time one of his wives, Kāminī, who regarded her husband as a god and was endowed with good qualities spoke to her husband:

Kāminī said:

24. O holy lord conversant with all holy rites, O master of all the contents of all the scriptures, O my lord, O blessed one, O highly intelligent one, listen to my words.

25. On the banks of Suvarṇamukharī frequented by multitudes of sages there is the sacred Veṅkaṭācala worthy of being served by Devas.

26. On that great mountain Veṅkaṭa, bowed down to by Suras and Asuras, there is an auspicious sacred Tīrtha which burns all sins.

27. O highly intelligent and blessed one, go to that Tīrtha in Pāpanāśa. Take your holy bath carefully therein accompanied by your wives and sons.

28. The greatness of that Tīrtha has been heard by me from Nārada during my childhood. The sage recounted it in the presence of my father:

29-32. "On the Veṅkaṭa mountain of great merit, which is destructive of all sins and subdues all miseries and which yields all types of riches, a devotee should take bath in Pāpanāśa, the great Tīrtha, with *Saṁkalpa* (i.e. a solemn pronouncement of the resolve). He should think about a Dharma (holy rite) that yields enormous prosperity and glory. The devotee should decide to make a gift of land, which is the most excellent of all excellent gifts. It takes the donor to heaven (after death). It yields whatever best things one craves for. Gift of land is glorified as the most excellent of all gifts. By making that gift a man obtains whatever is most wished for."

33. On hearing the words of Nārada my father, a Brāhmaṇa, became delighted in his mind and went to Śeṣādri.

34. After going there (my father) the blessed one made over a gift of land to an excellent Brāhmaṇa well-versed in the Vedas—a gift that bestows all prosperities and glories.

35. Thereupon my father became endowed with all fortunes, O learned one. He attained happiness in this world and after death went to Viṣṇu's city.

36. You too, O blessed one, go to Veṅkaṭādri, the most excellent mountain. Make the gift with determination—the gift of land that bestows all desired things.

Kāminī glorifies the Gift of Land

37. Listen with great attention to the greatness of the gift of land.[1] In the whole of the world none can describe it fully, O holy lord.

38. There had never been a greater gift than the gift of land before (i.e. in the past) nor will it be in future. There is no doubt about this that a donor of land attains the greatest salvation.

39. By giving as a gift even a smallest piece of land to a person well-versed in the Vedas, who maintains the sacred fire, one attains the world of Brahmā, from which there is no return to this world.

40. A bestower of land is said to be a bestower of everything. The person who makes a gift of land shall attain liberation. Making a gift of land on Vṛṣādri is destructive of all sins.

41. A person may have committed great sins, he may have committed all sins, but by gifting away a piece of land measuring ten *hastas* or cubits (a cubit = 18 inches) he becomes liberated from all sins.

42. He who donates land to a deserving person shall obtain the benefit of all gifts. In the whole of the universe consisting of the three worlds there is no one else on a par with a donor of land.

43. If anyone makes the gift of a splendid land to a Brāhmaṇa without means of livelihood, even Śeṣa will never be competent to recount his meritorious benefit.

---

1. The importance of land grants is described in Mbh and Purāṇas (*vide* Kane, HD II.ii.862ff. and also verses quoted in Appendix pp. 1271-77), Kane, however, has noted the restrictions on such gifts.

44. He who gives even the smallest piece of land to a Brāhmaṇa of good conduct (but) without any means of sustenance is Viṣṇu himself. There is no doubt about it.

45. He by whom a meadow or a land full of sugarcane or wheat or areca-palms etc. is given as a gift is Viṣṇu. There is no doubt about it.

46. By making a gift of land, even if it be very small, to a poor Brāhmaṇa burdened with a family but devoid of a means of livelihood, one attains *Sāyujya* with Viṣṇu.

47. If a forest land is given to a Brāhmaṇa devoted to worship of gods, one gets the benefit of taking holy bath in Gaṅgā for three days.

48. Listen to the benefit one derives by making a gift of a land yielding one Droṇikā[1] (119 kg.) to a Brāhmaṇa of good conduct but without means of sustenance.

49. He gets that great benefit which a man obtains by performing hundreds of horse-sacrifices on the banks of Gaṅgā in accordance with the injunctions.

50. If a person gives a land yielding a *Bhāra* of foodgrains (i.e. about 100 quintals) to a poor Brāhmaṇa, I shall speak of the merit of that person, O my lord, O holy lord.

51. He shall obtain that benefit which one derived after performing thousands of horse-sacrifices and hundreds of Vājapeyas on the banks of Gaṅgā.

52-55. A gift of land is a great gift. It is glorified as surpassing all gifts. It subdues all sins. It yields the benefit of salvation. Even a person who hears about this (land gift) with great faith shall attain the benefi. of gifting away a land.

On hearing these words of his wife with citations from a legendary story the gentle Bhadramati, devoted to all holy rites, became delighted. He mentally meditated upon the Lord residing on Śeṣācala. He already began to proceed to the excellent Krīḍācala mentally. (At the outset) he went to the city named Suśāli accompanied by his wives.

1. *Droṇikā* also means a valley between two mountains, but a land yielding so much corn or foodgrains is preferred in this context.

Sughoṣa Attains Heaven Through the Gift of a Land to Bhadramati

56-61. The Brāhmaṇa went to an eminent Brāhmaṇa named Sughoṣa endowed with all prosperities and glories, and begged for a land-strip measuring five hands (i.e. cubits in length).

On seeing that Brāhmaṇa having a large family Sughoṣa who strictly adhered to (the path of) righteousness, became pleased in his mind. He honoured him and spoke thus:

"O Bhadramati, I am blessed. My life is fruitful. My family has become sinless since you have become one acceptable to me."

After saying thus Sughoṣa of great intellect and devoted to virtue honoured him duly and gave him the land five hands in length, reciting the Mantra: "The earth belongs to Viṣṇu and is (hence) sacred. It is protected by Viṣṇu. May Janārdana be pleased with me for making a gift of land."

O great Brāhmaṇas, Sughoṣa worshipped that prominent Brāhmaṇa, regarding him as Viṣṇu himself, and gave him that much land.

62-63. O Brāhmaṇas, that intelligent Brāhmaṇa (Sughoṣa) donated the requested (piece of) land to Bhadramati who was a devotee of Hari and was well-versed in the Vedas and had a large family.

Accompanied by a crore members of his family, Sughoṣa attained Viṣṇu's abode, after going where no one experiences grief. It was on account of the gifting of the land that he went there.

Bhadramati Goes to Veṅkaṭādri on the Banks of Pāpanāśana for Gifting Lands

64-65. Accompanied by his sons and wives, Bhadramati went to the great mountain Veṅkaṭa that is bowed down to by Suras and Asuras, that is resorted to and served by Gandharvas, Yakṣas, presiding deities of mountains and others—Veṅkaṭācala who is the son of Meru, that is divine, that has come from Vaikuṇṭha and is called Krīḍāśaila, the excellent mountain (near Svāmipuṣkariṇī).

66-67. In the pure, sacred and splendid water of Svāmisaras he took his bath along with his wives, sons and others preceded by the rite of *Saṁkalpa.* He bowed down to the white Boar, the uplifter of Earth, on its western bank in accordance with the injunctions and went to the abode of Śrīnivāsa.

68. There the highly intelligent devotee of Viṣṇu had the vision of Veṅkaṭeśvara served by Brahmā and other Devas. He along with his sons and others visited the Lord.

69-71. After devoutly bowing down so Śrīnivāsa, the Lord of Devas, the storehouse of mercy, he went to Pāpanāśana accompanied by his wives, sons and others.

He took his bath in accordance with the injunctions. He performed all the requisite holy rites. The highly intelligent one made the splendid salvation-yielding gift of land to a certain Brāhmaṇa well-versed in the Vedas and a devotee of Viṣṇu as well, considering him to be Viṣṇu himself.

Bhadramati Realises the Lord by the Power of Land Gift

72-74. At that time the Lord manifested himself holding the conch, the discus and the iron club, seated on Garuḍa and adorned with garlands of sylvan flowers. The Lord appeared before him on the banks of Pāpanāśana by the power of land gift. Then the gentle Bhadramati began to eulogize (the Lord):

75. "Obeisance, obeisance to you, the cause of everything. Repeated bows to you, the protector of everything. Obeisance, obeisance to you, the leader of the immortal ones. Obeisance, obeisance to the suppressor of Daityas.

76. Obeisance, obeisance to the Lord who is fond of devotees. Repeated obeisance to the Lord dispelling sins. Obeisance, obeisance to the destroyer of vicious people. Hail to that Lord of the universe!

77. Obeisance, obeisance to the Lord who incarnated as Dwarf for the sake of a cause. Obeisance to Nārāyaṇa of unmeasured valour. Bow to the Lord holding the Śārṅga bow, the discus, the sword and the iron club. Hail to that Puruṣottama!

78. Obeisance to the Lord residing in the ocean; obeisance to the immutable Lord of Lakṣmī; bow to the Lord of unmeasur-

ed splendour excelling the sun etc. Obeisance, obeisance to the Lord of meritorious arrival and departure.

79. Obeisance, obeisance to the Lord with the sun and the moon as his eyes. Hail to you, the bestower of the fruit of Yajñas; obeisance to the Lord shining with Yajñāṅgas (i.e. the requisites of a sacrifice). Bow to you, the lover of good people.

80. Obeisance, obeisance to the cause of causes. Obeisance to the Lord devoid of (or beyond the objects of senses such as) sound etc. Obeisance to you, the bestower of happiness desired. Obeisance, obeisance to the Lord who is fascinating unto the devotee.

81. Obeisance, obeisance to you, the wonderful cause. Bow to you, the supporter of Mandara (i.e. the Divine Tortoise). Obeisance to you called Yajñavarāha ('Boar in the form of sacrifice'). Obeisance to the tearer of Hiraṇyakaśipu.[1]

82. Obeisance to you who assumed the form of a Dwarf (Vāmana). Bow to you, the destroyer of the dynasties of Kṣatriyas (Paraśurāma). Obeisance to you, the suppressor of Rāvaṇa (Rāma). Hail to you, the elder brother of the daughter of Nanda (i.e. Śrīkṛṣṇa)!

83. Bow to you, the lover of Kamalā (Lakṣmī). Obeisance to you, the bestower of happiness. Hail to you, the destroyer of the agony of those who resort to you! Obeisance, obeisance, again and again."

84. On being eulogized by that Brāhmaṇa Lord Śrīnivāsa, the storehouse of mercy, fond of devotees, spoke these words out of affection:

85-86. "O dear one, welfare unto you. I am delighted, O Brāhmaṇa, by this great eulogy. You will be endowed with all worldly pleasures in the company of sons, grandsons etc. After obtaining (enjoying) happiness in this world, attain salvation after death."

After saying this Lord Viṣṇu vanished there itself.

---

1. Here the reading: *Hiraṇyākṣa-vidārakāya*, is defective. If accepted it becomes an adjective of Varāha. But the author intends to give us the series of Viṣṇu's incarnations and the incarnation next to Varāha is Nṛsiṁha (Man-lion). If the reading is emended as *'Hiraṇyākhya-vidārakāya'*, it means Nṛsiṁha, the incarnation after Varāha and preceding Vāmana.

87. Thus, O Brāhmaṇas, the greatness of Pāpanāśana has been recounted to you all. The greatness of land gift on its banks is also described.

CHAPTER TWENTYONE

The Greatness of Ākāśagaṅgā

The Episode of Brāhmaṇa Rāmānuja[1]

Śrī Sūta said:

1. O ye ascetics, all residents of the Naimiṣa forest, I shall recount the greatness of Ākāśagaṅgā Tīrtha.

2-3. Near Ākāśagaṅgā a certain devotee of Viṣṇu, well-known as Rāmānuja, performed penance. He was a master of all the contents of all scriptures. He had conquered all his sense-organs. He was a virtuous soul closely following the advices of anchorites. During summer he seated himself in the middle of five fires and engaged himself in the meditation of Viṣṇu.

4-5. He repeated the eight-syllabled Mantra[2] (*Oṁ namo Nārāyaṇāya*) and meditated on Janārdana in his mind. During rainy season he stayed out under the open sky and during (early) winter he constantly remained in water. He thought of the welfare of all living beings. He had perfect control over the sense-organs. He was free from (the effect of) all the mutually opposed pairs (such as pleasure-pain). For many years he lived on old and decaying leaves.

6. For some time he took only water as his food. For many years only air was his intake.

---

1. This is a mythological person different from the founder of Viśiṣṭādvaita school of Vedānta. The personal name Rāmānuja was popular in Tamil Nadu in the 11th and 12th centuries CE, which may give some clue to the date of this Māhātmya.

2. This is the Pañcarātra Mantra; may be due to the influence of that system on this chapter.

Pleased with Rāmānuja's Penance the Lord Manifests Himself on the Bank of Ākāśagaṅgā

7-9. The Lord, affectionate to his devotees, was delighted by his penance. He appeared directly before him holding the conch, the discus and the iron club. His eyes were like the petals of a full-blown lotus. His lustre was equal to that of a crore of suns. He rode on Garuḍa. He was rendered splendid by means of the umbrella and the chowries. He was bedecked in necklace, armlets, crown, bracelets etc. He was surrounded by Viṣvaksena, Sunanda and other attendants.

10. Nārada and others who played on flutes, lutes, Mṛdaṅga-drums and other instruments sang songs in his praise. He shone in his yellow robes.

11. On his chest Lakṣmī shone brilliantly. He had the blue lustre of a cloud. On his either side he was attended upon by Sanaka and other great Yogins.

12-13. With his gentle smile he fascinated the three worlds. Honouring (everyone) he rendered all the ten directions brilliant with his refulgence. Thus Lord Veṅkateśa, the storehouse of mercy, easily accessible to good devotees, appeared before that great sage Rāmānuja.

14-15. On seeing Śrīnivāsa, the storehouse of compassion, the Lord clad in yellow robes, who appeared before him then, the great sage attained great delight. Endowed with the greatest devotion, he eulogized the Lord of the universe.

Hymn to the Lord Composed by Brāhmaṇa Rāmānuja

Rāmānuja prayed:

16. Obeisance to the over-lord of Devas holding the conch, the discus and the iron club. Bow to you, the eternal one, the purest one, the Lord of Veṅkaṭa.

17. Obeisance to the dispeller of the agony of devotees. Hail to you, having the form of *Havya* and *Kavya*! Obeisance to you of three forms, the cause of creation, sustenance and dissolution (of the universe).

18. Obeisance to the greatest Lord, Bow to the Lord of great bounty and abundance. Obeisance to the Lord of Lakṣmī,

to the creator. Hail to the Lord with the sun and the moon for his eyes! Obeisance to you respectfully bowed to by Brahmā and others.

19. Obeisance to that destroyer of Daityas who has none of these diversities, such as name and caste and other things, who is devoid of all defects and who dispels the fears of the entire universe.

20. Obeisance to the Lord who can be known only through the Upaniṣads. Obeisance to the Lord of Ramā, to the resident of Vṛṣādri, to the father of Brahmā. Obeisance, obeisance to the dispeller of the agony of all the people. Obeisance to Nārāyaṇa of unmeasured valour.

21. Obeisance to you, to Lord Vāsudeva wielding the Śārṅga bow. Repeated obeisance to you, to the resident of Veṅkaṭādri.

22. After eulogizing Śrīnivāsa, the Lorb of Veṅkaṭa, the preceptor of the universe thus, sage Rāmānuja, the excellent Brāhmaṇa, remained silent.

23. On hearing this eulogy of that noble soul, pleasing to the ears, the Lord of Veṅkaṭācala who was eulogized, attained deep satisfaction.

24-25. The delighted Lord Śauri embraced the sage with his four arms and spoke to him, "Let the boon be chosen. O great sage, I am delighted at your penance, eulogy and obeisance. I am pleased. I have come here as the bestower of boons on you."

Brāhmaṇa Rāmānuja's Request to the Lord

Rāmānuja said:

26-27. O Nārāyaṇa, O Lord of Ramā, O Śrīnivāsa identical with the universe, O Janārdana having the universe for your abode, O Govinda, O slayer of Naraka, I am satisfied and blessed on seeing you. O crest-jewel of Veṅkaṭādri, persons of virtuous nature bow down to you because you are the protector of virtue.

28. I know you, the Supreme Soul whom neither Bhava (Śiva) nor Brahmā know, nor do the three Vedas know. What else is greater than you?

29. I see the Supreme Soul whom Yogins do not see and whom those who are exclusively devoted to the performance of religious rites do not see.

30-31. I am contented and blessed with this, O Veṅkaṭeśa, the Lord of the universe, that I perceive Janārdana, merely by recollecting whose name men of very great sins attain salvation. Let my devotion to your lotus-like feet be firm and steady.

The Auspicious Time for Holy Bath in Ākāśagaṅgā as Described by the Lord

Śrī Bhagavān said:

32-36. Let your devotion to me be firm and steady, O Rāmānuja of great intellect. Listen to another statement of mine, O Brāhmaṇa. Those people who take their holy bath at the time of the transit of the Sun to the Zodiac Aries in conjunction with the Constellation Citrā or on the Full-Moon day in (Ākāśa) Gaṅgā, attain the highest region from which there is no return.

You do stay, O Brāhmaṇa Rāmānuja, near Viyadgaṅgā (i.e. Ākāśagaṅgā). When this body (of yours) that has begun (to experience the results of Karmas) perishes, you will attain my form (i.e. *Sārūpya* type of liberation).

Of what avail is much talk? All those people who take their holy bath in the auspicious waters of Viyadgaṅgā are excellent Bhāgavatas ('Devotees of the Lord'). O tiger among sages, there need be no doubt in this.

Rāmānuja said:

37. What are the characteristics of Bhāgavatas? By what action are they known? I wish to hear this since I am very eager and earnest.

The Characteristics of Bhāgavatas as Described by the Lord

Śrī Veṅkaṭeśa said:

38-40. Listen to the characteristics of Bhāgavatas,[1] O excel-

1. VV 38-61 detail the chracteristics of a Bhāgavata or a devotee of Bhagavān or Viṣṇu.

lent sage. Even in crores of years their power cannot be described.

Those who are devoid of hostility and jealousy, those who are wise, calm and free from vulgar desires and those who wish for the welfare of all living beings are indeed excellent Bhāgavatas.

41. They never give pain to others physically, verbally and mentally. They habitually refrain from accepting gifts and owning properties. They are indeed excellent Bhāgavatas.

42. Indeed those whose Sāttvika intellect is engrossed in listening to stories of saintly people and who are devoted to my lotus-like feet are excellent Bhāgavatas.

43. Those excellent men who render service to their parents, those who are engaged in worshipping gods, those men who aspire for godliness and those who rejoice on seeing worship of the deity are indeed excellent Bhāgavatas.

44. Those who sincerely render service to religious students and ascetics and those who never indulge in censuring others are indeed excellent Bhāgavatas.

45. Those who always speak words conducive to the welfare of others, those excellent men in the world who accept (and appreciate) the good qualities of others are indeed excellent Bhāgavatas.

46. Those excellent men who see all living beings as their own selves, those who behave equally towards enemies and friends are indeed remembered as (i.e. said to be) Bhāgavatas.

47. Those who expound *Dharmaśāstras* (Codes of Laws and Ethics), those who are devoted to truthful statements, and those who render service to them are indeed excellent Bhāgavatas.

48. Those who expound the Purāṇas, those who listen to them and those who are devoted to the expounders of Purāṇas are indeed excellent Bhāgavatas.

49. Those men who perpetually render service to cows and Brāhmaṇas and those who are devoted to pilgrimages are indeed excellent Bhāgavatas.

50. Those men who rejoice at the prosperity of others and those who are devoted to (recitation of) the names of Hari are inde ed excellent Brāgavatas.

51. Those who are engaged in growing and developing parks and gardens, those who maintain lakes and those who build and dig wells and lakes are indeed excellent Bhāgavatas.

52. Those who make big water-reservoirs, those who build shrines for deities, those who are engaged in repeating the Gāyatrī Mantra are indeed excellent Bhāgavatas.

53. Those who rejoice on hearing the names of Hari, those who are overjoyed on hearing the names of Hari and get the hair on their body stand through thrill of joy are indeed excellent Bhāgavatas.

54. Those men who bend down their heads on seeing a bed of holy basil plants and those who place a small piece of holy basil on their ears are indeed excellent Bhāgavatas

55. Those who are delighted in inhaling the fragrance of the holy basil and those who smear themselves with the mud taken from its root are indeed excellent Bhāgavatas.

56. Those who are engaged in the conduct of life ordained for their stage in life and those who worship guests and those who expound the meanings of Vedic passages are indeed excellent Bhāgavatas.

57. Those who explain to others the scriptures known to them and those who appreciate virtues everywhere are indeed excellent Bhāgavatas.

58. Those who are engaged in making gifts of water, those who are engaged in making gifts of food and those who are devoted to the holy rites of Ekādaśī (i.e. fast etc. on the eleventh lunar day) are excellent Bhāgavatas.

59. Those who are engaged in gifting cows, those who are engaged in making gifts of virgins (by way of marriage) and those who are engaged in activities for my sake are indeed excellent Bhāgavatas.

60. Those whose minds dwell on me, those who are my devotees, those who eagerly desire (to perform) my worship, and those who are absorbed in remembering my names are indeed excellent Bhāgavatas.

61. Of what avail is much talk? I shall tell you succinctly. Those who strive for virtuous deeds are indeed excellent Bhāgavatas.

62. Of those Brāhmaṇas who are Bhāgavatas a few have been glorified here. They cannot be described even by me in the course of hundreds of crores of years.

63. O Rāmānuja of exalted magnificence, O highly intelligent one, the characteristics of my devotees have been spoken out of love and affection for you, my devotee.

Śrī Sūta said:

64. Thus, O Brāhmaṇas, Śaunaka and others of great prowess, the excellent greatness of Viyadgaṅgā Tīrtha on Vṛṣādri has been spoken to you all.

CHAPTER TWENTYTWO

Qualifications of Those Who Are Fit to Receive Charitable Gifts

The sages said:

1-2. O holy omniscient Sūta, expert in the Vedas and the Vedāṅgas! To whom should charitable gifts be given? What is the proper time for making gifts? Who is eligible to receive them? It behoves you to tell everything to us.

Śrī Sūta said:

3-4. O excellent Brāhmaṇas, in the holy spot named Veṅkaṭa which bestows great merits, a Brāhmaṇa is the great preceptor unto all the castes. Charitable gifts are to be made to him. That learned man will redeem (all persons). A Brāhmaṇa can accept monetary gifts. A Brāhmaṇa can receive gifts from everyone except an avarṇaka (i.e. a disreputable person) (explained below).[1]

5-8a. What is given to (and by)[2] an impotent fellow, one

1. VV 5-14 give a list of persons not eligible to receive a gift (cf. Manu 4.193-200; Mbh, Vana 200.5-9).

2. Lines 10b-11a show that the restrictions mentioned herein are applicable both to donor and receiver.

devoid of sons, one of hypocritical conduct, one hating the Vedas and Brāhmaṇas, one who has forsaken his special rites and duties becomes fruitless.

What is given by a person fondly attached to another man's wife or covetous of another man's wealth becomes fruitless. If a Brāhmaṇa is a (professional) singer, what is given (to and) by him becomes fruitless. What is given by a Brāhmaṇa whose mind is filled with jealousy, who is ungrateful, deceitful and devoid of knowledge becomes fruitless.

8b-12a. What is given by one who perpetually indulges in begging, who is violent towards the weak, who sells his name and fame, Vedic passages, Smṛti texts and holy rites becomes fruitless.

If a person habitually oppresses others, what is given by him becomes fruitless. One should not accept anything from or give anything to those who are engaged in sins or who are censured by the people of good activities.

Gifts should be given only to a person regularly engaged in good activities, who is well-versed in the Vedas, who maintains the sacred fires, who is poor and devoid of means of livelihood and has a large family.

12b-15. Gifts must be given by making special efforts to a person absorbed in the worship of gods or to a person who narrates the stories of the Purāṇas. O Brāhmaṇa, charitable gifts must particularly be made to a poor man.

Of what avail is much talk? Listen, O excellent Brāhmaṇas. Gifts can always be made to all Brāhmaṇas.

If anything is given to the husband of a barren woman, the man is reborn as a donkey.

One should never make obeisance to an unbeliever,[1] a person who has transgressed the limits of decorum, a person without a son, a person who is sluggish and knavish, and (to) one who indulges in gambling and stealing.

16. One should never bow to a heretic, to a fallen man, one who has lost his caste, a person who sells the Vedas, an ungrateful person and a person engaged in sinful activities.

17. One should not make obeisance to a person engaged in bathing, a person with sacrificial twigs and flowers in his hand, a

1. VV 15-23 give a list of those whom one should not pay obeisance.

person holding a water-pot as well as a person engaged in taking food.

18. One should not bow to a person engaged in arguments, an angry and ferocious person, a person who is vomiting, one standing in the midst of people, a person holding food received as alms and a person lying down (or asleep).

19. One should never bow to a barren woman, a woman in menses, an adulteress, a woman in the lying-in-chamber, a woman who has had an abortion, a woman who spoils holy rites as well as a fierce woman.

20-23. Individual obeisance in an assembly, in a sacrificial hall and in temples destroys earlier merit.

One should not make obeisance to a person employed in the holy rites of Śrāddha, one who is engaged in the worship of a deity and one who is engaged in the performance of Yajña and Tarpaṇa.

If a person does not salute in return to a person who makes obeisance, he should be known as undeserving to be saluted like a Śūdra. Hence on all occasions an intelligent excellent Brāhmaṇa shall abstain from making obeisance to husband of a barren woman or a cruel Brāhmaṇa.

The Greatness of Ākāśagaṅgā

Śrī Sūta said:

24-27. In this connection I shall relate the legendary story of the intelligent Puṇyaśīla as recounted by Nārada to sage Sanatkumāra. I shall recount it, O excellent sages. Listen attentively.

Formerly on the banks of Godāvarī there was an excellent Brāhmaṇa (named) Puṇyaśīla. He was devoted to all holy rites. He was truthful in speech. He had conquered his sense-organs and was merciful to all living beings. He worshipped gods, Brāhmaṇas and the fire. He was pure by birth as well as by activities. He was engaged in doing service conducive to the welfare of his parents; he was devoted to preceptors and elders. He was courteous and chivalrous. He was hospitable to Brāhmaṇas and honoured by good people.

Conversion of Puṇyaśīla's Face into that of a Donkey by Inviting a Barren Woman's Husband (to Śrāddha)

28-30. A certain Brāhmaṇa who was a master of the Vedas and Vedāṅgas and who was endowed with good qualities like these came to the house of the intelligent Puṇyaśīla. Immediately he was requested to take part in the Śrāddha of the Pitṛs by Puṇyaśīla.

After employing that quiescent Brāhmaṇa well-versed in the Vedas for the holy Śrāddha of the Pitṛs, the righteous-souled (Puṇyaśīla) performed the excellent annual Śrāddha.

31. Then after some time a hideous deformity resembling the face of a donkey, came over the face of Puṇyaśīla.

32-33. Thereupon that extremely righteous Puṇyaśīla became dejected at heart. Heaving heavy sighs, the deeply depressed Puṇyaśīla came to the hermitage of Yogī Agastya. It was extremely divine and yielded all desired benefits. It was on the banks of Suvarṇamukharī and was resorted to by multitudes of sages.

34-35. In that hermitage he saw the noble-souled Agastya who wished for the welfare of all the worlds, being attended upon day and night by prominent sages. Seeing him the excessively miserable Brāhmaṇa with the face of a donkey bowed down to him.

Puṇyaśīla said:

36-38. Obeisance to you, O Agastya, storehouse of penance, who are served by sages. Save me, O storehouse of mercy, save me, a great sinner with a despicable face. By what fault has my face become hideous and ugly. O excellent sage, O blessed one speak it out of love for me.

Agastya said:

39. O excellent Brāhmaṇa of great distinction, O Puṇyaśīla of great intellect, listen attentively to (the cause) of the ugliness of your face, O Brāhmaṇa.

INELIGIBILITY OF A BARREN WOMAN'S HUSBAND FOR INVITATION TO A ŚRĀDDHA

40-45a. You had (once) engaged a Brāhmaṇa who was a storehouse of good qualities, master of the Vedas and Vedāṅgas and conversant with sacred learning, though he was sonless. It is on account of that great sin that there is ugliness in your face, O Brāhmaṇa.

Those who employ a Brāhmaṇa, husband of a barren woman, in offering *Havyas*, *Kavyas* etc. attain donkey-facedness. One should never invite the great sinner, husband of a barren woman, in any auspicious rite or in the rites concerning the Manes, O Brāhmaṇa.

O prominent Brāhmaṇa, a person who wishes for welfare and felicity should never invite at a Śrāddha ceremony husband of a barren woman, an exceedingly cruel person and husband of a Śūdra woman.

Even if he be well-conversant with the Vedas, scriptures etc., even if he be of noble birth and even if he be engaged in the performance of religious rites, O excellent Brāhmaṇa, husband of a barren woman must be avoided in the Śrāddha rite at all costs by one desirous of welfare.

45b-50. An excellent Brāhmaṇa should avoid husband of a barren woman in the Śrāddha rite, even if he be competent to perform sacrifices such as Jyotiṣṭoma and others, in holy observances and austerities.

If a deserving Brāhmaṇa is not available, one should invite a Brāhmaṇa of good conduct having a son, though he may be sustaining himself merely on the sacred thread(?) [symbolising his Brahminhood].

In the absence of such a person, O excellent Brāhmaṇa, one should engage one's son or younger brother or oneself but should refrain (from inviting) husband of a barren woman in the Śrāddha rite. O illustrious Puṇyaśīla, it is proclaimed with arms lifted up that one should not at any cost engage a sonless person for the Śrāddha rite.[1]

1. Śrāddha signifies and is intended for the continuity of the family. An issueless person is naturally regarded as ineligible for it. Hence this tirade against husband of a barren woman.

If the person performing a Śrāddha engages a Brāhmaṇa who is husband of a barren woman, that Śrāddha should be known as *Āsura* (demoniac) and the person who performs it shall go to hell.

THE DEFORMITY OF PUṆYAŚILA DISPELLED BY MEANS OF HOLY BATH IN ĀKĀŚAGAṄGĀ

51-54a. Of what avail is much talk? I shall mention to you the means of dispelling that defect and sin. On the auspicious banks of Svarṇamukhī there is the highly meritorious Veṅkaṭācala which is resorted to by multitudes of Devas. It is the son of Meru and it bestows all desired benefits.

There is a very great Tīrtha named Viyadgaṅgā on that prominent mountain Veṅkaṭa, bowed to by Suras and Asuras. It suppresses all sins and increases longevity and health.

54b-55. You go to the mountain Veṅkaṭa and take your holy bath in the waters of Svāmipuṣkariṇī with due performance of the holy rite of *Saṁkalpa*. Thereafter go to Gaṅgātīrtha. After going there, O highly intelligent one, you take your holy bath in it in accordance with the injunctions regarding Tīrthas.

56-57. Merely by having the holy bath, O highly intelligent one, the ugliness of this face will disappear instantaneously. There is no doubt about it.

On being told thus by the noble-souled Agastya Puṇyaśīla bowed down to that noble-souled (sage) and then went to Veṅkaṭādri.

58-59. After going there the blessed one took his holy bath with due observances in the waters of Svāmipuṣkariṇī. Then he went to Viyadgaṅgā. By taking his holy bath there the righteous-souled one, Puṇyaśīla, attained a face comparable to the face of Kāma (god of Love). Thanks to the greatness of the Tīrtha.

Śrī Sūta said:

60. Thus, O Śaunaka and other Brāhmaṇas of great prowess, what was told by Nārada to sage Sanatkumāra has been recounted to you.

CHAPTER TWENTYTHREE

Great Efficacy of Cakratīrtha

Śrī Sūta said:

1-3. Now I shall narrate, O eminent Brāhmaṇas of truthful speech, the greatness of Cakratīrtha that destroys all sins.

Those who listen to the greatness of Cakratīrtha of great merit go to the abode of Viṣṇu from which there is no return into this world, i.e. *Saṁsāra*.

Those who are averse to the charitable gift of food as well as that of water, those who are averse to the charitable gift of cows, become pure by taking their holy bath here.

4. Hence Cakratīrtha, the excellent Tīrtha, is excessively meritorious.

Performance of Penance by Brāhmaṇa Padmanābha

Śrī Sūta said:

5. Formerly Padmanābha of Śrīvatsa Gotra, who had conquered his sense organs, performed a great penance on the banks of Cakrapuṣkariṇī.

6. He was endowed with mercifulness. He abstained from food. He was truthful in speech and had conquered his sense-organs. He looked at all living beings as his own self. He was free from desire for sensual pleasures.

7-9a. He wished (and strove) for the welfare of all living beings. He controlled his mind. He was free from the (effects of) mutually opposed pairs (such as pleasure and pain etc.). For a few years he maintained himself by eating old (fallen) leaves. For some time his sole diet was water; for a few years he subsisted on air only. Thus for twelve years the great sage Padmanābha performed a severe penance very difficult to be performed even by Devas.

Delighted by the Penance Performed by the Brāhmaṇa Named Padmanābha at Cakratīrtha the Lord Appears Before Him

9b-11. On being satisfied and pleased by his penance the Lord of Kamalā, holding the conch, the discus and the iron club became visible to him. His eyes resembled the petals of a full-blown lotus. He had the lustre similar to that of a crore of suns.

He (Padmanābha) opened his eyes and saw Śrīnivāsa, the Lord of Veṅkaṭa, the calm and quiescent storehouse of mercy, holding the conch and the discus.

On seeing the noble-souled Lord he began to eulogize.

Hymn to Śrīnivāsa Composed by Brāhmaṇa Padmanābha

12. "Obeisance to the over-lord of Devas, to the Lord of Veṅkaṭa wielding the Śārṅga bow. Bow to you, to Śrīnivāsa, resident of the Nārāyaṇa mountain.

13. Obeisance to Viṣṇu, the son of Vasudeva, the destroyer of sins. Hail to you, Śrīnivāsa, resident of the Śeṣācala mountain.

14. Obeisance to the Lord of the three worlds, the omnipresent witness. Obeisance to you, to Śrīnivāsa worthy of being saluted by Śiva, Brahmā and others.

15. Obeisance to the Lord with lotus-like eyes. Obeisance to you lying on the Milk Ocean. Hail to you, Śrīnivāsa, the slayer of wicked Rākṣasas.

16-18. Obeisance to the Lord fond of the devotees, to the Lord of Devas. Obeisance to you, to Śrīnivāsa, the destroyer of the agony of those who bow down (to you).

A bow to the Lord of Yogins, to Viṣṇu, to be always known through the Vedas. Obeisance to you, to Śrīnivāsa, the dispeller of the sins of devotees."

19. Thus was eulogized Śrīnivāsa, the auspicious one who is immanent in the universe, by the sage named Padmanābha who was a resident of Cakratīrtha.

The Lord Directs Padmanābha to Stay at Cakratīrtha Permanently

20-21. After having attained the greatest delight Puruṣottama, the Lord of Veṅkaṭa, the storehouse of mercy, spoke these nectar-like words to Padmanābha, the excellent Brāhmaṇa, who was calm and devoted to holy rites:

Śrīnivāsa said:

22. O excellent Brāhmaṇa, O blessed one, O worshipper of

my lotus-like feet, you stay on the banks of Cakratīrtha to the end of the Kalpa worshipping me.

23-24a. After saying this Lord Viṣṇu vanished there itself. When Lord Śrīnivāsa, the sire of the universe, vanished, (the Brāhmaṇa) of great intellect stayed on the banks of Cakratīrtha.

24b-25. Then after some time a certain Rākṣasa of a terrible appearance who was very cruel and was afflicted with hunger, came there to devour that sage named Padmanābha who was devoted to Nārāyaṇa.

26-30. The Rākṣasa caught hold of the Brāhmaṇa with great force. On being seized by him with great force, the Brāhmaṇa, a master of the Vedāṅgas, yelled loudly to Nārāyaṇa, the discus-bearing deity, the greatest resort of persons in distress, an ocean of mercy. He repeatedly cried: "Save me, save me. O Lord of Veṅkaṭa, O ocean of mercy, O protector of those who seek refuge in you, O tiger among men, save me. I have been overcome by a Rākṣasa. O Hari, O Viṣṇu, O Lord of Lakṣmī, O Garuḍa-emblemed Lord, O Vaikuṇṭha, protect me. I have been seized by a Rākṣasa. Save me in the manner you saved the elephant attacked by the crocodile.[1] O Dāmodara, O Lord of the universe, O suppressor of Hiraṇyāsura, save me as you saved Prahlāda (as I am) exceedingly afflicted by the Rākṣasa."

The Lord Despatches His Discus for Slaying the Demon about to Kill Padmanābha

31-34. As Padmanābha eulogized thus, O Brāhmaṇas, Cakrapāṇi, the storehouse of mercifulness, realized the danger of his devotee. He despatched his own Discus for protecting the devotee.

On being hurled by Viṣṇu, the powerful one, that Discus of Viṣṇu, came to the banks of Cakrapuṣkariṇī speedily. It shone like infinite number of suns. It had the lustre equal to that of infinite number of fires.

1. This refers to the episode of Viṣṇu's saving an elephant from a crocodile given in BhP VIII, Chs. 2 and 3.

On seeing Viṣṇu's Sudarśana of great refulgence and loud sound, capable of suppressing great Asuras, the Rākṣasa fled.

The Discus Despatched by the Lord Slays the Asura

35-36. Even as the Rākṣasa fled, Sudarśana which was unapproachable on account of clusters of sparks and flames, suddenly cut off his head. On seeing the Rākṣasa fallen on the ground, the excellent Brāhmaṇa rejoiced excessively and eulogized Sudarśana.

Padmanābha said:

37-41. O Viṣṇu's Discus, obeisance to you. You are prepared for protecting the universe. Salute to you, to the ornament of the lotus-like hand of Nārāyaṇa. O Sudarśana, of great sound, O destroyer of the agony of devotees, obeisance to you, efficient in the destruction of Asuras in the course of battles. Save me. I am extremely frightened. Save me from all sins, O Lord and Master Sudarśana! Be ever present at the Cakratīrtha for the welfare of the universe desirous of salvation.

On being prayed thus by that Brāhmaṇa that Discus of Viṣṇu, O great sages, spoke to that (Brāhmaṇa) named Padmanābha, delighting him with great friendliness:

Granting of Boons by the Discus at the Request of the Brāhmaṇa

42-47. "O Padmanābha, I shall stay here permanently with a desire for the welfare of all the worlds at this most excellent and highly meritorious Cakratīrtha.

On pondering over your distress caused by the wicked Rākṣasa, O Brāhmaṇa, I have been despatched by Viṣṇu and I hastened to this place. This wretched Rākṣasa, your tormentor, has been killed by me. You have been liberated from fear as you are a permanent devotee of Hari.

In the Cakratīrtha of great merits, destructive of all sins, O Brāhmaṇa, I shall be present near you forever for the sake of protecting the worlds.

Due to my presence here, hereafter no harassment caused by evil spirits and demons shall disturb you or other Brāhmaṇas. Since I am present here it will become famous by the name Cakratīrtha.

48-50. The sons and grandsons, indeed all the persons born in the family of those who take their holy bath in Cakratīrtha that bestows salvation, shall become rid of their sins. They will go to the greatest region of Viṣṇu."

After saying this, O Brāhmaṇas, even as Padmanābha and all other Brāhmaṇas stood watching, that Discus of Viṣṇu suddenly entered Cakrapuṣkariṇī that is destructive of sins.

Śrī Sūta said:

51-53. O Śaunaka and other great Brāhmaṇas of great prowess, the greatness of Cakratīrtha that is destructive of sins has been completely narrated to you all.

A Tīrtha on a par with Cakratīrtha has never been (before) nor will there be any (in future). O Brāhmaṇas, by taking their bath here men shall undoubtedly be liberated.

He who narrates this chapter or listens to this with great concentration and purity of mind attains the excellent benefit of taking the holy bath in Cakratīrtha.

CHAPTER TWENTYFOUR

The Episode of the Gandharva Sundara

The sages said:

1. O holy lord Sūta, the most excellent one among those conversant with the Purāṇas, who was this Rākṣasa who tormented the noble-souled Brāhmaṇa, a devotee of Viṣṇu?

Śrī Sūta said:

2. O Brāhmaṇas, I shall narrate the story of that cruel Rākṣasa and how as a result of the curse of sages he became a Rākṣasa. Listen with concentration.

3-4. Formerly in Śrīraṅga,[1] the temple of Viṣṇu on a par with Vaikuṇṭha, all the devotees of Viṣṇu, of great prowess, the chiefs of whom were Vasiṣṭha and Atri, came to reside and began to worship Śrīraṅganātha, the Lord of Devas, the bestower of immunity from fear on the devotees. They worshipped him for salvation.

5-6. Once a certain Gandharva named Sundara, powerful son of Vīrabāhu (came there), O great Brāhmaṇas. He was deeply attached to the assembly of lecherous people. Accompanied by a hundred young women, he entered the water-pond without any clothe on. He joyously sported with naked young women.

7-9. Vasiṣṭha was desirous of performing Mādhyāhnika (Mid-day) religious rites. From the temple of Śrīraṅga he went to the holy Tīrtha of the river Kāverī along with the other sages.

On seeing those sages those young women became frightened. They immediately wore their clothes but not Sundara who was over-bold and rash. Thereupon, Vasiṣṭha became angry and cursed that shameless fellow.

Vasiṣṭha said:

10-12. Since, O Sundara, O Gandharva, even after seeing us the clothes were not put on by you out of natural shame, become a Rākṣasa instantaneously.

When this was imprecated by Vasiṣṭha, the women bowed down to him with palms joined in reverence and mind humble due to devotion. They spoke to Vasiṣṭha in the midst of the multitude of sages thus:

The young women said:

13-16. O holy lord, O son of Brahmā, conversant with all holy rites, O ocean of mercy, in our presence it does not behove you to be angry. It is the husband who is mentioned to be the greatest ornament of women. A woman without a husband, even if blessed with a hundred sons, is called a widow in the world, O sage. Her life is purposeless. Hence, O sage, be pleased with our husband. One offence should be pardoned by the sages. the seers

1. Seringapatam on Kāverī in Mysore.

of Truth. Forgive, O ocean of mercy. Be merciful to Sundara, your disciple.

Śrī Sūta said:

17. When requested thus by the womenfolk of Sundara, Vasiṣṭha, the excellent Brāhmaṇa, became pleased once again and spoke these words:

THE REMEDY FOR TERMINATING SUNDARA'S RĀKṢASAHOOD AS SUGGESTED BY VASIṢṬHA

Vasiṣṭha said:

18. O ladies of beautiful eyebrows, my words will never be false. I will recount to you the means (to get out of the curse). Listen with attention and faith.

19-21. The curse in the case of your husband will certainly be effective for a period of sixteen years. During this period of sixteen years, Sundara will have the form and features of a Rākṣasa. O celestial ladies, once he will, by chance, go to Veṅkaṭa, the auspicious mountain that dispels all sins. He will then go to Cakratīrtha. Padmanābha, a prominent sage and a great Yogin, stays there. This Rākṣasa will rush at that sage for devouring him.

22-24. Thereafter, the excellent Discus despatched by Viṣṇu for the protection of the Brāhmaṇa, will undoubtedly sever his head from his body. Thereafter, that Sundara, your husband, will be released from the curse and will regain his own form. He will return to heaven once again. There is no doubt about it. Thereupon, after reaching heaven, O beautiful women, Sundara, your husband, will delight you all in his beautiful dress.

Śrī Sūta said:

25. After saying thus to those excellent women of Sundara, Vasiṣṭha, a devotee of Śrīraṅgeśvara, went to his hermitage immediately.

26. Then those young women who were grief-stricken and immersed in the middle of the ocean of misery, embraced their husband Sundara and lamented.

27-30. Even as they were watching thus, Sundara became a Rākṣasa with a huge body and big curved teeth. His hair and beard were red in colour. On being frightened at his sight the beautiful women went to heaven.

Then this Sundara in the form of a Rākṣasa of terrible form and features, began to eat living beings. He wandered from land to land and forest to forest with the speed of wind. He roamed over the excellent mountain Veṅkaṭādri. The great sinner entered Cakratīrtha and then went away. Thus sixteen years elapsed while he continued his wanderings.

31-33. Then, at the close of the sixteenth year, O great sages, this Rākṣasa rushed at Padmanābha, a resident of Cakratīrtha, with the velocity of wind, in order to devour him.

He (Padmanābha) then eulogized Janārdana. On being eulogized by the Yogin, Viṣṇu hurled his Discus in order to protect that Padmanābha who was terribly harassed by the Rākṣasa. Hari's Discus came and removed the head of the Rākṣasa.

Liberation of Sundara from Rākṣasahood and Restoration of His Original Form

34-35. Then he abandoned the body of Rākṣasa. Sundara got back his divine body and got in an aerial chariot. He was showered with flowers. With palms joined in reverence he bowed down to and saluted that Sudarśana. With great respect he eulogized him with excellent words pleasing to the ears:

Sundara said:

36. O Sudarśana, obeisance to you, O sole ornament of Viṣṇu's hand. Obeisance to you, the destroyer of Asuras, to the (weapon) having the refulgence of a thousand suns.

37. It was by your grace that I cast off the body of Rākṣasa and regained the original form of mine. O missile Discus of Viṣṇu, salute to you.

38. O favourite of Viṣṇu, permit me to go to heaven. My wives are bewailing me due to the grief of separation.

39. O Discus, grant me such a form as to enable me to think about you as long as I live. Obeisance to you.

40. On being thus eulogized devoutly by Sundara, O great

sages, the Discus of Viṣṇu at once blessed him saying, "Let it be so."

41. Permitted by the Missile Discus, Sundara, the Gandharva, bowed down to the excellent Brāhmaṇa and permitted by him went to heaven.

42-46. When Sundara had gone to heaven, the prominent sage Padmanābha prayed to the Discus:

"O missile of Viṣṇu, obeisance to you. O weapon Discus, the suppressor of great Asuras, I bow down to you. Be pleased to be present in this splendid Cakratīrtha devoid of impurities. By your presence destroy the sins of all the sinners who take their bath here. Grant them eternal salvation. Let this Tīrtha become famous by the name Cakratīrtha in the world. Henceforth let the fear of the sages living here be dispelled. O noble weapon Discus, obeisance to you. Let there be no fear from evil spirits, vampires and ghosts, O Lord."

47-49. On being prayed to in this manner by Padmanābha, the Yogin, the Discus said, "So be it" and vanished in that Tīrtha.

Śrī Sūta said:

Thus, O Brāhmaṇas, the greatness of Cakratīrtha has been recounted by me with (reference to) the origin of the Rākṣasa. It dispels all impurities. On hearing it men on the earth are liberated from all sins.

CHAPTER TWENTYFIVE

The Greatness of Jābālitīrtha

Śrī Sūta said:

1-2. O ye all ascetics, O residents of the Naimiṣa forest, I shall describe the greatness of Jābālitīrtha on the Veṅkaṭādri of great merit and destructive of all sins. O Brāhmaṇas, (a sinner) named Durācāra became liberated by bathing there.

The sages enquired:

3-4. O Sūta, knower of the exact nature of reality, who was this person named Durācāra? What sin had been committed by that Durācāra, O sage? How was he liberated from the sin, due to the greatness of the bath in this Tīrtha? O sage, we are desirous of hearing this. Relate it to us in detail.

The Episode of the Brāhmaṇa Named Durācāra Who Lived on the Banks of Kāverī

Śrī Sūta said:

5. O sages, let the sin of that Durācāra be heard. So also (listen) how he was liberated from the sin by taking his holy bath in Jābālitīrtha.

6. There was a certain Brāhmaṇa named Durācāra who had resorted to the banks of Kāverī. This Brāhmaṇa who was a sinner, was always engaged in cruel activities.

7. O Brāhmaṇas, this sinner was defiled due to his frequent associations with Brāhmaṇa-slayers, liquor-drinkers, thieves and defilers of preceptor's bed. He always lived with them.

8. O excellent Brāhmaṇas, the Brahminical power of this sinner was entirely destroyed on account of the evil of association with great sinners.

9-11. If a Brāhmaṇa eagerly stays with great sinners for one day, one part (i.e. one fourth) of his Brahminhood will undoubtedly be lost at that very moment. By serving them, touching them, seeing them, lying with them and taking food with them in the same row, by remaining for two days with great sinners thus, O Brāhmaṇas, a second part (i.e. one half) of his Brahminhood is undoubtedly lost.

12. If the association lasts for three days a third part (i.e. three fourths) is lost undoubtedly. If it lasts for four days, (the last) fourth part is certainly obliterated.

13. If any person associates with great sinners beyond this period by sitting, lying or taking food with them, he shall become a sinner of (their) equal grade.

14. Therefore, the Brāhmaṇa named Durācāra became completely bereft of Brahminhood. He was haunted by an evil

spirit. It was as though he was swallowed by a powerful and terrible snake or beast of prey.

15-21. Excessively afflicted by that vampire, he became distressed. He wandered from country to country and from forest to forest. Due to his previous merit and his good luck, that Brāhmaṇa reached the highly meritorious Veṅkaṭādri (which was) destructive of all sins. He was pursued there by the vampire (the ghost).

Durācāra and the Vampire Get Rid of Their Sins by Taking Holy Bath in Jābālitīrtha

The Brāhmaṇa closely pursued by the evil spirit came to the mount Veṅkaṭa. The vampire immersed the Brāhmaṇa who was associated with great sinners, in Jābālitīrtha that is destructive of great sins, O great Brāhmaṇas. Within a moment he was released by the vampire and he stood up (free).

Getting out of that holy Tīrtha, O Brāhmaṇas, that Brāhmaṇa regained composure. He pondered, 'I was residing on the banks of Kāverī. How have I come to a place near Svarṇamukhī?'

With these thoughts agitating him, Durācāra bowed down to the excellent Tīrtha of Jābāli as well as Jābāli, the noble-souled excellent great Yogin. After approaching him he spoke:

22-24. "O holy lord, O Brāhmaṇa, I do not know what this mountain is. Tell me. I am a resident of the banks of Kāverī. My name is Durācāra. Kindly tell me how I happened to come here?"

On being asked thus by Durācāra that sage of good holy rites, the storehouse of mercy, meditated for a short while and spoke to Durācāra:

Narration of the Defect of Non-Performance of Pārvaṇa Śrāddha as Described by Jābāli

Jābālī told:

25-29. On account of your contact with great sinners formerly, O Durācāra, your Brahminhood got destroyed. Then a vampire seized you. Because you were possessed by him, you became helpless and deluded in your mind. In that confounded state you came here. The vampire immersed you in this extremely sacred Tīrtha. Merely by taking your bath here you became rid of the sins.

If men take their holy bath in Jābālitīrtha, all the heaps of their five types of sins perish. It is true. Merely by the bath in this holy Tīrtha which is the cause of good holy rites, your sin due to your association with great sinners has perished. The vampire that seized you was formerly a Brāhmaṇa.

30-31. He did not perform the Śrāddha rite unto the Manes on the day of death in accordance with the Pārvaṇa rite. So he was cursed by his Manes and he attained the state of vampire.

Due to the power of taking the holy bath in the waters of Jābālitīrtha, he cast off his vampirehood and attained the world of Viṣṇu.

32. A man who does not perform the Śrāddha unto his father and mother (every year) on the day of death becomes a vampire immediately and falls into hell later.

Śrī Sūta said:

33-34. Merely by taking his holy bath in this Tīrtha, Durācāra, the great sinner, attained the world of Viṣṇu from which no one returned (to Saṁsāra). Thus the holy story of the liberation of Durācāra has been recounted to you all. Hence this Tīrtha is the most sacred (of all Tīrthas). It is auspicious and destructive of all sins.

35-39a. Durācāra was liberated merely by a bath therein. This holy Tīrtha shall destroy even those sins which have no other way of expiation. If a Brāhmaṇa bows to a Liṅga or the idol of Viṣṇu (once) worshipped by a Śūdra no means of expiation has been laid down for him in the Smṛtis by the great sages. But even that sin of his shall perish in the Tīrtha named (after) Jābāli.

There is no means of atonement for those who censure Brāhmaṇas. Similarly there is no expiation for those who commit breach of trust, those who are ungrateful and those who carnally approach the wives of their brothers. But due to their holy bath in Jābālitīrtha they will become pure.

39b-40. Thus, O Brāhmaṇas, the greatness of Jābāli's Tīrtha has been described to you all. On hearing this men on the earth become liberated from all sins.

•

CHAPTER TWENTYSIX

The Greatness of Tuṁburu (Ghoṇa) Tīrtha

Śrī Sūta said:

1-3. Here I shall recount the greatness of Ghoṇatīrtha that is destructive of all sins, O Śaunaka and other (sages) of great prowess.

It is the fruit of a penance of previous birth that people get the opportunity of taking bath therein. On the Full-Moon day in conjunction with the Constellation Uttarāphālgunī, when the Sun is in the Zodiac Pisces, Gaṅgā and all other Tīrthas in the three worlds come there in the afternoon.[1]

The sages asked:

4-5. O holy lord Sūta, O omniscient one, O master of all the contents of all scriptures, why do all the rivers Gaṅgā etc. take bath in the exceedingly sacred Ghoṇatīrtha when the Sun is in the Zodiac Pisces?

Śrī Sūta replied:

6-11. The Tīrthas Gaṅgā etc. think like this: 'All men who have committed sins, scrupulously take their holy bath in us. Those people cast off their sins in us and go away with their object achieved. How is this mass of sins accumulating in us to be destroyed?'

After thinking thus they remembered the divine, fascinating words of the noble-souled son of Brahmā, Nārada (for) absolving all sins. They go to Śrī Veṅkaṭa, the mountain that dispels

1. The special day of this Tīrtha is the Full-Moon day in Phālguna when the Sun is in the Zodiac Pisces.

the sins of Brahmin-slaughter etc. They take their holy bath in the waters of Svāmipuṣkariṇī, the excellent Tīrtha. Thereafter, O Brāhmaṇas, all those Tīrthas take their bath (i.e. flow into) in the exceedingly sacred Ghoṇatīrtha on the Full-Moon day in conjunction with the Constellation Uttarāphālgunī when the Sun is in the Zodiac Pisces. Who is capable of knowing (completely) the greatness of that Tīrtha in the entire universe consisting of the three worlds?

A Description of the Great Sins of those who are Averse to the Holy Bath in Ghoṇatīrtha

12. Hence, O excellent Brāhmaṇas, Ghoṇatīrtha is the most meritorious Tīrtha.

13. They call a person who has abandoned Ghoṇasnāna ('holy bath in Ghoṇatīrtha') one who cruelly destroys parks and gardens (i.e. he incurs the sins of such acts), one who sells horses and virgins, one who slays Brāhmaṇas.

14. They call one who has discarded Ghoṇasnāna, a destroyer of the property of deities, a person who takes back what is gifted away, a person who is a Brāhmaṇa-slayer.

15. Learned men call one who has avoided Ghoṇasnāna, a destroyer of lakes, bridges and dams, one who ardently longs for sexual union with other men's wives, one who steals.

16. Learned men know the person who has abstained from Ghoṇasnāna as a base non-believer who promises a Brāhmaṇa "I shall give" and afterwards (does not give it), as a person who habitually drinks liquor.

17. Learned men call the person who has abandoned Ghoṇasnāna, a person who is worthy of being hated by preceptors, Brāhmaṇas and (other) people, one who is given to self-praise, who steals.

18. Brāhmaṇas call the person who has discarded Ghoṇasnāna, a consumer of food that has not been consecrated, a consumer of the remnants of food offered to the Manes and a thief.

19. Learned men call the person who has abandoned Ghoṇasnāna, a person who offers (to others) the remnants of food offered to the Manes, a person who is antagonistic to his mother and father, and is a thief.

20. They say that the person who has abandoned Ghoṇasnāna is one who is habitually engaged in sexual union with other men's wives, who is fond of sexual dalliance with his brother's wife and is a defiler of the preceptor's bed.

21. They say that the person who has abstained from Ghoṇasnāna is one who talks to a Cāṇḍāla, who is a Brāhmaṇa always bereft of Darbha grass in his hand and is a sinner of the fifth class (i.e. one who associates with sinners who have committed the four types of major sins).

22. They say that the person who has abandoned Ghoṇasnāna is one who takes his food after hearing the voice of a woman in her menses, of a Cāṇḍāla or of a horse, and who is a sinner of the fifth class with their association.

23. They call the person who has abandoned Ghoṇasnāna, a person who causes obstacles in the holy rites of expounding the Purāṇas, celebrating marriage, investiture with the sacred thread and other rites and who kills animals.

24. Learned men say that the person who has avoided Ghoṇasnāna is a slayer of one who has sought refuge, who is averse to all the Tīrthas and who causes abortion.

25. They call the person who has abandoned Ghoṇasnāna, a person who has abandoned Pitṛyajña (i.e. performance of śrāddha), who has deserted his wife, is the meanest in the family and who kills cows.

26. O excellent Brāhmaṇas, sins on a par with the major sins and minor sins resort to the person who has abandoned Ghoṇasnāna.

The Power of Bath in Ghoṇa to Dispel All Sins

27-36. O eminent Brāhmaṇas, the fascinating Ghoṇatīrtha sanctifies all these sinners through the holy bath, drinking (its) water etc. Wonderful indeed is the greatness of the Tīrtha!

The following are the sinners sanctified:[1] One who is engaged in committing major sins, one who cooks dog's meat, the meanest in the family, the cruel, destroyer of the family, the mischievous one, one who has not gifted anything, one

1. This list of 'sins' includes all unsocial acts detested at the time of this Purāṇa.

who has stopped performance of holy rites, a killer of animals, a tormentor of others, one who has resorted to a backbiter, one who habitually speaks lies, a hypocrite, one who is attached to the wives of others, one who is treacherous to friends, an ungrateful one, a destroyer of foetus, a heinous sinner, a sinner cohabiting with other men's wives, an informant about the assets of other men, an untruthful person, one who is engaged in agricultural activities, a traitor to the master, a fraudulent one, a covetous one, a patricide, one who is averse to all gods, one who praises himself, a rogue who causes obstacles to pious activities, one who wastes money over undeserving persons, one who causes split among persons who receive favour and concession, one who cuts off or uproots trees laden with excellent fruits, one guilty of breach of faith, one who is bent on massacring warriors, one who does not maintain the sacred fire, one without a son, one who administers poison, a sinner who makes the preceptor hate him, one who causes estrangement between husband and wife, one who acts as a tyrant in administering a village or a temple trust, one who teaches (Vedas) for salary, a Brāhmaṇa absorbed in cruel activities, one who has made committing of sins his second nature, one who is solely devoted to commit multitudes of sins secretly, one who commits sins due to ignorance, one who commits vicious deeds knowingly and all other persons of a similar nature.

Story of a Gandharva Called Tuṁburu

Śrī Sūta said:

37. In this connection I shall relate an ancient legend that is destructive of sins, that absolves one from sins, that yields the benefit of salvation.

38. Formerly Gārgya, an omniscient Brāhmaṇa of great refulgence, expert in all lores, who was just and master (subduer) of his sense-organs said as follows:

39. He bowed down to the noble-souled Devala and requested him with delighted mind:

"O (sage) of exalted magnificence, be merciful unto me. Recount to me the greatness of Ghoṇatīrtha that is auspicious and destructive of all sins."

Devala said:

40-41. A Gandharva named Tuṁburu cursed his chaste wife. He took his bath here and worshipped Veṅkaṭeśa, the storehouse of mercy. Thereby he attained Viṣṇu's world from which no one can return (to Saṁsāra).

Gārgya asked:

42-43. O Sage Devala, why did the Gandharva named Tuṁburu, an expert in all lores, curse his beautiful wife? What was the fault of his wife endowed with all good qualities? O (sage) of exalted magnificence, tell me the same. I am eager to hear.

Tuṁburu Instructs His Wife about the Procedure in Taking Holy Bath in the Month of Māgha

44-45. The Gandharva named Tuṁburu told his wife lovingly: "For a period of three Māghas take the bath along with me. It dispels all impurities and sins. In the month of Māgha, when the Sun has risen, smear with cowdung the bank that dispels all sins, for the sake of the worship of Viṣṇu.

46. In this month of Viṣṇu that bestows auspiciousness render service unto me through Raṅgavallī etc. (? colourful designs as a mark of auspiciousness), designs of white lotus, Svastika etc. drawn by means of minerals.

47. In this Māgha offer *Dīpavartikā* (i.e. a lamp and a wick) to Mādhava. In front of Hari offer devoutly fire with incense.

48. Cook food unto the noble-souled Mādhava, remaining pure (in mind as well as in body). In the month of Māgha perform circumambulation and obeisances along with me with great devotion.

49. Perform the religious rites and services to Viṣṇu, the Lord of Devas, everyday. Listen to the Purāṇa of Viṣṇu everyday without any lethargy.

50-51a. Take bath scrupulously everyday and drink Hari's *Pādodaka* (i.e. the water with which Hari's feet are washed). Repeat continuously (his names such as) O Kṛṣṇa, O Viṣṇu, O Mukunda, O Nārāyaṇa, O Janārdana, O Acyuta, O Ananta and O Viśvātman.

51b-52a. Abandon anger, rivalry, jealousy, greediness etc. and observe a vow. Thereby you will attain liberation and permanent residence in Viṣṇu's world."

Tuṁburu Curses His Wife: The Means of Redemption Therefrom

52b. On hearing what was spoken thus by her husband, the beloved wife of the Gandharva angrily spoke to her husband (words) that were unbearable and leading to hell (or misfortune):

53. "O sinless one, when the chillness increases in the morning, when the sun rises very slowly, how can one bathe in the month of Māgha that gives agony due to chillness?

54. The rites mentioned by you cannot be performed by me constantly. O husband, I will not take bath in the morning along with you.

55-56a. If my death takes place due to excessive cold, you will not come to my rescue."

On hearing the words spoken thus, in spite of his being calm and quiet, the Gandharva, the loving husband, cursed his wife who spoke unpleasantly and offensively.

56b-60. He thought thus: 'One shall immediately punish by means of curses a son who is averse to virtue and piety, a wife who speaks unpleasantly and a king unfavourable to Brāhmaṇas.' Prompted by this maxim he cursed his chaste wife then: "Become a mere (ordinary) frog, O foolish woman, in a dry place without water, in the hollow of a holy fig tree near Ghoṇatīrtha on Veṅkaṭa mountain of great merit and destructive of all sins."

On hearing this imprecation of her husband the beloved wife of the Gandharva, the chaste woman, fell at his feet and requested Tuṁburu. Afterwards Tuṁburu, the husband, indicated the redemption too from the curse:

61-64. "Agastya of exalted magnificence, the ascetic who has conquered his sense-organs, will take his holy bath in the excellent Ghoṇatīrtha on the great day of Full Moon. The excellent Brāhmaṇa will then relate the greatness of Ghoṇatīrtha to his disciples near the Aśvattha tree. At that time you shall be within the hollow of the holy fig tree. Listen to the greatness of Ghoṇatīrtha that bestows liberation with great attention. You shall then get rid of all your sins and sport with me."

On being told thus the chaste and pious wife ceased (to speak).

65-69. On account of the curse of her husband she took up the terrible and hideous body of a frog. The woman slowly went to the hollow of the holy fig tree on the peak of Śeṣādri to the south of Ghoṇatīrtha. She stayed in the hollow of the holy fig tree for a period of ten thousand years.

Then after a lapse of time (on one occasion) Agastya went to the fascinating Veṅkaṭādri. With all due holy observances he took his bath in Svāmitīrtha. He bowed down to Varāha, the deity to the south of the Tīrtha. He then went to the abode of Veṅkaṭeśa and bowed down to Śrīnivāsa, the storehouse of mercy, the Lord of Devas who can be known only through the Vedas, the eternal Lord of large eyes. Thereafter, Agastya of exalted magnificence went to Ghoṇatīrtha.

70-72. The most excellent one among Yogins took his bath in the excellent Tīrtha along with his disciples. With great devotion Agastya, the most excellent one among Yogins, the holy lord and sage, described to his disciples under the shade of the holy fig tree the greatness of Ghoṇatīrtha that is destructive of the sin of Brahmin-slaughter, that is meritorious, bestower of all auspiciousness and that grants all prosperity.

On Seeing Agastya in Ghoṇatīrtha the Wife of Tuṁburu is Liberated from the Form of a Frog

73-75. On hearing it the frog fell at the feet of that Yogin after knowing the greatness of the sage through the light of knowledge. She regained her original form, the charming form of a woman. She spoke to him thus:

"O Agastya, the most excellent one among Yogins, save me, save me, O storehouse of mercy. O Brāhmaṇa, kindly protect me though I opposed the words of my husband."

Saying thus the lady of large eyes ceased (to speak) thereafter.

Agastya asked:

76. Who are you, O lady of ample, fine buttocks? Welfare unto you. There was committed a sin in the previous birth that gave you the birth of a frog. What is that? Tell me. Do not delay.

The woman said:

77. There is a Gandharva named Tumburu. He is an expert in all lores. O Brāhmaṇa, O Agastya served by sages, I am his wife.

78. O excellent sage, my husband Tumburu who is conversant with all Dharmas said to me: "You are a charming (lady). Always perform all holy rites along with me."

79-80. On hearing the words of my husband, which would help in the other world, I uttered unbearable and very harsh words that would lead to hell. O dear one, O excellent sage, those words were uttered by me on account of my vicious intellect.

The Duties of a Chaste Woman as Described by Agastya

Agastya said:

81. Your husband of keen intellect cursed you angrily. Such a curse is proper in regard to a woman who acts contrary to the words of her husband.

82. A woman who dishonours the utterance of her husband and does as she pleases, falls into a terrible hell (where she remains) as long as the moon and the stars shine.

83-84a. Women have no freedom; husband's words or directives should not be transgressed. Women go to the region of Viṣṇu due to chastity and the merit of serving their husbands and not through other holy rites.

84b-86a. Learned men know (and assert) that husband is everything unto women, viz. mother, Viṣṇu, Brahmā, Śiva, preceptor and the holy Tīrtha. If a woman disobeys the directive of her husband, even if she is always engaged in the performance of all other holy rites, she shall never be pure even once.

86b-87a. A woman without husband (i.e. a widow) shall perform holy rites that bestow virtuous benefits on being bidden (and permitted) by preceptors conversant with Dharma.

87b. If a woman is directed by her husband, she should devotedly engage herself in obeying the order of her husband.

88. She who takes bath in the Tīrtha of (i.e. holy water flowing from) the lotus-like feet of her husband is a favourite of Hari. Undoubtedly, it is as good as a bath in all the Tīrthas, Gaṅgā etc.

89-91. Hence the sin committed by you yields the fruit thereof. While you were reaping the fruit of your own action, you heard the greatness of Ghoṇatīrtha. You were liberated. You regained the auspicious form of that lady. Hence this Ghoṇatīrtha has become famous as Tumbutīrtha in the world. What a (wonderful) greatness of the Tīrtha!

Those who take Their Holy Bath in Ghoṇatīrtha Attain Different Kinds of Benefits

Śrī Sūta said:

92-98. O (sages) of great prowess, O Śaunaka and others, if people take their bath on the Full-Moon day in Ghoṇatīrtha of great merit and destructive of all sins, they will attain the meritorious benefit of sacrifices. They will have the benefit of ten thousand Tīrthas.

By taking the holy bath in Tumburutīrtha one shall attain that benefit which is obtained by one who makes a gift of a thousand *Kapilā* (tawny) cows everyday.

By taking a plunge in Ghoṇatīrtha one attains that benefit which is obtained by one who makes a gift of thousands and crores of precious stones everyday or thousands of elephants in rut or ten thousand horses.

From the sacred Ghoṇatīrtha one attains that benefit which is said by sages to be the fruit of a gift of a crore of virgins.

By the greatness and power of Ghoṇatīrtha one attains that benefit which is obtained by one who makes a gift of a thousand golden robes in Kurukṣetra.

By the great power of Ghoṇatīrtha one attains that benefit

which is obtained by one who casts off his body for the sake of the preceptor, or a Brāhmaṇa or his own master.

99. From the Ghoṇatīrtha that merit accrues that is obtained by those who dispel the agony of persons in extreme distress or those who are eagerly devoted to the visits of holy Tīrthas or those who forever adhere to truthfulness.

100. From the holy Ghoṇatīrtha one attains that benefit which is obtained by those who perform Śrāddhas to Pitṛs on the New-Moon day.

101. From the holy Ghoṇatīrtha one attains that benefit which is obtained by a man who takes his holy bath in all the Tīrthas, in Gaṅgā, in Narmadā, in Sarayū, in Candrabhāgā and others.

102. Hence learned men know that Ghoṇatīrtha is the most meritorious of all the Tīrthas.

103. If a person listens to this chapter which dispels all sins, he will have the benefit of Vājapeya and a permanent stay in the world of Viṣṇu.

CHAPTER TWENTYSEVEN

Śrī Veṅkaṭācala Contains All the Tīrthas

The sages said:

1. O Sūta, the most excellent one among those conversant with the Purāṇas, how many Tīrthas are there on Veṅkaṭādri of great merit and destructive of all calamities and distresses?

2. Tell us their number. How many of them are important? There too, O excellent sage, tell us the most important among them.

3-4. How many among them produce interest in righteousness? How many are the most important among them? Which are those that bestow knowledge? Which are those that bestow devotion and detachment? Which are those that bestow salvation? Tell us, O sage engaged in holy rites.

Śrī Sūta said:

5. Here, on this excellent mountain, there are sixty-six crores of holy Tīrthas. Among them, O (sages) of holy rites, one thousand and eight are very important.

6-7. There are one hundred and eight Tīrthas that inspire interest in righteousness. They are more important than the other thousand Tīrthas. They are separate from them. Among the one hundred and eight (Tīrthas) sixty are those that bestow devotion and detachment.

The Time for Holy Bath in the Six Tīrthas Including Svāmipuṣkariṇī[1]

8-9. There are six Tīrthas on the top of Veṅkaṭācala that bestow salvation, viz. Svāmipuṣkariṇī, Viyadgaṅgā, Pāpavināśa, Pāṇḍutīrtha, Kumāradhārikā Tīrtha and Tuṁburu Tīrtha.

10-12a. On the Full-Moon day in the month of Kuṁbha (when the Sun is in Aquarius), when the constellation Maghā comes in conjunction, O Brāhmaṇa, all the Tīrthas fall into Kumāradhārikā.

He who takes his holy bath there, O eminent Brāhmaṇas,

---

1. There are six important Tīrthas on the Veṅkaṭa hill. Their special important days are mentioned below:

Tīrtha	*Important day*
1. Svāmipuṣkariṇī	Bright half, 12th day of Mārgaśīrṣa
2. Viyad (Ākāśa-) gaṅgā	Full-Moon day of Caitra (with the Sun in the Zodiac Aries)
3. Pāpavināśa	Sunday, bright half of Āśvina, 7th day when the Moon is with Uttarāṣāḍhā and 12th day when the Moon is with Uttarābhādrapadā
4. Pāṇḍu Tīrtha	Tuesday or 11th or 12th day of Vaiśākha (both in dark and bright half with the Sun in Taurus)
5. Kumāradhārikā	Full-Moon day of Māgha (with the Sun in the Zodiac Aquarius)
6. Tuṁburu	Full-Moon day of Phālguna (with the Sun in the Zodiac Pisces)

shall acquire the benefit of Rājasūya sacrifice. He shall attain salvation too. There is no doubt about it.

O Brāhmaṇas, one should make gift of food there, along with monetary gifts.

12b-18a. On the Full-Moon day in conjunction with the constellation Uttarāphālgunī, when the Sun is in the Zodiac Pisces, all the Tīrthas come to Tuṁburutīrtha in the afternoon. One who takes the holy bath there, is not re-born (i.e. becomes liberated). Investiture with the sacred thread and marriage rite should be performed there along with a gift of money.

When the Sun is in the Zodiac Aries, on the Full-Moon day in conjunction with the constellation Citrā, (all the Tīrthas) fall into Viyadgaṅgā. By taking his holy bath therein a man immediately derives the benefit of a hundred sacrifices. Gold must be given as gift there. Gift of a virgin (i.e. giving her away in marriage) is particularly (recommended).

O Brāhmaṇas, when the Sun is in Vṛṣabha (Taurus) on the eleventh or twelfth day of the lunar fortnight either in the bright half or in the dark half in conjunction with (i.e. when it is) Tuesday, all the Tīrthas in all the three worlds beginning with Gaṅgā fall into Pāṇḍutīrtha. By taking the holy bath therein and by offering a cow as gift one is liberated from obstacles.

18b-20. On a Sunday in the bright half of the month of Āśvayuj (September-October), on the seventh day (when the Moon is) in conjunction with the constellation Uttarāṣāḍhā or on the twelfth day in conjunction with Uttarābhādrapadā constellation, the devotee shall come to Pāpavināśana and take his holy bath as enjoined (in the scriptures). Thereafter he should make a gift of a Śālagrāma stone. He is liberated from all sins arising from (i.e. committed in) crores of births.

21-24. In the month of Dhanur (when the Sun is in Sagittarius), on the twelfth day in the bright half, during early dawn, all the Tīrthas fall into the waters of Svāmipuṣkariṇī. A man who takes bath therein shall undoubtedly attain salvation instantaneously. One gets the opportunity to take the holy bath only as a result of one's merit acquired in the course of thousands of births. Other persons who are not self-controlled will never have that chance. One shall make gifts there in accordance with one's capacity and in accordance with the injunctions. Particularly one should make gifts of a Śālagrāma stone and a cow.

The Special Merit of Listening to the Purāṇas[1]

25. Those who always listen to the story of Viṣṇu that sanctifies the universe, do indeed become devotees of Viṣṇu in this world of human beings.

26. If he is not able to listen always to the story that sanctifies the universe, the man should listen to it for a *Muhūrta* (48 minutes) or for half that time or even for a moment. If a man devoutly listens to the excellent story of Viṣṇu, he does not have any mishap or bad luck.

27. By listening to the Purāṇas once one obtains that merit which one derives from all the Yajñas and all types of charitable gifts.

28. Particularly in Kaliyuga excepting listening to the Purāṇas there is no greater holy rite for men nor there is any greater thing that yields salvation.

29. Listening to the Purāṇas and repeating the names of Viṣṇu—these two alone are the two great fruits of the tree of merits to human beings.

30. By drinking the nectar with great effort only one shall be rid of old age and death. But the nectar of the story of Viṣṇu shall make the entire family free from death and old age.

An Expounder of the Purāṇas Worthy of Being Worshipped by All

31. Whether he be a boy or a young man or an old man, whether he be poor or wretched, a man conversant with the Purāṇas should always be respected by meritorious persons.

32. One should never think about a person conversant with the Purāṇas to be mean or lowly, since the word that comes out from his mouth is a (veritable) wish-yielding cow (Kāmadhenu) unto all embodied beings.

1. VV 27-30 describe the benefits derived from listening to Purāṇas.

33. It is he who grants the chance of never returning (to the world) to those persons who have become dejected and distressed by frequent compulsion to take thousands and crores of births. Who else can be a better, a greater preceptor?

34. When a Brāhmaṇa-expounder of the Purāṇas occupies the seat of Vyāsa, he shall not bow down to anyone till the conclusion of the story or discourse.

35. The intelligent one shall not expound the holy story (of Purāṇas) in a place infested with vicious men, Śūdras or beasts of prey, or in a gambling house.

36. The intelligent one should sermonize the (Purāṇa) story in a good village peopled by good men, a holy spot, a temple or on the sacred banks of rivers.

37. The listeners who are endowed with faith and devotion, who are not hankering after any other activity, who are restrained in their speech, are pure and are not unduly excited shall earn merit.

38. If vile and mean persons listen to the holy story without devotion, they will never have the merit. They will be miserable in every birth.

39. Those who honour and adore a Purāṇa by means of offerings of Tāmbūla (betel leaves) etc. and then listen to the story with devotion, shall never be poor or sinners.

40. If men go out elsewhere while a Purāṇa is being expounded, their wives and wealth shall perish in the midst of their enjoyment.[1]

41. Those who listen to the holy story (Purāṇas) with a turban on their heads, will be born as foolish sinners, the meanest of men.

42. Those who listen to the sacred story even as they chew betel leaves, shall fall indeed into a hell and swallow the filthy ordure of dogs.

43. Those hypocrites who listen to the story while occupying a higher seat, shall undergo everlasting tortures in hells and then will be reborn as crows.

44. Those who sit on their hams in the posture of Vīrāsana,

1. VV 40-50 describe the restriction on the listeners of Purāṇas.

and those who occupy thrones and listen to the holy story shall become Arjuna trees.

45. Those who begin to listen without bowing down at the outset, shall become poisonous trees. Those who listen to the story while lying down, shall become pythons.

46. He who listens to the story while occupying a seat on a level with that of the expounder, shall incur a sin on a par with that of defiling the preceptor's bed and fall into a hell.

47. Those men who censure a person conversant with the Purāṇas or the holy story that dispels sins, shall indeed be reborn as dogs a hundred times.

48. Those who make impertinent remarks while the discourse is being held, shall be reborn as donkeys and chameleons thereafter.

49. Those men who never listen to the holy story, undergo tortures in hell and are reborn as wild pigs.

50. Those who create disturbance while the story is being told, undergo the tortures of hells for a crore of years and are reborn as village pigs.

51. Excellent men who encourage the narration of holy stories, shall attain the imperishable eternal region, even if they do not listen.

52. Those men who expound the holy story of the Purāṇas (to others), dwell in the region of Brahmā for more than hundred crores of Kalpas.

53-54. Those men who give a seat to a person conversant with the Purāṇas, or give him blankets, deerskins, clothes or a couch, shall attain heaven after enjoying all desirable pleasures. After residing in the world of Brahmā and others they go to a place devoid of ailment (i.e. salvation).

55-57. Those who offer excellent and new thread (to tie) a Purāṇa, shall enjoy pleasures in every birth and become endowed with perfect knowledge.

Those who have committed major sins, those who have committed minor sins—all these attain the highest region only through listening to the Purāṇas.

After hearing about the greatness of Veṅkaṭādri those sages worshipped and duly honoured Sūta who was richly endowed with the favour of Vyāsa and was the most excellent one among those conversant with the Purāṇas. They derived matchless delight.

CHAPTER TWENTYEIGHT

In Praise of Kaṭāha Tīrtha[1]

THE GREATNESS OF KAṬĀHA TĪRTHA

The sages said:

1-2. O Sūta conversant with the truth of all subjects and objects, O master of the Vedas and Vedāṅgas, it is heard that there is an extremely sanctifying Tīrtha named Kaṭāha on Śrī Veṅkaṭācala. Its greatness is proclaimed in all the three worlds. Recount this kindly to us, O disciple of Vyāsa.

3-5. Formerly the glorious son of Brahmā, the holy sage Nārada, the most excellent Brāhmaṇa, came to the Naimiṣa forest. On seeing that son of Brahmā all these sages duly worshipped him with splendid *Arghya*, *Pādya* etc. They offered him a seat with great devotion. They bowed to him with their necks lowered due to modesty. All those sages requested him thus:

6-8. "O glorious Nārada, excepting you there is no other instructor of *Dharma* to us. There is none among the great sages. On the mountain Veṅkaṭa of great merit, served by all the Devas, the divine mountain that has come from Vaikuṇṭha and is attended upon by Siddhas and Gandharvas, there is a holy spot called Kaṭāhatīrtha. Describe the greatness of Kaṭāhatīrtha to us, the forest-dwellers."

1. The Kaṭāha Tīrtha is attached to Śrī Veṅkaṭeśvara's sanctum on its northern side in the *Vimāna-pradakṣiṇā* (circumambulation passage around the temple). It contains the Abhiṣeka Tīrtha of Veṅkaṭeśa collected after the holy bath.

Śrī Nārada replied:

9-11. Listen ye all sages of great prowess headed by Śaunaka! Who knows the greatness of Kaṭāhatīrtha (adequately) in all the three worlds? Only Mahādeva understands the greatness of that Tīrtha. All those sacred Tīrthas within the Cosmic Egg, Gaṅgā and all the other Tīrthas, resort to the Kaṭāha Tīrtha, O excellent Brāhmaṇas, in order to dispel their own sins.

12-13a. A foolish person may think thus: 'All people touch this water—Brāhmaṇas, Kṣatriyas, Vaiśyas, Śūdras and people of other castes too.' Thinking thus he may not drink it. Indeed that foolish one will become a Cāṇḍāla and he will fall in Kuṁbhīpāka hell.

13b-15a. Whether he be a religious student, a householder, a forest-dweller or an eminent ascetic, by serving that Tīrtha he attains the highest state. In Śrutis, Smṛtis and Purāṇas there are many passages praising that Tīrtha which destroys the five major sins.

15b-17. It is exceedingly wonderful, O Brāhmaṇas; it is the only sanctifying thing in all the worlds. By serving and resorting to that Tīrtha ten thousand sins of Brahmin-slaughter, ten thousand sins of liquor-drinking, ten thousand sins of carnally approaching the preceptor's wife, ten thousand sins of the theft of gold and crores of the sins of associating with the great sinners, immediately become dissolved.

18. By resorting to this Tīrtha all those different kinds of sins which have no means of expiation, perish.

19-20a. This Tīrtha of great merit has issued from the feet of the Lord. If a person suffering from leprosy and other diseases drinks the water of this everyday, he shall get rid of that disease and go to the world of Viṣṇu.

Those Who have no Faith in the Greatness of Kaṭāhatīrtha Will Fall into Great Hells

20b-21. In the course of his (revelation) of secret experiences Lord Śaṅkara formerly spoke to Pārvatī about the greatness of that Tīrtha. No one should entertain any doubt about what has been said before.

22-24. It should never be uttered that it is mere laudatory statement. Those who say that this is mere eulogy are atheists in the core of their heart. The servants (of Yama) will place red-hot axe at the tips of their tongues. Hence the Tīrtha called Kaṭāha-tīrtha should be scrupulously served and resorted to. It suppresses all miseries and bestows the benefit of salvation. By drinking (its waters) devoutly a man shall realize all his desires.

25-27. O Sūta, the most excellent one among those conversant with the Purāṇas, after saying thus (to us) the glorious Nārada of exalted magnificence went to Kāśī that sanctifies all the three worlds. That holy lord spoke everything briefly in the Naimiṣa forest. Now we wish to know the greatness of Kaṭāha in great detail. Kindly tell it to us, O Sūta.

THE PROCEDURE OF DRINKING THE WATERS OF KAṬĀHA TĪRTHA

Śrī Sūta said:

28. O ye all ascetics living in the Naimiṣa forest, O excellent Brāhmaṇas, listen to the greatness of Kaṭāha Tīrtha.

29. O Brāhmaṇas, Kaṭāha Tīrtha is well-known in all the worlds. It causes all prosperity. It is pure and destructive of all sins.

30. It annihilates (the effects of) evil dreams. It is destructive of great sins. It suppresses great obstacles and brings about great peace (of mind) to men.

31-36. Merely by being remembered it nullifies all the sins of men. One should drink its enchanting waters after repeating the eight-syllabled Mantra.[1] Or he should mutter the names of Keśava etc. and sip water after each name. Or he should drink the water that bestows auspiciousness after muttering three names (Keśava, Nārāyaṇa, Mādhava) (together). Or he shall repeat the eight-syllabled Mantra of Veṅkaṭeśa and drink (the water of) Kaṭāha Tīrtha. That yields worldly pleasures as well as salvation.

1. The mantra is : *Oṁ namo Veṅkaṭeśāya.*

If any Brāhmaṇa wishes to drink at the excellent Tīrtha without a Mantra, he should always say "Destroy quickly all the great sins of mine committed in all the previous births" and drink the water. It is the sole means leading to salvation.

The following three are very rare in all the three worlds: bath in Svāmipuṣkariṇī, vision of Lord of Śrī in the form of Varāha and drinking of (the water of) Kaṭāha Tīrtha.

Of what avail is much talk? It is destructive of all sins like that of slaying a Brāhmaṇa etc.

The Episode of a Brāhmaṇa Named Keśava

37-38. Formerly, out of delusion, a Brāhmaṇa named Keśava viciously killed Bahuśruta and incurred the sin of Brahmin-slaughter. He drank the excellent water of this great Tīrtha. The great sinner named Keśava was liberated from the sin of Brahmin-slaughter.

The sages asked:

39. Whose son was this (Brāhmaṇa) named Keśava? How did he incur the terrible and exceedingly formidable sin of Brahmin-slaughter? It behoves you to tell it to us.

Śrī Sūta narrated:

40. There was a great Agrahāra (i.e. village donated to Brāhmaṇas) named Vedāḍhya on the beautiful banks of Tuṅgabhadrā resorted to by Gandharvas.

41-43. In that beautiful place Vedapura all the Brāhmaṇas were masters of the Vedas. They were devoted to the Science of Words (i.e. Grammar). All of them were promotors of the Science of Astrology. They were conversant with Nyāya and Mīmāṁsā systems of Philosophy. All of them were expounders of Vedānta. They were devoted to the treatises on Ethics and Law Codes. They were always engaged in making gifts of food. All the great residents of the Agrahāra were blessed with sons. (There was a Brāhmaṇa) well-known as Padmanābha in that Agrahāra (named) Vedāḍhya.

Keśava, a Brāhmaṇa Hankering after Harlots, Incurs the Sin of Brāhmaṇa-slaughter[1]

44-48a. He had a son named Keśava who had been banished from all holy rites. He abandoned his mother, father and his wife also who was a chaste woman. He was attached to harlots and he always visited brothels. The Brāhmaṇa enjoyed the company of a prostitute for two days and handed over to her the two gold coins due to her. Then he went away happily. When he had no money he was discarded by the woman of ill fame. Since he was desirous of sexual union with her, he began to steal much money frequently. He handed over the same to her and sported with her for a long time. He took food in her house. He drank wine with her from the same goblet.

48b-50. Once that Brāhmaṇa assumed the guise of a Kirāta (hunter) and went to the house of a certain Brāhmaṇa along with other Kirātas in order to rob him of his wealth. Keśava, the unworthy Brāhmaṇa, took a sword in his hand. He rashly attacked the Brāhmaṇa who was the master of the house and killed him with his sword. He brought much wealth from there and entered the prostitute's house.

51-52. The awful and hideous Brahmahatyā followed him as he went along. She was terrible in her blue robes and very red hair. She roared with boisterous laughter shaking heaven and earth. Being pursued by her the Brāhmaṇa wandered all over the earth.

53. While wandering all over the earth the vicious, unworthy Brāhmaṇa went to his village with excessive fright, O Śaunaka and other (sages) of great prowess.

54. He was terrified on being chased by her and went to his own house. Brahmahatyā who pursued him went into the house along with him.

55. Saying, "Save me, save me" Keśava sought refuge in his father. The father said, "Do not be afraid" and attempted to save him.

---

1. The motif of redemption from the sin of Brāhmaṇa-slaughter by the water of a sacred place is previously used in the case of Sumati who, as per advice of Durvāsas, is absolved by the waters of Svāmipuṣkariṇī (vide Supra Ch. 12.5-46) and the same is used here about Keśava who through Bharadvāja's advice imbibes the water of Kaṭāha Tīrtha.

56-58. As Padmanābha endeavoured to protect his son, the cruel demoness Brahmahatyā spoke to the father:

Brahmahatyā said:

O excellent Brāhmaṇa Padmanābha, do not accept him (and give him shelter). He is addicted to drinking liquor. He is a thief and Brāhmaṇa-slayer. He is a great sinner. He is treacherous to his mother and father. He is vicious in his mind. He has deserted his wife and is over-fond of harlots. Leave off this wicked one.

59-60. O Brāhmaṇa, if you shield in vain your son who is a great sinner, I will swallow your wife, this man's wife, you, your son and the entire family. Hence leave off this wicked one. If you abandon your son now, I will release you all.

61. O highly intelligent one, it does not behove you to get the whole family destroyed for the sake of one (member).

On being told by her thus Padmanābha spoke to her thus:

Padmanābha said:

62. Affection for my son torments me. How can I forsake my son?

On hearing it Brahmahatyā spoke to the Brāhmaṇa:

Brahmahatyā said:

63-64. This son of yours has become fallen. He is excommunicated from the pale of castes and stages of life. Do not love this son. His very sight is despicable.

After saying this Brahmahatyā struck his son named Keśava with her hand even as Padmabābha was watching.

65. Calling his father frequently he lamented, "O father! O father!" The father, mother and wife of that wicked one, all lamented.

The Means of Liberation from Brahmahatyā as Advised by Bharadvāja to Padmanābha

66. At that time Bharadvāja, the great sage of exalted magni-

ficence, the great Yogin, chanced to come there, O Śaunaka and sages of great prowess.

67. On seeing Bharadvāja the great sage Padmanābha bowed down to him and eulogized him. He sought refuge in him for the sake of his son:

68-74. "O Bharadvāja of exalted magnificence, you are a part of Viṣṇu himself. Persons without merits will never see you. My son has become murderer of a Brāhmaṇa, liquor-addict and a thief. The terrifying Brahmahatyā has come to strike my son. Advise me the means whereby my son shall become liberated from great sins and this terrible Brahmahatyā shall be destroyed quickly. Take pity on my son. O sage, I have only one son. I have no other son. If this son dies, my family will become extinct. Then there may not be anyone to offer rice-balls to the Pitṛs. Therefore, O sage, be kind to us."

On being appealed thus Bharadvāja who was a part of Nārāyaṇa himself, meditated for a long time and spoke these words to Padmanābha:

Bharadvāja said:

75-76. O Padmanābha, very formidable sins have been perpetrated by your son. Even by means of ten thousand atonements his sins will not be quelled. Still I shall recommend some expiation for absolution of the sins of your son. O Brāhmaṇa Padmanābha, listen.

77-78. O Brāhmaṇa, two hundred Yojanas (2400 kms) to the south of Gaṅgā, five Yojanas to the west of the Eastern Sea, on the northern basin of Suvarṇamukharī and only one Krośa from it, there is the mountain well-known as Veṅkaṭādri.

79-80. It is bowed to by all the worlds. It is the son of Meru. It is of great merit. It is saluted to by all the Devas. It has been brought from Vaikuṇṭha by the fast moving (vehicle) Garuḍa. It is the great mountain of sport of Viṣṇu. Now it is there on the auspicious banks of Svarṇamukhī. It is adored by groups of Devas and groups of sages.

81-83. On that prominent mountain Veṅkaṭa Nārāyaṇa himself dwells along with Goddess Lakṣmī, Goddess Bhū (the Earth) and Goddess Nīlā. Veṅkaṭeśa is the direct bestower of salvation. To the north of the temple of Veṅkaṭanātha, O great

Brāhmaṇa, there is the holy spot Kaṭāhatīrtha that bestows auspiciousness. It destroys the sins like that of Brāhmaṇa-slaughter. It yields all desired objects.

84-85. O eminent Brāhmaṇa, along with your son drink the charming holy water (of that Tīrtha).

On hearing the words of Bharadvāja, which are on a par with the words of Vedas, he bowed down his head to him and went to the Veṅkaṭa mountain.

By Drinking the Holy Water from Kaṭāhatīrtha as per Advice of Bharadvāja Keśava is Liberated from the Sin of Brāhmaṇa-slaughter

86. After going to the mountain Veṅkaṭa the eminent Brāhmaṇa took his holy bath with due holy observances in the waters of Svāmipuṣkariṇī along with his son.

87-88. He bowed down to Lord Varāha and went to the shrine of Śrīnivāsa. He circumambulated and bowed down to Vimāna (palatial Temple). Along with Keśava, his son of great wickedness, Padmanābha drank (the water.of) Kaṭāhatīrtha that is destructive of the sin of Brāhmaṇa-slaughter.

89-91. Thereat Brahmahatyā was dissolved immediately. Thereafter the leading Brāhmaṇa Padmanābha went to Veṅkaṭeśa, the storehouse of mercy, along with his son and visited the Lord. Then Veṅkaṭeśa, the storehouse of kindness, appeared before them on being delighted by their drinking (the water of) Kaṭāhatīrtha. He spoke these words:

The Lord Addresses Padmanābha who was Accompanied by His Son Liberated from Brahmahatyā

Śrī Bhagavān said:

92-95. O Padmanābha of great wisdom, O master of Vedas and Vedāṅgas, at the instance of Bharadvāja you came to the Veṅkaṭa mountain. After drinking (the water from) Kaṭāhatīrtha you have undoubtedly become blessed with your object achieved. Your son named Keśava has been released from Brahmahatyā. Hence Kaṭāhatīrtha should be resorted to with great effort. O Brāhmaṇa of great fortune, after drinking the excellent water in that Tīrtha even sinners become blessed and contented. It is true. It is (really) true. There is no doubt. Come to my world and be happy, O highly intelligent one.

96. After saying this Veṅkaṭeśa vanished from there.

Śrī Sūta said:

97-98. Hence, O ye all ascetics, Śaunaka and others of great prowess, the greatness of Kaṭāhatīrtha along with the legendary story has been recounted well in the manner it had been heard by me.

CHAPTER TWENTYNINE

Arjuna Proceeds on a Pilgrimage[1]

The sages said:

1. The power of all the holy places as also of the rivers, mountains, holy shrines and lakes has been related by you.

2. It has been described by you, O sinless one, that at the instance of Brahmā the river Suvarṇamukharī was brought to the earth by Agastya.

3. Now a desire has arisen to hear about its origin and power as well as of the groups of Tīrthas depending on it. It behoves you to recount that to us.

4. Sūta who was thus requested by the sages, bowed down to Śaṁbhu, the Lord Nandī, the six-faced Lord Skanda and Vyāsa. Then he began to recount.

1. From this chapter begins the sub-section of the glorification of river Suvarṇamukharī (see Supra p. 6, Fnt 2).

Śrī Sūta said:

5-6. O blessed ones, what has been asked by you is relevant and conducive to the good. This narrative bestows the Siddhi that comes from listening to the Vedas.

Listen attentively. I shall recount to you the divine story that is destructive of sins. It had been narrated by Bharadvāja to Arjuna.

7. After getting Yājñasenī (i.e. Draupadī) from the wise king Drupada the sons of Pṛthā went to the splendid city of Hastināpura at the bidding of Dhṛtarāṣṭra.

8. They were honoured there by Bhīṣma as well as by the son of Aṁbikā (i.e. Dhṛtarāṣṭra). They lived there for five years along with Duryodhana and others.

9-10. As advised by Bhīṣma and others, Dhṛtarāṣṭra of great fame, who was himself delighted in his mind on account of their services, granted to the sons of Pāṇḍu the excellent city named Khāṇḍavaprastha along with half the kingdom in the presence of Vāsudeva and all the elderly members of the family.

11. After taking leave of the Kurus headed by Dhṛtarāṣṭra, the sons of Pāṇḍu went to that city of Khāṇḍavaprastha accompanied by Kṛṣṇa.

12. Residing in that city named Indraprastha which was well guarded by Viśvakarman, Dharmaputra (Yudhiṣṭhira) ruled over the kingdom in the company of his brothers.

13. After Kṛṣṇa had gone back to his city, the sons of Pṛthā, well-conversant with Dharma took a vow (i.e. made an agreement) regarding Draupadī at the advice of Nārada.

Prelude to the Pilgrimage of Arjuna[1]

14-16. The agreement was as follows: Kṛṣṇā (i.e. Draupadī) should stay with each one of them (Pāṇḍava-brothers) in due order, with great respect, for one year, with this proviso that if any one of them were to see the daughter of Pāñcāla staying in

1. The story here is based on Mbh, *Ādi*, Chs. 211 and 212. But our author being a good storyteller, wove out an interesting story out of the facts stated in Mbh without borrowing any verses from that text.

another brother's house, he would proceed on a pilgrimage for a period of one year.[1]

Having taken a vow thus, those sons of king Pāṇḍu spent their time carefully in all those activities common to everyone in the world.

17. Once a Brāhmaṇa from the rural areas came and stood in the palace courtyard and lamented loudly many times, "My cow has been taken away by thieves."

18. After consoling that Brāhmaṇa Dhanañjaya (Arjuna) hurriedly entered the arsenal to take out his weapons.

19. There he saw Pāñcālī and Dharmaputra seated (together). Though he was fully aware of the vow, he entered the apartment and took out the bow along with the quiver.

20. That Prince went to fight with the thieves, killed them in battle, retrieved the cow and gave it to the Brāhmaṇa with due respect.

21. Thereafter Phālguna intimated to Dharmaputra (Yudhiṣṭhira):

"Pilgrimage has to be undertaken by me, because I have broken the stipulations in the vow."

22. On hearing the words of his younger brother the wise king Dharmaputra, the most excellent one among those conversant with righteousness, eagerly spoke thus:

Yudhiṣṭhira said:

23. If for the sake of cows and Brāhmaṇas one were to tell a lie, it is truth itself. If for the same purpose one were to commit an evil act, it is appropriate indeed.

24. It is for the sake of a Brāhmaṇa as well as for the sake of a cow that you have done like this. How can it become a vile deed? Tell me, O (brother) of good holy rites.

25. The duty of a king is the protection of his subjects. If he is indifferent to thieves, he will incur the sin of Brāhmaṇa-slaugh-

1. In Mbh, *Ādi* 204.28, the penalty for intrusion in privacy was remaining celibate for 12 years in a forest:

draupadyā naḥ sahāsīnamanyonyaṃ yo'bhidarśayet/
sa no dvādaśa-varṣāṇi brahmacārī vane vaset//

Here the penalty is limited to one year only.

ter. If he punishes the thieves, he shall enjoy the benefit of a horse sacrifice.

26. Even after knowing that they are uncontrollable enemies, if the thieves who oppress the people of his own country are not punished by the king, he will not be entitled to welfare and peace.

27. What has been done by you is an act conducive to the good and welfare of us, the kings, as well as of all the classes of the public. Therefore there is no fault on your part.

Śrī Sūta said:

28. On hearing the words of Dharmaputra, Dhanañjaya who was always virtuous, joined his palms in reverence and submitted once again:

Arjuna said:

29-30. O King, do not speak like this (to approve) a thing that involves the breaking of one's own vow.

A vow should never be broken by a person who knows everything about Dharma, who is himself the brilliant Dharma incarnate, who is conversant with what should be done and what should not be done (and especially by one) who is competent. A vow that has been proclaimed before by oneself should never be broken.

31. It is a way out for weaklings to forsake their duty on being prompted by the words of kinsmen and elders by casting off their own pledges announced by themselves previously.

32. If out of compassion my noble (brother) were to dissuade me from undertaking the pilgrimage, who can prevent the people from decrying me as one who has broken his vow?

33. My mind is extremely eager for going on a pilgrimage. My duty based on the behest of Nārada has been remembered by me.

34. Hence be pleased, O great King, in the matter of undertaking the pilgrimage. The vow of servants should be honoured by masters.

35. Arjuna was given permission by saying "So be it". Along with his brothers he delighted his elder brother by means of his humility, obeisance etc.

36. The son of Pāṇḍu took leave of his brothers Bhīmasena and others. Holy rites for his welfare during his travels were performed by excellent Brāhmaṇas.

37-38. At the bidding of Yudhiṣṭhira[1] many persons followed him, viz. Brāhmaṇas conversant with the Purāṇas, astrologers, physicians, artisans, servants, bards and heralds. Affectionate and well-behaved officers of the treasury followed him taking with them sufficient wealth for the sake of Arjuna's pleasures as well as charitable purposes.

Arjuna's Arrival at Suvarṇamukharī after taking His Holy Bath in Gaṅgā and Other Tīrthas[2]

39. At the outset the Prince went to the river Bhāgīrathī. He visited the holy places of Gaṅgādvāra, Prayāga and Kāśī.

40. Visiting various Tīrthas and travelling by the path along the banks of Gaṅgā he reached the southern ocean agitated by high waves.

41. After visiting Mahānadī of great merit, the well-known shrine of Puruṣottama (i.e. Jagannātha) and Siṁhācala he attained great contentment (and peace).

42. Thereafter the son of Kuntī saw the holy river Godāvarī whose greatness is increased on account of its power of dispelling all the masses of sins.

43. He duly took his bath in its waters. The son of Pāṇḍu delighted others by means of different kinds of charitable gifts such as lands and gold.

44. After visiting the river named Malāpahā he experienced splendid pleasure. Then he reached Kṛṣṇaveṇī, the excellent river.

45. He visited Śrīparvata, the permanent residence of Śiva. It has four entrances and there are many Tīrthas there.

---

1. In Mbh, *Ādi,* Ch. 206, Brāhmaṇas and others followed Arjuna of their own accord. Here it is Yudhiṣṭhira who orders such useful artisans and artists and treasury officers to accompany Arjuna.

2. Arjuna's route from Indraprastha to Veṅkaṭādri is as follows: Indraprastha→Gaṅgādvāra→Prayāga→Kāśī→the sea along the banks of Gaṅgā → Coastal route → Mahānadī → Jagannātha Purī → Siṁhācala → crossed Godāvarī→Malāpahā? → Kṛṣṇā → Śrīparvata (Śriśailya)→ Pennar river→ Veṅkaṭācala. The author has a fairly good knowledge of Indian East Coast.

46. He crossed the river Pinākinī (modern Pennar) and proceeded ahead. Then he saw Veṅkaṭācala, the favourite abode of Nārāyaṇa, frequented by celestial sages.

47-48. With great devotion he worshipped the famous Hari, the sole leader of all the worlds stationed on the lofty peak of this mountain. He worshipped the Lord for the attainment of the good. He got down from the peak of the great mountain Veṅkaṭa and saw the river named Suvarṇamukharī that had been brought by the Pot-born Sage (i.e. Agastya) and that is frequented and resorted to by groups of Siddhas and Sages.

CHAPTER THIRTY

Description of the Hermitage of Bharadvāja

DESCRIPTION OF SUVARṆAMUKHARĪ[1]

Sūta said:

1. That great river heightened the pleasure of the son of Pṛthā (Arjuna) who had come there after visiting all the Tīrthas.

2. In the bowers on the banks of that river Siddhas and their women rejoice happily, being served and attended upon by winds cool on account of water-spray.

3. With its lofty waves coming into contact with the clouds, it appeared as though the river had flung up its arms to embrace the (heavenly) Gaṅgā flowing through the sky.

4. The penance groves on its banks were marked by the columns of smoke rising up from *Āhutis* (offering of ghee into the Sacred Fire) and the bark garments hanging from the branches of the trees.

5. The divine Liṅgas of the Trident-bearing Lord installed all round by prominent sages and excellent Suras were seen on the banks of that river.

---

1. A beautiful description of the river, esp. note the comparison of the river with a woman (vv 8-10). It speaks highly of the poetic gifts of the author.

6. Having taken rest in their abodes among the sands on the banks of that river, swans, the most excellent ones among birds, forget the Mānasa lake, their (original) home.

7. That river increases the productivity of grain-bearing plants and is capable of protecting people by its waters flowing through canals, thereby dispelling the anguish due to drought.

8-10. This river, the beloved of the Ocean, shone like a woman of an extraordinarily wonderful form. The Cakravāka (ruddy goose) birds were her protruding breasts. They were adorned with *Patravallīs* (lines or figures on the body drawn by means of fragrant colourful substances). She shone with the sandy banks as her buttocks and the eddy as her navel. The full-blown lotus was her face. The moving fish were her pair of eyes. She shone with the foams as her garments. She was charming with the gait of swans. The chirping sound of the aquatic birds was her voice and talk. She caused much delight to the eyes.

11-12. On the western bank of the river that flows in between, Dhanañjaya (Arjuna) saw a lofty mountain named Kālahastī. Many lofty peaks of this mountain scraped the region of the sky. The bottom rock of this mountain is firmly fixed beneath all the seven Pātālas.

Arjuna's Opportunity of Visiting and Worshipping Kālahastīśvara and Other Deities Stationed on the Banks of the Suvarṇamukharī

13. After taking his bath in that great river Arjuna visited the deity named Kālahastīśa,[1] worshipped by all the Suras on that mountain.

14. With his mind infused with devotion, he worshipped Mahādeva accompanied by the daughter of the Lord of Mountains. Thereby he derived full contentment.

15. With a desire to see special features that had never existed before (in other places), Arjuna wandered over that great mountain, the sole abode of mysteries.

---

1. This is in North Arcot District, one mile from Renugunta Railway Station. The deity is regarded as the *Vāyu* (Wind) form of god Śiva. It is reported that the lamp over the head of the Liṅga oscillates while other lamps in the temple are steady (De 84).

16. He saw Siddhas who accompanied by their womenfolk lived on the peaks and ridges of the mountain and sang the anecdotes of the Lord of Devas.

17. He looked at the Gandharvas with great respect as they were seated in the bowers of flowers accompanied by the Apsaras-maidens and excited and inebriated on account of the (imbibed) liquor extracted from the flowers.

18. In secluded spots he saw divine Yogins who were deeply engrossed in meditating on Śiva and full of respect and delight.

19. All around he saw quiet and peaceful hermitages and penance-groves. The son of Pāṇḍu saw the courtyard at the entrance (to the various abodes) resplendent with the Nīvāra grains offered as oblations.

20. He saw the sages abstaining from food, or taking in only air, or eating leaves, or consuming sunlight. All of them were calm with all their sense-organs perfectly controlled.

21-22. Lotus-ponds that rendered the quarters fragrant with the sweet smell of the full-blown flowers, gave delight to his eyes.

He saw Kirātas (Hunters) accompanied by their womenfolk, searching for deer, engrossed in thoughts of hunting and walking about with well-strung bows.

Arjuna Goes to Bharadvāja's Hermitage Situated on the Banks of Suvarṇamukharī

23-28a. Walking through the charming southern portion of the mountain, the descendant of Kuru saw the holy hermitage of Bharadvāja. It was rendered splendid by trees[1] laden with fruits and flowers, such as plantains, coconut palms, mango trees, black pepper, Campaka, Sandal trees, Takkola, Aśoka, Hintāla, Tāla, Ketakī, Dāḍima (Pomegranates), Jambū (Rose apple), Kadamba, Kaṭaka, Khadira, Arjuna, Pāṭala (Trumpet flower tree), Nāga, Punnāga, Sarala, Devadāru (Cedar), Karañjaka, Lavaṅga

1. Standard description of the forest.

(Clove tree), Luṅga (a kind of citron), Lavalī, Priyaṅgu, Tilaka, Vibhīta, Śrīphala (Bilva), holy fig tree, Madhūka, Plakṣa, Kesara, Pūga, Jambīra (a kind of citron), Nāraṅga (Orange), Nimba (Margosa), Āmalaka (Embylic Myrobalan) and Kauśika (coconut?) trees.

28b. It was surrounded by the creepers of Vāsantī, Kunda, Jāti etc. (varieties of Jasmine).

29-33a. Various lakes and tanks brought glory and magnificence to it. Being attracted by uncommon and unprecedented fragrance, bees hovered all round.

Birds like ruddy geese, cranes, storks, swans, Kāraṇḍava ducks etc. resorted to them. The lakes were marked with various flowers, such as red lotuses, blue lotuses, lilies etc. The lakes and ponds were full of water, sweet like nectar. The hermitage was a unique place of curious things.

It was full of animals of various kinds like lions, elephants, tigers, bears, deer, antelopes etc. All of them were friendly and helpful to one another. The gardens and parks therein far surpassed Nandana, Caitraratha and other divine parks. It was the cause of supreme bliss (to everyone). It was charming beyond the power of thinking of minds and the power of expression through words.

33b-44. Parrots of sweet voice revealed to their young ones the excellent meanings of the divine Śivāgamas.

The sky above the hermitage was rendered dark by means of the thick columns of smoke arising from the sacred fires when the offerings of ghee were poured therein. Seeing the same, peacocks had the erroneous notion of untimely clouds (spreading over the sky).

When the lions got tired after their continuous sport in the forests, the elephants approached them there of their own accord and showered water on them through their trunks to give their bodies some relief from the strain.[1]

---

1. This shows how, due to the *Sāttvika* influence of the hermitage, natural animosity of forest animals was forgotten.

Seeing that penance-grove, the son of Pāṇḍu got struck with wonder. He praised the power of the ascetics.

Preventing all his followers from straying here and there, he entered the hermitage along with his friends and excellent Brāhmaṇas.

Arjuna Pays His Respects to Bharadvāja

In front of him the son of Kuntī saw Sage Bharadvāja shining with the refulgence of blazing fire. He was surrounded by many excellent sages. He had smeared the whole of his body with ash. A deerskin constituted his upper garment. He was as resplendent as Kailāsa encircled by a fresh cloud. He was brilliant with his matted hair of golden splendour hanging down like the autumnal cloud with permanent streaks of lightning. He appeared as though the meanings of Śrutis, Smṛtis and Purāṇas had come collectively and adopted his form. He was (as it were) the receptacle of great auspiciousness, of divine knowledge and wisdom. He was permanently attended upon by (virtues like) fortitude, forbearance, kindness, contentment and peace, as though by loving wives. He had unimpaired Brahmanical splendour. The son of Pṛthā (Arjuna) approached him slowly and prostrated before his lotus-like feet with (his) eight limbs touching the ground.

Bharadvāja Extends His Hospitality to Arjuna

45. The eminent sage raised up the son of Pṛthā who had come (there and fallen at his feet) and blessed him with his mind extremely delighted.

46. After duly honouring him as a beloved guest with *Arghya* and other materials, he offered him a seat. As he sat thereon, he enquired about his welfare.

47. After getting due honour and hospitality from the sage, the middle one among the Pāṇḍava brothers entertained the eminent sage through pleasing words.

48. Then Bharadvāja remembered the Celestial Cow yielding everything one desired. She distributed various kinds of foodstuffs lavishly.

49-52. The son of Pṛthā took food along with his followers. After paying respects to the sage, he spent the remaining portion of the day discoursing on interesting stories.

Then he performed the rites connected with the evening prayer and performed *Homa* in the Sacred Fire.

Then he went to his abode in the hut accompanied by Brāhmaṇas and ministers. There he sat after being blessed by the eminent sage. He rejoiced when the cool breeze blew from the river and delighted him. Then he thought of hearing about the power of the river by asking the sage thus: "By whom was she brought here? From which mountain does she rise? How did she get superior power?"

CHAPTER THIRTYONE

Agastya's Departure to the South

Prompted by His Desire to Know the Power of Suvarṇamukharī Arjuna Asks Bharadvāja About the Same

Śrī Sūta said:

1-2. The prominent scion of the family of Bharata (Arjuna) bowed down to the leader of sages who had concluded his evening holy rites. He had a splendour like that of fire and was comfortably seated. He was pleased by his gladdening (words) of nectarine sweetness and cooling fragrance. Then he uttered the following words of decorous gravity full of humility:

Arjuna said:

3. O most excellent sage, I am the only blessed one in this world, since I have been enthusiastically honoured by you as though I am not at all different from your own son.

4. My mind, the curiosity of which has been aroused by your affection and encouragement, strongly urges me to imbibe the divine nectar of your words.

5. From which mountain has this great river originated? By whom was it brought? What is the merit obtained if the holy rites of bath, charitable gift etc. are performed there?

6. It behoves you, O good sage, to recount to me, your humble (follower), the origin and power of this (river). A devotee has to be blessed by you.

7. On hearing the words of Arjuna Bharadvāja, the excellent Brāhmaṇa, a skilled speaker, looked at his face and spoke these words:

Bharadvāja said:

8. O mighty-armed Arjuna, you are the sanctifier of the family of Kurus. You are specially worthy of my honour because you are the younger brother of Dharmaputra.

9. Many kings have been seen (by me), but, O Phālguna, they are not endowed with grace, rectitude, kindness, liberal-mindedness, courage and sagacity like you.

10. Nobility (of birth), learning and affluence are (usually) the cause of haughtiness in strong men. But in the case of excellent persons like you they are the cause of (greater) modesty and courteousness.

11. In spite of the abundant pleasures and vast kingdom, O descendant of Kuru, who else other than you can resist the tendency to deviate from normal decenc

12. O son of Kuntī, I am overcome by your extraordinary good qualities. What is it that should not be disclosed to you, O (noble one) with a mind full of such keen curiosity?

13. O king, listen to the divine story heard by me from a sage. On hearing this story all creatures are liberated from the afflictions born of sins.

Story of Śaṅkara's Marriage as Narrated by Bharadvāja

14. Formerly the Goddess, the daughter of Dakṣa, was subjected to insult by her father. After forsaking that body she became the daughter of the Snow-clad Mountain (Himālaya).

15. The Mountain (Himālaya) was approached and requested by the Seven Sages. Hence he was ready to give his daughter in marriage to Mṛtyuñjaya (Śiva).

16. The Bull-emblemed Lord of the universe came to the residence of Himavān, named Oṣadhīprastha,[1] in order to marry Sarvamaṅgalā (Pārvatī).

17. At his bidding all the living beings, both mobile and immobile, came there to rejoice in the felicity and prosperity of the Lord of Bhūtas (goblins).

18. The earth in the northern region became heavily burdened with their weight and caved in to such an extent that it reached the nether worlds.[2]

19. The southern region became very light because there was no burden on it. Hence it went up, on seeing which everyone became frightened.

20. On realising this change in the position of the earth, Maheśvara turned towards Agastya and said, "Come here, O highly intelligent one." Then he spoke these words:

21-22. "Since all the Bhūtas have come down here, the earth has become over-burdened by their weight. It has undergone a great alteration. Hence it behoves you, O highly intelligent one, to level up the earth. How can this be done by anyone other than you?

23. Indeed you are born of my splendour. You are engaged in the protection of the worlds. Hence, O my dear one, at my instance level up this earth.

24-26. You must not stay here among all those persons who have come down here eager to witness my marriage celebration. If you stay here, no one will be competent to set right the change in the level of the earth. Hence, O sinless one, you must go. Wherever you stay, I shall reveal unto you this form of mine resplendent in my marriage with the daughter of the Mountain."

---

1. A significant name as Himālaya has been traditionally famous for medicinal plants, some luminous even by night, (vide *Kumārasaṁbhava* I.10).

2. Imbalance of the earth is a novel reason in this Purāṇa for sending sage Agastya to the South.

Agastya's Departure to the South of the Himālaya for the Levelling of the Earth

27. After saying this Maheśvara embraced him and bade farewell to him. Saying "So be it", the sage bowed down to him and went in the direction of South.

28. When Agastya, a tiger among sages, went to the southern region after crossing the Vindhya mountain, the earth became level.

29. Suras, Gandharvas and Kinnaras experienced the thrill of delight (at it) and eulogized the Pot-born Sage who stayed on there (even) after removing the imbalance of the earth.

30. He then proceeded from that place and saw a lofty mountain standing upright in front of him, sustaining the earth by means of its extensive foothills.

31. It appeared like a veritable mine of great medicinal herbs and all types of gems and jewels, all with unimpaired brilliance and created by the Self-born Lord (Brahmā).

32. By means of its lofty peaks having extensive currents of water it appeared to hold up the sky permanently (preventing it from) falling upon the earth.

33. Agastya, the eminent sage, slowly climbed up the mountain and decided to reside in the beautiful region of its summit.

34-37. He built his excellent hermitage on a charming piece of land on the northern bank of a lake on that (mountain) with water that could be compared with nectar. The lake was surrounded by many trees and had the brilliance of clusters of lilies and lotuses.

He propitiated the Pitṛs, the celestial sages and the presiding deity of architecture in accordance with the injunctions.

Accompanied by multitudes of sages, he stayed there for a long time on that mountain frequented by Devas, Siddhas, Gandharvas and celestial damsels.

As the Pot-born Sage stayed in a penance grove with his mind engrossed in penance, the mountain became possessed of excellent sublimity and therefore acquired the name Agastyaśaila.[1]

CHAPTER THIRTYTWO

The Birth of Suvarṇamukharī

AN ETHERIAL VOICE URGES AGASTYA TO CAUSE A RIVER TO FLOW THERE

Bharadvāja said:

1. Once that excellent sage concluded the holy rites of forenoon and entered the temple to propitiate Śiva.

2. The Goddess of Speech of invisible form brilliantly revealed herself in clear syllables and it was heard by that noble-souled sage equipped with wonderful (power).

3-8. The etherial voice spoke to Agastya, the most excellent one among those who performed *Japa*:

"Indeed this land devoid of a river does not look nice, although it is famous. (It is) like a Brāhmaṇa who is averse to knowledge and wisdom, though he may have (Brāhmaṇical) features; (or) like the initiation (in a holy rite) without monetary gifts; (or) like the night without moonlight.

O excellent Brāhmaṇa, this piece of land without a river does not appear splendid. With a desire for the welfare of all the worlds, cause a river to flow.

It shall have power to release (everyone) from the fear arising from great sins. This is conducive to the welfare of multitude of Devas. This is what is sought by excellent sages. This is beneficial to human beings. Kindly do this, O sage of good holy rites. Cause a great river to flow—a river that is conducive

1. The genesis of the name Agastyaśaila of the mountain where Suvarṇamukharī rises.

to the welfare of Devas, excellent sages and people of the earth, a river that will destroy the mire of sins."[1]

Śrī Bharadvāja continued:

9. On hearing those words the Brāhmaṇa became engrossed in thought for a short while. After concluding the worship of the deity he came to the quadrangular spot in the courtyard and sat there.

10-12. He then brought together all those sages residing in that hermitage. To them he related the utterance made by the Divine Speech.

On hearing that wonderful utterance the sages became delighted in their minds. After saluting Maitrāvaruṇi (Agastya), the excellent sage, they spoke (these words):

The Great Sages Request Agastya to Create Suvarṇamukharī

The sages said:

13. O storehouse of mercy, your acts are divine and splendid. Your life is the greatest wonder of all wonderful mysteries. It is the most auspicious of all auspicious things.

14. Merely by your *Huṁkāra* (i.e. a noisy grunt of anger) Nahuṣa was brought down from the overlordship of Devas.[2] He then attained the state of a worm. There is nothing more wonderful than that.

15. Is there anything more wonderful than that (by you) the entire ocean was made a mouthful of water, the ocean that encircles the whole of the earth and strikes the sky with its waves?

16. The Vindhya mountain that attempted to obstruct the path of the Sun was subdued by you. What can be greater than this?

---

1. It seems that according to old tradition the birth of the river is due to human effort. Here the credit is given to Agastya.

2. This refers to Agastya's curse to Nahuṣa who made him carry his palanquin to Indra's wife.

17. Who is competent to praise adequately your wonderful activities on the earth? It is by my (our?) good luck that you have come here in this embodied form.

18. We have become the greatest of all blessed ones in the three worlds, O great sage, that we stay here in the precincts of this hermitage with you as our leader and guide.

19. (*Defective Text*) Though this land is worthy of being praised, it is far from being excellent, O excellent Brāhmaṇa. Though it is full of all (desired) objects, it does not shine, as it is devoid of a river.

20. Of what avail is this damned life that has not obtained the opportunity to bathe in a river? Not being born at all is far better than residing in a land without a river.

21. The time of fructification of our fortune is imminent, since you have been directed by Devas to cause the great river to flow.

22. When will we take our holy bath, and be blessed, in the great river caused to flow by you in this land, O sinless one?

23. Of what avail is much conjecturing and deliberation? Let the endeavour be made certainly to bring down the excellent river that is worthy of taking refuge in and that should be saluted by the entire universe.

Śrī Bharadvāja said:

24. That great Brāhmaṇa honoured their sincere words (of request) and made the resolve, 'I will bring the river'.

Agastya's Penance for Making Suvarṇamukharī Flow Out

25-26. He was (formally) accorded permission by the eminent sages. He worshipped Suras after performing a special worship of Śiva. He undertook an intensive observance of holy rites, unbearable on account of the excessive strain involved. With a great effort he performed a very severe penance (which is) not at all easy for anyone else.

27. During the hot and fierce days of summer he stayed in the midst of four fires with his eyes fixed on the Sun. Still he did not experience any strain or fatigue.

28. During rainy days he was lashed at by torrential downpours of rains accompanied by unbearable violent gusts of wind. Yet he did not feel disturbed in the heart.

29. During early winter he stood in the waters coming up to his neck and proceeded ahead with his *Japa* and meditation. Yet there was no change in his (steadiness or mental peace).

30. On realizing that there was delay in achieving what he desired, he adopted a procedure still more intense, that terrified all the worlds.

31. He controlled all his mental activities. He abstained from taking food. He conquered his sense organs. Without being conscious of external (world) he stood like a stone.

32. While he was thus engaged in penance, a terrible fire sprang up from all his limbs. Blazing with furious flames it scraped the sky.

33. All the quarters were covered with mysteriously wonderful clusters of flames. Greatly tormented by fear multitudes of people cried out.

34. After bowing down to him Devas informed the Lotus-born One about such a terribly great agitation of the whole universe that had taken place.

Arrival of the Four-Faced Lord to the Hermitage of Agastya

35. Brahmā reassured them. He was attended upon by Siddhas and Gandharvas. He appeared in front of the Pot-born Sage who was engaged in penance.

36. On seeing that Brahmā the great (Lord) had come, the Brāhmaṇa bowed to him. With his mind fixed on him alone he propitiated him with different kinds of hymns and prayers.

37. Then looking at Agastya who bowed to him humbly, the Lotus-born Lord, with his countenance beaming with great delight, spoke these sacred words:

***Brahmā said*:**

38. O sinless one, I am highly pleased with your penance (which is) very difficult to be performed. Choose your boon. O

(sage) of good holy rites, I shall grant you whatever is desired by you.

Agastya said:

39. By your favour, O Lord, everything is readily accomplished by me. If you desire to give me whatever I wish, I beg for this unhesitatingly.

40. On seeing this region devoid of a river my mind is pained as (it would be) at the repetition of the Vedic passages almost without understanding the meaning.

41. O Lord of Devas, be pleased to grant a great river that has power to sanctify and protect the earth. This alone is what I desire.

At the Request of Agastya the Four-Faced Lord Urges Gaṅgā

Śrī Bharadvāja said:

42. On hearing the words of Agastya Brahmā said: "It will so happen." He then remembered the river flowing through the celestial path (i.e. Gaṅgā).

43. Then the celestial Gaṅgā appeared and stood in front of Brahmā resplendent with her crown and palms joined in reverence.

44. Brahmā then spoke these words to that mother of all the worlds who had come to him at his bidding and (stood there) with the head bent down in humility.

Brahmā said:

45. O Gaṅgā, you have to be directed by me in a matter that is helpful to all the worlds. Like me you too invariably stand ready in all matters concerning the protection of the worlds.

46. The Pot-born Sage wishes to cause the flow of a river for the sake of the welfare of all the worlds in this land devoid of rivers.

47. Hence you descend down to the earth. Sanctify the people of the earth with a portion of yours. You go to the earth by the path pointed out to you by this (sage).

48. When the current of water begins to flow in the terrestrial world, all those who desire for spiritual achievement, the excellent Suras and the leading sages will resort to it.

49. Be the most excellent one among (all) the rivers; protect the people resorting to you; do what is pleasing to Agastya. O gentle one, go ahead happily.

Bharadvāja said:

50. After saying this, Brahmā vanished. He was specially honoured and adored by that river and that (sage) by obeisance, veneration and eulogies.

In the Presence of Agastya Gaṅgā Accepts the Responsibility of Causing the Flow of a River as Her own Part

51. Then Gaṅgā revealed in front of the eminent sage a divinely resplendent form born of her own part and spoke these words:

Gaṅgā said:

52. O dear sage, a part of mine will come to the earth after assuming the form of a river and will fulfil your desire.

Bharadvāja said:

53. After saying this the heavenly river went away. The river urged by Gaṅgā asked the sage, "Which way should we go?" The sage replied to her:

Agastya said:

54-56. O auspicious one, I shall go in front of you and show you the way to be followed. You may flow after me.[1]

On being told thus by the sage that auspicious river said delightedly: "O sinless one, I shall do as you please."

1. It seems that Agastya had detonated powerful explosives to reach the water-level.

The sage with great joy in his mind brought her who had taken the form of that river down from the great mountain with its peaks scraping the sky. He went ahead showing her the approved path.[1]

CHAPTER THIRTYTHREE

The Efficacy of Suvarṇamukharī

Śakra and Others Eulogize Suvarṇamukharī

Bharadvāja said:

1-2. Then the Heaven-dwellers, the chief of whom was Śakra, seated in the divine aerial chariots, followed that great river which followed Agastya. With the palms joined in reverence all the great sages followed that divine river that had newly descended and attended upon her with prayers.

3-4. Siddhas, Cāraṇas and Gandharvas who had gathered together in thousands, praised that eminent sage and that river with splendid hymns.

The people of the earth eagerly said: "Fortunately this water that is free from impurities and comparable to nectar has been obtained." They expressed their delight and enthusiasm thus.

5. At the bidding of the Lotus-born Lord, the Wind-god spoke these words within the hearing of all the Devas:

The Derivation of the Name Suvarṇamukharī as Explained by the Wind-God (Vāyu)

Vāyu said:

6. To the good fortune of the worlds this river was brought by Agastya to the earth like *Suvarṇa* (gold) making the quarters reverberate (*mukharīkṛta*).[2]

---

1. Cf. Mbh. *Vana*, Ch. 109 where Bhagīratha leads the river Gaṅgā to some channel prepared for the flow of the river in advance.

2. A popular derivation of the name of the river.

7. Hence it will be well-known by the name *Suvarṇamukharī* praised by all the worlds in the abode of the Lord who has salvation as his asset (i.e. the bestower of salvation).

8. This Suvarṇamukharī is the most excellent of all the rivers. It should be served and resorted to. This is the directive of Brahmā.

AGASTYA DESCRIBES THE GREATNESS OF SUVARṆAMUKHARĪ BROUGHT BY HIMSELF

Bharadvāja said:

9. On hearing these words uttered by Wind-god thus, the Pot-born Lord became delighted. He was overwhelmed with surprise within himself. He experienced thrill all over his body (making the hair stand on end).

10. Thus this divine river caused great happiness to men by providing for bathing and drinking and other purposes. It attained great renown in the world.

11. At the behest of the Lotus-born Lord it is the celestial river Suvarṇamukharī by name itself that sanctifies all those who resort solely to it.

12. This excellent river crosses many huge mountains, forest regions and diverse lands in due order. It is nourished by many great rivers arising from those mountains.

13. Its waters are the sole means of curing the seriously sick and those who are attacked by diseases and of restoring them to normal health. They dispel all the distressing sensations, internal as well as external. They cause great welfare.

14. Excellent elephants engrossed in sports strike hard with their trunks whereby columns of water sprays are raised. It appears as if the river makes flower offerings to the Sun-god thereby with great delight.

15. Its waters are excessively pure and they support (i.e. they contain) fragrant white and red lotuses and lilies that render the faces of the quarters fragrant with their sweet scent. Those flowers are the sole receptacles of the good luck of bees.

16. Heavenly damsels are enthusiastic to take a plunge sportingly into the water of this river. The saffron applied in the parting line of the hair on their head renders the waters pink in

colour. The Pārijāta flowers slipping down from their braids of hair make the waters fragrant with their sweet scents.

17. The waters cause auspiciousness. They are tasty and devoid of mud. They are exceedingly free from impurities. They are comparable to nectar. They dispel the sins of even the son of Indra.[1]

18. That river rises from the Agastya Śaila (mount Agastya). It has been brought to the earth by the Pot-born Sage. It is rendered splendid with many praiseworthy holy spots. Thus she falls into the Southern Ocean.

19. The waves of the Ocean came forward[2] favourably disposed to receive the river. They welcome it scattering the auspicious raw rice grains in the form of water sprays and holy lamps in that of gems and jewels.

20. Embracing her with his hands (in the form) of billows the Lord of Rivers honoured that river. The rumbling sound of the waves constituted his speech of welcome. Thus the Ocean delighted the River.

21. When the favourably inclined (River) came near his (Ocean's) shore, the water (line) of the Storehouse of Waters increased along with the delighted waves.

22. Thus Agastya united that River with the Ocean. After eulogizing her and taking leave of her, the sage who had fulfilled his objective, went away as he pleased.

Arjuna said:

23. O holy Sir, the origin of the great river has been told by you. Now I am eager to hear about its efficacy.

The Greatness of Suvarṇamukharī as Described by Bharadvāja

Bharadvāja said:

24. It (i.e. the river) is destructive of sins. It is the sole cause of all welfare and prosperity. Listen to its greatness, O son of Pāṇḍu. I shall tell it to you.

1. The only sin recorded against Jayanta is that he assumed the form of a crow and pecked at Sītā for which he had to lose his eye.

2. VV 19-22 give a romantic description of the confluence of the river and the sea.

25. When all the Karmas perish and the Jñānins (i.e. those who have acquired spiritual wisdom) come to their final birth, they get the opportunity to take their holy bath in Suvarṇamukharī. That shall bring about their identity with Brahman.

26. By remembering this Suvarṇamukharī even from hundreds of Yojanas away one shall be liberated from all sins. There is no doubt about it.

27. The bones of creatures deposited in the waters of Suvarṇamukharī become the steps for climbing up to the world of Brahmā.

28. Even when men take their bath in other waters (e.g. tanks, lakes or rivers) wherever they may be, if they remember Suvarṇamukharī at the time, they derive excellent benefit.

29. Men are assailed by crores of sins only until they get the auspicious opportunity to take their holy bath in Suvarṇamukharī.

30. All the Tīrthas of heaven, firmament and the earth remember the river Suvarṇamukharī everyday in the morning for their own fulfilment.

31. Merely by being remembered Suvarṇamukharī that rises from Agastyācala and falls into the Southern Ocean, shall destroy sins.

32. With their innermost heart yearning for bath in Suvarṇamukharī Śakra and other Devas desire for birth in the human species.

33. Those who regularly consume the grains and vegetables nourished by the waters of Suvarṇamukharī are never afflicted with great sins arising from hundreds of consumptions of faulty foodstuffs.

34. The waters of Suvarṇamukharī weighing a *Niṣka* (about 15 grams) when drunk shall immediately destroy the sins of embodied souls, sins as huge as mountains.

35. Even after attaining human birth if people do not take their holy bath in the waters of Suvarṇamukharī, their birth is fruitless.

36. One bath taken in Suvarṇamukharī in accordance with the injunctions is on a par with crores of baths in Gaṅgā during the *Parvans* (Full-Moon day, New-Moon day etc.).

37-40. Among all the rivers Suvarṇamukharī is the most

excellent one like Govinda among Devas, the Moon among luminaries, a king among men, Kalpaka (wish-yielding tree) among trees, like the sky among the great elements, like Māyā among all powers, like Gāyatrī among Mantras, like thunderbolt among weapons of Devas, *Ātman* among all the ultimate reals, like Rudrādhyāya among the Yajus Mantras, like Anant among serpents, like Himācala among mountains, like the shrine of Potrin (Varāha) among all holy spots and like mind among the organs of sensation.[1]

41. One who aspires for purity, welfare, auspiciousness etc. shall always remember, salute, glorify and mentally adore the splendid Suvarṇamukharī.

42-44. The following two Mantras should be recited: "I resort to you, O Suvarṇamukharī rising from Agastyācala, falling into the Southern Ocean and destroying all the sins. O mother of the universe, with your waters I wash my body burned and scorched by sins. Bestow on me excellent welfare." One should recite these two Mantras perfectly after observing holy rites. By taking the holy bath then he shall become pure. He shall rejoice then.

45. Suvarṇamukharī was formerly created by Brahmā. It was brought (to the earth) by Agastya. It is the excellent embodied form of Mandākinī herself.

46. This divine (river) of such efficacy should be glorified by those who seek auspiciousness with a mind full of devotion. Those who desire splendid welfare must take their bath therein.

47. The holy rites of bath, charitable gifts etc. performed on the banks of Suvarṇamukharī during the lunar and solar eclipses shall be of unmeasurable benefit, O son of Pṛthā.

48. If the holy bath in Suvarṇamukharī is taken during the transit of the Sun from one Zodiac to another, at the time of holy *Ayana* (i.e. northern or southern transit of the Sun) or on the day of *Vyatīpāta* (a particular astronomical position), it shall redeem a crore of the members of the family.

49. By taking bath in the waters of Suvarṇamukharī during

1. Cf. BG X, *Vibhūti-yoga*, for the list of such topmost persons and things.

the rise of one's birth-star or on one's birthday in accordance with the injunctions one obtains welfare, good health, happiness and glory.

50. By taking the holy bath in the waters of Suvarṇamukharī one gets over the sin that causes evil dreams and obstacles, evil spirits, adverse Planets, Planets in maleficent positions etc.

51. By gifting a land as small as the space occupied by cow's hoof on the banks of Suvarṇamukharī one shall obtain that benefit which is obtained by gifting away the entire earth.

52. By gifting in accordance with the injunctions a cow along with clothes and ornaments to a Brāhmaṇa on the banks of Suvarṇamukharī one attains the eternal Brahman.

53. For the sake of attaining benefits here and hereafter all types of charitable gifts should be offered on the banks of Suvarṇamukharī during auspicious occasions.

54. *Japa*, *Homa*, penance, charitable gift, rites unto the Manes and the worship of Devas performed on the banks of Suvarṇamukharī shall become hundred times more efficacious.

55. I shall tell you another excellent holy rite that should be performed every year on the banks of Suvarṇamukharī by those who seek happiness.

56-57. During the season of clouds after being hidden by the rays of the Sun when the sage Agastya gloriously rises once again (i.e. when the star Canopus is seen), the devotees should with great purity and concentration perform holy ablutions (and other rites) in this river, O scion of the family of Kuru. They dwell in the celestial abode for the period of a Kalpa.

58. Those who offer a gold replica of Agastya at that time in accordance with the injunctions attain the eternal Brahman, O son of Pṛthā.

Arjuna said:

59. What is that prescribed procedure whereby this holy rite should be performed, O great sage? Tell everything to me who am eager to know.

The Prescribed Procedure Regarding Making a Gift of an Idol of Agastya

Bharadvāja said:

60. A man of perfect mental control should calculate the day of the rise of Agastya (Star Canopus). In accordance with his capacity he should get gold image of that great sage prepared.

61. He should have brilliant golden appearance with matted hair tied up. In his lotus-like hands he holds a rosary of beads and a water pot.

62. He wears a soft bark garment. His form is gentle, beautifully marked and smeared with ash. Rudrākṣa beads constitute his ornament.

63. After making the replica thus the devotee should take his holy bath with perfectly controlled mind. He shall adorn the preceptor with scents, flowers etc. in accordance with the injunctions.

64. An *Āḍhaka* (256 handfuls) of rice grains should be formed into a heap and the gold replica of Agastya should be placed upon it along with two clothes. The devotee should worship the image.

65-67. He shall then recite the following Mantra: "Let Lord Agastya be highly pleased with this charitable gift—Agastya who paralysed Vindhya, who gracefully reduced the ocean into a mouthful of water, who became exceedingly refulgent by means of the brilliance of all the Devas beginning with Brahmā, the Pot-born Sage, my Lord who was bowed down to by all the Devas and Asuras."

After reciting this Mantra, he should make over the gift with a stream of water poured over it. He shall be liberated from all sins and he shall attain (union with) the eternal Brahman.

68. There is no doubt about this that he will be liberated from all major and minor sins, whether committed in the previous births or in the current one.

69. All the Devas beginning with Brahmā, the great sages beginning with Sanaka, and the living beings both mobile and immobile, shall become delighted undoubtedly.

70. After performing this holy rite of Agastya, the great

sage, one shall feed Brāhmaṇas in accordance with one's capacity for the delight of the holy sage. Monetary gifts too shall be made.

71. A person who is not able to perform that rite, should devoutly propitiate Brāhmaṇas by gifts of gold, food-grains etc. according to his capacity.

72. That day shall not be allowed to pass off in vain. The devotee should celebrate it scrupulously. One should certainly perform some holy rite (on that day).

73. The river Suvarṇamukharī shall be glorified by Suras and Asuras. It is the mature fruit of the penance of the great sage Agastya.

74. Thus the origin as well as the efficacy of the great river has been fully recounted to you. Tell me, what more do you wish to hear?

CHAPTER THIRTYFOUR

The Miraculous Power of Agastya Tīrtha and Agastyeśvara

Arjuna said:

1-3. Even after frequent drinking of the nectar of your statements through the ears as though in handfuls, my mind, being desirous of hearing further, does not become satiated. I am desirous of hearing more of your words. This repeated act (i.e. of requesting you for elucidation and narration) of mine shall not cause any distress in your mind, since your heart is filled with mercy. Now I wish to hear, O great sage, as to what are those holy places on this river capable of destroying sins and where are they located.

4. What are the different holy rivers that flow into this river, O sage? Where are the people to take their holy bath so that they can dispel sins and cease to be afraid of Yama?

5. What are those meritorious and sacred shrines and holy spots of Hara, Acyuta and other Devas situated on both the banks of this river?

6. What is the benefit that is obtained by those men who duly perform auspicious rites such as holy bath, charitable gift etc. in those holy spots?

7. A great desire has cropped up, O most excellent one among those who are conversant with the Vedas, to know all these things along with the associated subsidiary tales and anecdotes. Narrate them in due order and in full details.

Bharadvāja said:

8. What is asked by you, O son of Pṛthā, is being related in due order and in its full details. The greatness of the group of sacred places is being told now beginning with Agastyatīrtha, the lord of all the Tīrthas.

9-11. The first place where the great river was brought down from the mountain to the earth by the noble-souled Agastya, worthy of being honoured by Suras as well as Asuras, who wished for the welfare of all the worlds by means of perfect knowledge, is called Agastyatīrtha.[1] By taking his holy bath there in the great river a person becomes blessed and has his objectives achieved. It is the most sacred one in all the three worlds. By taking their holy bath there even great sinners become purified.

12. People who (regularly) take their holy bath there, dispel the mass of great sins committed in the course of their many births, and they rejoice in heaven.

13-14. If ascetics and persons of perfect control over their sense-organs take their holy bath in that Tīrtha and make great charitable gifts of cows, lands, gingelly seeds, gold etc., O Arjuna, they obtain full hundred times of the benefit of the charitable gifts made by people of great purity and concentration at Gaṅgā-dvāra (place where Gaṅgā enters the plains).

15-16. Lord Īśa is also here. He is well-known by the name Agastyeśa. The Liṅga had been installed by sage Agastya who caused happiness to all the worlds. Those who take their holy bath in the great river and worship that Liṅga, acquire the benefit of ten horse sacrifices.

---

1. VV 9-16 describe the glory of Agastya Tīrtha.

Time Prescribed for Holy Bath in Suvarṇamukharī

17-19. When the Sun leaves the sign of Zodiac Sagittarius and enters that of Capricorn,[1] that holy period is called *Uttarāyaṇa* (Northern Transit). People who take their holy bath in that river on that day with perfect self-control, concentration and mental purity, and visit the Lord of Pārvatī, Agastyeśa, worshipped by Suras, get the benefit of a thousand Agniṣṭomas and a hundred Vājapeyas. They rejoice in heaven and are honoured by multitudes of Devas.

20. At the time of the transit of Mṛga (i.e. when the constellation Orion is associated with the Sun) all persons seeking their welfare must certainly visit Agastyeśa.

The Greatness of Devarṣipitṛtīrthas

21. To the north-east of that Tīrtha, O Arjuna, in a place extending to a *Krośa* (3 kms), there are three Tīrthas named after Devas, Ṛṣis (Sages) and Pitṛs (Manes).

22. Devas, Sages and Pitṛs were worshipped there by that sage. Delighted in their minds, they granted him all the desired objects.

23. At that time it was spoken in his presence by Devas, Ṛṣis and Pitṛs: "These three Tīrthas should be honoured by our names in this order."

24. Those who take their holy bath in those three Tīrthas and perform the *Tarpaṇa* rite (water libations) are liberated from the three-fold debt and they attain everlasting stay in heaven.

The Confluence of Veṇā and Suvarṇamukharī

25. In the land to the north-east of it, within 2 Yojanas, a great river named Veṇā joins Suvarṇamukharī.

---

1. This generally falls on the 14th January (or a day on either side according to some almanacs).

26. With increased force of its current it causes the trees on the banks to fall down. It floods the forests (and fields) through the waters gushing out through its canals.

27. On its raised banks flocks of ruddy geese play about and make them noisy and full of excitement. There are the pleasant humming sounds of the swarms of bees inebriated by the fragrance of lotuses.

28. It crosses many lofty mountains and has plenty of sweet water. Thus it joins Suvarṇamukharī.

29. Those who take their holy bath in the confluence of the two rivers in accordance with the injunctions shall derive full benefit of ten horse-sacrifices.

30. The sacred river Suvarṇamukharī flows northwards after its confluence with Veṇā. It goes through the impassable mountainous track.

31. The river then flows for about 4 Yojanas (=50 kms.) through the rugged path amongst mountains and appears charming.

32-33. For about one and a half Yojanas the great river flows to the east. There is the well-known Liṅga of Śiva named Agastyeśvara on its fascinating northern bank. Its remembrance removes all the sins of Devas as well as of human beings.

34-35. Men who exercise great control over their sense organs and take their holy bath in the great river and then visit the Lord of Pārvatī installed by Agastya, dispel the mass of sins accumulated in the course of their innumerable previous births. They then rejoice in heaven for an everlasting period.

36. Thereafter Suvarṇamukharī flows northwards for about half a Yojana. That strip of land contains many Tīrthas.

The Confluence of Suvarṇamukharī with the River named Vyāghrapadā[1]

37. It is at this place which is very charming on account of Hintāla, date-palms and resin-bearing Śāla trees that the river named Vyāghrapadā joins Suvarṇamukharī.

1. Vyāghrapadā is modern Vāghurā. VV 37-41 describe the confluence of Suvarṇamukharī and Vāghurā.

38-41. It gracefully flows preventing many inevitable sins. On either side there is a dense growth of canes and reeds adorning the banks.

Young females of Siddha and Gandharva families plunge into its waters regularly. It sparkles with the flowers and oblations offered into it by daughters of ascetics.

Its surroundings are exciting and noisy on account of the cackling and chirping sounds of swans, Kāraṇḍava and Krauñca birds (cranes). It flows eastwards through forests and mountains.

Excellent men who take their holy bath in the confluence of the two rivers shall get the full benefit of ten horse-sacrifices.

Śaṅkhatīrtha[1]

42-46. On the banks of the river named Vyāghrapadā that dispels the dirt (sins) of all the worlds, stands the excellent Śaṅkhatīrtha that annihilates all sins.

It is a permanent abode of Brahminical Sages. It is frequented by Suras and Gandharvas. It gives immeasurable pleasure by its sight, holy ablution therein and drinking and using in various ways of its water.

Lord Īśa resides there, O Phālguna, by the name Śaṅkheśa. The Liṅga was installed by a great sage named Śaṅkha.

Those who take their excellent bath there and visit the Bull-vehicled Lord, obtain the merit accruing from ten horse-sacrifices. They then go to heaven.

After joining the river named Vyāghrapadā (Suvarṇamukharī) flows to a distance of about a Yojana and reaches the mountain named Vṛṣabhācala. It is resorted to by eminent sages. Its waters are splendid and free from dirt.

---

1. VV 42-46 describe Śaṅkha Tīrtha. It appears that the author has personally followed the course of Suvarṇamukharī.

CHAPTER THIRTYFIVE

The Confluence of Kalyā with Suvarṇamukharī

Bharadvāja said:

1. Like Kālindī that joins Gaṅgā the auspicious and sacred river named Kalyā joins Suvarṇamukharī there.

2. Kalyā that rises in Vṛṣabhācala, that stands like the sovereign of all the Tīrthas and that is the most excellent of all the rivers, is destructive of masses of sins.

3. Both of its banks are adorned by different kinds of trees and creepers. It is a pleasant abode of multitudes of sages. It is conspicuous on account of holy hermitages.

4-5. Its banks are marked with Darbha grass and raw rice-grains gracing the *Arghyas* (water libations etc.) offered by Brāhmaṇas. Its waters are muddy (only) because they wash the musk-unguents from the breasts of celestial damsels.

It is rendered fragrant by the liquid ichor oozing from the temples of huge elephants. It is full of hundreds of sacrificial posts fixed by Brāhmaṇas and kings.

6-11. By means of a perennial supply of water that is never turbid, it has satisfied (thoroughly) the entire mankind. Of these two rivers even one by itself is capable of dispelling sins. Who is competent to eulogize (adequately) the greatness of both of them joined together?

In the middle of the river there is a rock named Brahmaśilā. Afterwards due to the penance of Agastya it will attain the (near) equivalence to Gayā. Those who take their bath there in the holy waters of both the rivers, shall obtain the benefit of a hundred *Pauṇḍarīka* sacrifices. The sins of Brāhmaṇa-slaughter etc. are destroyed in the case of those who are sanctified by their holy bath in the confluence of the two rivers.

United with Kalyā then, which is destructive of Saṁsāra,[1] Suvarṇamukharī shines like the sanctifying Kṛṣṇaveṇī.

---

1. As there is no river called Bhavanāśini joining Kṛṣṇaveṇī *bhavanāśinyā* is taken as an adjective to the word *Kalyayā*.

Śrī Veṅkaṭācala Situated on the Banks of Suvarṇamukharī

12. To the north of the great river (Suvarṇamukharī) about half a Yojana away stands the famous Veṅkaṭācala about a Yojana in height.

13-14a. This excellent mountain is the support of all Tīrthas. The following are the groves of this mountain: Añjana, Ananta, Vṛṣabha, Nīla, Kesari, Potrin, Nārāyaṇa and Veṅkaṭa.

14b-15a. This mountain is glorified as Varāhakṣetra by noble men, because it was formerly accepted (as a resort) by the Slayer of Madhu after he assumed the form (body) of Boar.

15b-16a. Accompanied by the daughter of the great Ocean Acyuta dwells here permanently on the well-known Veṅkaṭācala on the banks of Suvarṇamukharī.

16b-18a. Siddhas, Gandharvas, sages, Dānavas and human beings attend upon (and worship) the Lord of Veṅkaṭa residing on that mountain along with Śrī. The desires and ambitions of the devotees who have dedicated their minds to Puruṣottama are realized immediately, O Arjuna, and their miseries perish.

18b-19. Those who remember the Lord of the universe residing on Veṅkaṭādri get all their defects and blemishes dispelled. They go to the permanent and immutable region.

Arjuna said:

20-22. How did Lord Kamalāpati (Lord of Lakṣmī), the Lord who is bowed down to by Suras and Asuras, manifest himself on Veṅkaṭādri of great merit?

To which blessed (devotee) did he reveal on being pleased his own wonderful form that bestows the benefits of worldly pleasures and ultimate salvation? O great Sage, I wish to hear about the greatness of Viṣṇu, the primordial Lord of Devas. Please recount it to me accurately and in detail.

The Greatness of the Lord Residing on Śrī Veṅkaṭācala

Bharadvāja said:

23-24. Listen to the greatness of Veṅkaṭanātha with great

concentration. It is not possible even for Brahmā to state it in great detail.

O dear one, O suppressor of enemies, you are blessed because you have the devout inclination to hear about the greatness of the Slayer of Madhu, of the Lord of Devas.

25. I too am meritorious, O son of Pṛthā, because the sacred activities of Hari, the Lord of all living beings, will be recounted by me now.

26-27. I shall recount to you, O son of Pṛthā, the story related by Vāmadeva formerly to the noble-souled Janaka on the banks of Gaṅgā, when that king who possessed pure and perfect knowledge, was engaged in sacrifice with due initiation. It is the story that destroys sins and is highly sanctifying because Viṣṇu is glorified therein.

28-30. Lord Nārāyaṇa is prior to all living beings. He is immanent in the universe. He is the creator of the universe. He is unsullied. He is of the form of consciousness and knowledge.

The lord is thousand (innumerable)-headed, thousand-eyed and thousand-footed. It is on account of his brilliance that this universe consisting of mobile and immobile beings shines.

There is no splendour greater than he. There is no penance greater than he. There is no knowledge greater than he. There is no other Yoga greater than he.

31. There is no Vidyā (Lore or Knowledge) greater than he, O son of Pṛthā, O leader of men. The Lord is always abiding in all the living beings.

32. All the living beings stay happily within him. He alone is Yajña, the performer of Yajña and the adjuncts of Yajña such as the ladle, the wooden spoon etc.

33. He is the fruit (of religious rites), the bestower of the benefit as well as the goal to be reached thereby. When the sacrificial fire is brought and one offers oblations with the animal sprinkled with sacred water, the animal sprinkled (with holy water) and those who resort to him, attain the goal (heaven/salvation) granted by him.

34. Those who make the bondage resulting from Karmas the sacrificial animal and consign it to the holy fire of Jñāna (i.e. spiritual knowledge) with Him as the aim, attain *Sāyujya* with Him.

35. Hari, Sadāśiva, Brahmā and Mahendra, the great ruler of heaven, all these are declared as the synonyms of that self-same Lord of all.

36. He who with concentrated mind ponders over the greatness of Nārāyaṇa, the Supreme Soul, is not reborn.

37. The attributeless one, of the nature of knowledge and bliss, the witness, the Ātman without limitation or condition, and the eternal one, assumes different forms as per His will.

38. He is the most sacred one of all sacred things; he is the greatest goal of the helpless; he is the deity unto all deities; he is the most excellent good of all the good.

39. He is the only *Bodhya* ('that which should be known') among of all *Bodhyas*; he is the most excellent *Dhyeya* ('that which should be meditated upon') of all *Dhyeyas*; he is the superior *Vinaya* (humility, good bearing, polite conduct) among all *Vinayas*; he is endowed with *Naya* (justice).

40. He is the splendour that produces other splendours and luminaries; he is the most excellent and intensive penance of all penances; he is the supporter of all living beings. Janārdana is without beginning and end.

41-42. Even Brahmā and others are at a loss to know his intrinsic nature. He is unborn yet takes incarnations. He is the soul of everyone and yet kills the enemies. Though he is independent, he functions as subservient to his devotees. That omniscient, Garuḍa-emblemed Lord is the witness of all actions (of all beings).

43-46. Sages with great concentration and mental purity seek his form. Four of his *Mūrtis* (forms) are famous,[1] viz. Saṅkarṣaṇa, Vāsudeva, Pradyumna and Aniruddha. *Praṇava* is proclaimed thereafter. His heart is refulgent. Vāsudeva is the Lord and this Mantra reveals him. He who repeats this *Mantrarāja* regularly, shall be the recipient of *Siddhis* due to the mercifulness of Viṣṇu.

---

1. This is the Pāñcarātra influence. These four manifestations are called *Vyūhas* in that system.

The Creation of Living Beings Evolved by the Lord[1]

47-51. Listen with concentration. I shall recount everything, how at the beginning of the Kalpa, Mādhava who wards off adversities and calamities, who provides (bestows) affluence and who bestows worldly pleasures and liberation, created living beings.

As he contemplated the process of creation the great and brilliant form of Hari resorted to *Rajoguṇa* and became well-known as Viriñca. From the mouth (face) of the Lord Śakra, the Deva, was born along with Pāvaka (the Fire-god). Śakra became the lord of the three worlds and Pāvaka became the lord of the process of cooking.

From his mind (which is) perpetually cool due to his mercifulness, came out the Moon. He is the permanent protector of waters, of all the medicinal herbs and of Brāhmaṇas.

From his eyes was born the Sun that illuminates the universe. He is the cause of cold, heat and rain, and causes the (various units of) Time and is the storehouse of refulgences.

52. From his vital airs was born Samīra (the Wind-god), the life essence of the universe, the exceedingly powerful supporter of planets, stars, celestial Gaṅgā and aerial chariots.

53. From the region of the navel of that noble-souled one was born the Intermediate Space (Antarikṣa). From his head issued forth Ākāśa (Sky/Ether) that is the cause of the origin of all elements.

54. From his lotus-like feet came out the earth, the support of the multitudes of living beings. All the directions issued forth from the ears of the Supreme Soul.

55-56. From his activity of recollection were born the Worlds *Bhūḥ*, *Bhuvaḥ* etc. as well as the (nether) worlds beginning with Rasātala and Yakṣas, groups of Rākṣasas etc.

O scion of the family of Kuru, he created Brāhmaṇas, Kṣatriyas, Vaiśyas, Śūdras and the others in due order from the mouth, the arms, the thighs and the feet.

---

1. This theory of evolution of the universe is to a great extent based on the Puruṣa Sūkta (RV X.90) with Purāṇic element, e.g. Viṣṇu's yogic slumber at the end of the Kalpa and creation of god Brahmā etc.

57. The Vedas, Yajña, horses, cows, goats and sheep and others originated from him, which is beyond all imagination.

58. By (mere) thought or will of the Lord of Devas the entire world of living beings, both mobile and immobile, was born. So also did Time, past, present and future.

59. Assuming the form of Vaḍavānala ('submarine fire') he drinks the waters of the ocean. At the end of the Kalpa he casts off everything that he holds within himself.

60. Adopting the form of the Sun and the Moon, he makes the sustenance of the living beings go on smoothly. He dispels darkness thereby and causes Time to function properly.

61. At the close of the Kalpa he places all the worlds within his belly and adopting the form of a child sportingly he lies on the leaf of a Banyan tree in the great ocean.

62. With the Lotus-aboded (Lakṣmī) as his second (companion) he indulges in the Yogic Slumber in the extremely comfortable and exalted couch of the body of the great Serpent.

63. The Lord of all the worlds created the Four-faced Lord of creation from the lotus rising from the lake of his navel.

64. This is a mere sport of Mukunda who works as he pleases. That Lord cannot be comprehended truly by anyone.

65-68. When there is loss of virtue (*Dharma*), when evil prevails, when groups of Devas undergo the greatest affliction, when the enemies of Suras become uncontrollable due to their haughtiness and increase in number, when great danger and fright befall the earth and the people of the earth, when there is inevitable misfortune causing endless agony to his devotees of excellent nature, he assumes eagerly the forms befitting (the particular occasion).[1] He destroys the evil immediately and causes the welfare of the universe.

69-70. With his *Rājasa* form he takes up the name *Vidhi* and creates. Adopting the *Sāttvika* form and the name *Hari* he sustains the universe. After adopting *Tāmasa* activity and the name Hara he destroys (the universe). There is none who knows the greatness of the Slayer of Madhu.

---

1. Cf. *yadā yadā hi dharmasya glānir bhavati. . . .tadātmānaṁ sṛjāmyaham//* (BG IV.7)

With the parts of *Yajña* all the limbs and joints of the form of Boar are constituted.[1] The Lord of the worlds assumes that form and takes up his residence on this mountain. I shall describe how it happened in detail, O son of the overlord of the Devas.

CHAPTER THIRTYSIX

Glorification of the Boar Incarnation (of Viṣṇu)

THE WAY VARĀHA LIFTED UP THE EARTH

Bharadvāja said:

1. Formerly at the end of the Night of the Creator the Slayer of Madhu woke up. In his mind he thought about the acts of living beings.

2. He suspected in his heart, 'Excepting the Earth no one else will be able to bear the burden of the flood (i.e. mass) of living beings.'

3. With abstract and profound meditation he saw the Earth in the neighbourhood of Pātāla. She was extremely frightened and was flooded with a vast sheet of water.

4-8. The Lord then adopted a form fit (to accomplish the task) of lifting up the Earth. *Upakarman* (subsidiary holy rite) was his lip; fire was his tongue, *Praṇava* was his loud grunt; the four Vedas were his four legs; expiatory rites his beautiful hoofs; *Prāgvaṁśa* (a sacrificial chamber with the columns or beams turned to the east) was his body; the shining Darbha grass constituted the hair on his body. *Pravargya* (a ceremony preliminary to the Soma Sacrifice) constituted the lock of hair curling backwards; the Dakṣiṇāgni (a type of sacrificial fire) was his belly. The wooden ladle *Sruk* was his snout; all the complete parts (of Yajña) constituted his limbs and joints. Divine hymns constituted

1. For the concept of *Yajña-varāha* see p. 1, ftn 2.

his manes; Supreme Brahman was his head. *Havya* and *Kavya* were his velocity; the pure sacrificial animal was his knee; Ukta, Atyukta and other metres were his pathways; Mantras constituted his strength. Thus the Lord adopted the form of divine Boar identical entirely with Yajña.

9-15. In order to find out the Earth he entered the waters of the Ocean. With the lustrous beams of his curved teeth resembling the Crescent Moon, he forcibly dispelled the dense darkness characterizing the close of the Kalpa. With the intense *Ghuru-ghuru* sounds that suppressed (drowned) the rumbling sounds of the clouds he made the cavity of the Cosmic Egg reverberate with sound.

Treading with his hoofs as sharp and tough as the arrow Khurapra, he made the body of the Lord of Serpents severely shattered and tossed it here and there. With his powerful breath-winds he made the interior of the Ocean come to the surface within the range of vision. With his long snout getting immersed in water and rising up again he stirred up the waters. Thus he went into the Ocean. He saw the trembling Earth stationed beneath the bottom of the seven nether worlds. She was agitated with fear. On seeing her he was delighted in his mind. He placed her on the tip of his curved teeth and rose up to the surface of the Ocean.

16-19. He rose up from the Ocean even as he was eulogized by the Sages residing in Janaloka.

When the Lord lifted up (married) the Earth with love the (water) of the Ocean falling down (from its surface) became the auspicious marriage screen for a short while. At the time of taking her across, O Arjuna, the Ocean, through its majestic thundering sound, performed the functions of the auspicious musical instruments unto the Lord in the form of the Boar.

Pearls scattered up by the sprays of water by the curling waves gave the impression of the *maṅgalākṣatas* (auspicious raw rice-grains showered over the couple in marriage).

Married (lifted up) by that Lord and dripping with the water (of the Ocean), the Earth shone as if her body was rendered wet due to the perspiration arising from intense love (for the Lord).

20-26. After lifting up the Earth from beneath the nether

worlds thus the Lord placed her firmly in the midst of the waters of the Ocean.

When the Earth was lifted up by him, the water that filled up the space between the Earth and the atmosphere became the inviolable line of demarcation of the boundary made by him.

After establishing the Earth thus he placed the Elephants of the Quarters, the King of Serpents and the Tortoise for giving her extra support. That receptacle of mercy (Hari) willingly applied his own *Śakti* (power) in an unmanifest form as a support for them all.

As Hari thus stood in the form of Boar after retrieving the Earth, the residents of Janaloka beginning with Sanaka eulogized him.

After propitiating Puruṣottama in the form of Boar and at his behest, Brahmā created the universe as before.

Arjuna enquired:

27-28. O great sage, how does this Earth stand when sunk within the watery expanse at the time of the close of the Kalpa beneath the seven nether worlds? What is her support? How long does the period of a Kalpa last? What is its function?

29. Explain all this in detail to me, O Brāhmaṇa, O sage.

The Incarnation of Śveta Varāha and Details of the Period of Kalpa

Bharadvāja explained:

30-34. Sixty *Vināḍikās* make one *Nāḍikā*.[1] Sixty *Nāḍikās* make a full day. Thirty days make a month which consists of two *Pakṣas* (fortnights). Two months make what is called a *Ṛtu* (season). Such six *Ṛtus* make one year. It is in the form of two *Ayanas* (transits of the Sun). It has (a cycle of) chillness, rains and heat.

Days and nights of Devas and Asuras are in opposition to each other. The two *Ayanas* of the Sun are the northern and the southern transits.

1. VV 29-34 give the measures of Time.

One *Mahāyuga* (a great Yuga, i.e. a set of four ordinary Yugas), O son of Pṛthā, consists of four hundred and thirty-two thousand human years. They are in the form of Kṛta etc. The period consisting of seventy-one *Mahāyugas* is one Manvantara. Listen to the Manus born in this Kalpa named Śveta-Varāha.

35-40. Svāyambhuva was the first Manu.[1] Then Svārociṣa became Manu. Afterwards came Uttama, Tāmasa, Raivata and Cākṣuṣa.

All these six Manus along with (their special) Indras, Suras and Sages have passed away previously. It is Vaivasvata who is the Manu now, O Arjuna. He is the seventh Manu. Ādityas, Vasus, Rudras and others are the groups of Devas in his regime. After performing a hundred horse-sacrifices the most brilliant one attained the position of Indra.

The Seven Sages, O Arjuna, are Viśvāmitra, I (i.e. Bharadvāja), Atri, Jamadagni, Kāśyapa, Vasiṣṭha and Gautama. The sons of Manu were extremely mighty. There were great warriors with Ikṣvāku as their Chief. They ruled over the Earth. They were always devoted to virtue. The five sons of Sūrya, Dakṣa, Brahmā, Dharma and Rudra called (respectively) Sūryasāvarṇi, Dakṣasāvarṇi, Brahmasāvarṇi, Dharmasāvarṇi and Rudrasāvarṇi together with Raucya and Bhauma are the seven future Manus.

41. In the course of a day of Brahmā there are fourteen Manus. This period is called a *Kalpa*. At the end of it there shall be night, the extent of it being equal to that (of the Day of Brahmā). Listen.

42. Towards the close of a day of Brahmā, O son of Pāṇḍu, a terrible drought lasting for a hundred years befalls the earth.[2]

43. In the course of that drought, when the earth becomes dry, O Dhanañjaya, the four types of living beings get perished.

44. At that time the Sun will be endowed with rays that will resemble fire. It will vomit sparks of fire and that will have hot flames like fiery tufts of hair.

---

1. VV 35-40 give the list of Manus.

2. The Purāṇic concepts about the destruction of the world at the end of a Kalpa are given in vv 42-55.

45. With the villages, cities, mountains, trees, forests etc. perished, the earth then becomes comparable with the back of a tortoise. It will resemble a red-hot ball of fiery iron.

46-48. Then from the limbs of the Creator great clouds will issue forth. They will cover up the sky. They will have loud roaring, thundering sound. They will be terrible with different colours such as white, yellow, red, black and variegated colour too. They will have the forms of mountains, elephants, mansions, trees etc. They will cause a great shower for a period of one hundred years. With that water the great fire caused by the Sun will be extinguished.

49. Again for a hundred years the great clouds will cause a fierce downpour. On account of that water all the oceans will be flooded and they will undergo change in form.

50-55a. That water poured down by the clouds at the close of the Kalpa spreads to all the worlds. A dense darkness envelops the worlds of ***Bhūḥ***, ***Bhuvaḥ***, *Svaḥ* and *Mahaḥ*.

The earth sunk under water goes down to the bottom of the nether worlds. It does not perish. It stays there somehow supported by the Śakti of Brahmā.

Then, O Arjuna, the wind issuing forth from the breath of Brahmā drives away all those great clouds rising at the close of the Kalpa.

The wind then blows incessantly for a period of hundred years without a break. Its velocity cannot be checked.

Shunning this fierce wind the Lotus-born Lord goes into Yogic Slumber and lies hidden within the lotus coming out from the navel of Hari in the vast sheet of water.

As the Lord of the universe is thus engrossed in Yogic Slumber, O son of Pṛthā, the night of the same extent as the day befalls him.

55b-59. When the night passes off, he gets up quickly and as before creates all the creatures at the behest of Hari.

Hari protects the universe in different Kalpas adopting befitting forms. In this Kalpa he had adopted the form of white Boar consisting of the parts of Yajña. Sporting about on the earth in the form of Boar, the Lord reached Veṅkaṭācala, his own stipulated previous abode.

While wandering over the banks of Svāmipuṣkariṇī for a

long time, Lord Viṣṇu saw the Lotus-based Lord endowed with great devotion.

Brahmā worshipped that sanctifier of living beings and requested:

60-62. "O Lord, resort to your own previous divine body." Accepting his request, the Lord abandoned the form of Boar and resorted to his own cosmic body that cannot be worshipped by anyone else. He stood thus with great earnestness and enthusiasm. Even after a long time no one was able to see him.

Arjuna said:

63-65. Hari thus became imperceptible and could not even be remembered. How then, O great sage, did he become manifest to human beings? Did anyone who, due to the good luck of the worlds, propitiated the Lord, reveal him here? Tell me this story?

You are conversant with all the Āgamas. Do recount the story of Hari, the hearing of which dispels sins. O excellent one among the sages, I have now attained the foremost place among meritorious persons.

CHAPTER THIRTYSEVEN

The Arrival of Śaṅkha, Agastya and Others at Śrī Veṅkaṭācala

The Story of the King Named Śaṅkha

Bharadvāja said:

1. Listen, O son of Pṛthā, I shall relate a wonderful story as to how the Lord revealed himself on this mountain.

2. There was a king named Śruta. He was a descendant of the family of Haihaya. He ruled over the splendid earth for a long time treating his subjects like his own children.

3. His son was the king named Śaṅkha. He was storehouse of good qualities. He was an expert in all the scriptural texts. He ruled over the earth.

4. He had steadfast devotion to Viṣṇu, the Lord of the universe with large eyes resembling lotuses. He had eschewed the support of everything else.

5-6. With a firm resolve he regularly meditated upon Puruṣottama, the Lord of Devas, the Lord of the universe, the infinite one of wonderful power.

He performed holy rites and gave various kinds of meritorious charitable gifts regularly for the sake of the pleasure of the Enemy of Madhu, the Lord who can be understood only through the Vedas.

7. He performed the sacrifices *Vājimedha* (Horse-sacrifice) etc. with him (Viṣṇu) alone as his object (of worship). By distributing monetary gifts as laid down he delighted every Brāhmaṇa.

8. With his heart permanently fixed on Keśava who is fond of his devotees, he performed all the holy rites of the nature of Iṣṭa and Pūrta.

9. He always remembered Govinda. He performed the *Japa* of Acyuta, the immutable one. He worshipped the Lotus-eyed Lord. He glorified the Śārṅga-wielding Lord.

10. The king used to listen to the sacred stories of Viṣṇu that redeem people from the ocean of worldly existence and that were expounded by persons well-versed in the Purāṇas.

11-13. He adored Brāhmaṇas for the sake of pleasing Hari. Though the king was tirelessly engaged in all these things wholeheartedly, he did not perceive Puruṣottama who possesses eternal prosperity and is self-determined. Unable to attain the vision of Viṣṇu identical with Yajña, he was overwhelmed with grief in his heart and immersed in great anxiety.

Śaṅkha said:

14. In the course of thousands of my previous births much sin has been committed by me and so the vision of Hṛṣīkeśa has not been obtained by me.

15-17. Indeed the vision of Viṣṇu, the slayer of Madhu, is the entire fruit of austerities performed in the course of many previous births. How will the Lord come within the range of my eyes? When will the bliss of hearing his words be obtained? Fie upon me who have committed sins, who am deprived of the fruit of holy rites, who am far removed from the grace of Nārāyaṇa and have become the victim of the sufferings of worldly existence!

Bharadvāja said:

18. When the king who was thus agitated in his mind became disinterested in life, Keśava of invisible form said thus within the hearing of everyone:

Śrī Bhagavān said:

19. Do not be grief-stricken, O king. Listen. I shall tell you what is conducive to your welfare. You have sought in me sole refuge. You are a good man. How will I forsake you?

20. This mountain named Veṅkaṭa is well-known in all the three worlds. Residence there is liked by me more than in Vaikuṇṭha.

21. Go to that excellent mountain and perform penance devoutly. When a thousand years pass off thus, I shall become visible to you.

22-23. Like you Agastya also endeavoured for the sake of acquiring my vision quickly. He asked the Four-faced Lord (Brahmā): "Where is Viṣṇu seen?" The Lotus-born Lord told, "It is possible for persons of controlled mind to get Hari on the Vṛṣabha mountain. Go there."

24. The Pot-born Sage being directed thus by the Lotus-born Lord will come to my residence, the Añjana mountain, in order to perform penance.

25. You too should fix your residence on that meritorious mountain. You be engaged in penance and propitiate me. You shall obtain my vision.

King Śaṅkha Goes to Śrī Veṅkaṭācala at the Suggestion of the Lord

Bharadvāja said:

26. On being commanded thus by the Lord, the enemy of Dānavas, matchless Śaṅkha attained matchless pleasure in his mind thinking, 'I am blessed'.

27. Entrusting to his son Vajra the work of protecting the subjects, he went to the Mountain Nārāyaṇa seeking the vision of Govinda.

28. On its lofty peak he saw the auspicious Svāmipuṣkariṇī full of divine waters comparable to nectar.

29-30. It was frequented by multitudes of Siddhas, Gandharvas, Devas and sages. It assuages the scorching heat of worldly existence and is the resort of all the Tīrthas. It was rendered noisy by water crows, storks, cranes, swans and Kāraṇḍava ducks. It was very charming with lilies, blue lotuses, red lotuses and white lotuses.

31-33a. On seeing that divine (river) abounding in lotuses he put up a hut on its banks. He was delighted by his holy ablutions, drinking of water etc. His mind was free from doubts and hesitation. He surrendered (the benefits of) all the holy rites to Janārdana, the Lord of the universe. He was permanently engaged in *Japa* and meditation. He performed a very severe penance.

AGASTYA COMES TO VEṄKAṬĀCALA FOR THE SAKE OF THE VISION OF THE LORD

33b-37a. At that very same time, at the behest of Parameṣṭhin, Sage Agastya too came there surrounded by hundreds of sages. Beginning with the western extremity, he endeavoured to circumambulate (the mountain). He wandered over the mountain for a long time seeing the meritorious holy spots. In different places he saw Brahmā, Guha, Śakra, Īśa, Viṣvaksena and others who were desirous of seeing Hari. He saw the following also: leading Yogins beginning with Sanaka, sages the chief of whom was Nārada, Siddhas, Gandharvas, Daityas, Yakṣas, Rākṣasas and serpents.

37b-40. By means of humble and loving conversations he was honoured by those different persons. He wandered over all those different wonderful places looking at them (with pleasure). He took bath in the different Tīrthas beginning with Skandadhārā. In the different places he worshipped Govinda, the Lord of the worlds. Thus the excellent sage wandered (for a long time). Even when a thousand years elapsed the sage could not see the Lotus-eyed Lord. He became anxious and grief-stricken.

Guru (Jupiter), Vasu and Others Address Agastya

41. At that time Dhiṣaṇa (Jupiter) and Uśanas (Venus) as well as the king Uparicara-Vasu came to that great sage. (They said:)

42-43. "Our life has become fruitful, O excellent sage, since you have been seen by us like another Nārāyaṇa. We were desirous of seeing Acyuta, O sage. What we had been told then by Brahmā, the Lord of the worlds, is being communicated to you.

44. 'There is in the southern region a mountain named Veṅkaṭa. This abode is liked by Hari more than Śveta Dvīpa.

45. On that mountain Govinda, the sire of the universe, will reveal his own form to Agastya as well as to Śaṅkha, the king.

46-49. At that time all the Devas, sages, Yakṣas, Rākṣasas and we too will have the vision of the Lord of Devas. That will take place ere long. Hence eschew all your sins and evils and go in search of Agastya on that Nārāyaṇa mountain.'

On being commanded thus by Brahmā we came to this place. It is our good fortune that we could see you of exalted magnificence and plenty of refulgence. Accompanied by you, we shall go to the banks of Svāmipuṣkariṇī and see Śaṅkha also, the excellent follower of the Lord."

Agastya and Others see the Various Beautiful Spots on Śrī Veṅkaṭācala

Bharadvāja said:

50. On being requested thus by Gīṣpati (Jupiter) and other important persons the Pot-born Sage (Agastya) cast off his mass of grief and quickly went along with them.

51. He saw great tall trees heavily laden with flowers and fruits and so bending down (under their weight). They had spread their great shade over all the quarters with multitudes of their branches.

52. In the middle of the various paths he saw various animals such as lions, elephants, tigers, boars, buffaloes etc.

53. The ridges holding clouds were seen by them. They were as splendid as gold, silver, copper etc. (They shone like them.)

54. Hundreds of streams were seen by them. They appeared to offer oblations unto the heaven-dwellers by means of the water-sprays raised by them. With their forceful currents they had dislodged many rocks.

55-57. Gentle wind that blew over the slopes and valleys of the mountain, wafted the fragrance of lotuses and increased their delight. The chirping and the cooing sounds of parrots and cuckoos were heard. They saw Siddhas seated on broad and large rocky slabs in different places singing songs of the greatness and good qualities of Kṛṣṇa.

58-61. All of them, the leading sages, the chief of whom was Agastya, went round and saw the divine Svāmipuṣkariṇī with water free from impurities. They saw the king Śaṅkha who had put up his residence on its banks. He had consigned all his activities, physical, verbal and mental, to Hari and stood by. On seeing the eminent sages of praiseworthy, holy rites suddenly, he offered them due adoration and reverence along with obeisances and eulogies. They honoured one another enthusiastically and took their seats. Engaged in glorifying Govinda, they attained great contentment.

CHAPTER THIRTYEIGHT

Manifestation of Lord Viṣṇu to Agastya and Others

Bharadvāja said:

1. Three days passed off while they were engaged in worship and prayers with their minds dedicated to Hari, the Lord of the universe.

2. On the third day while they were asleep at night they saw an excellent dream at the end of the fourth watch (Yāma = period of 3 hours).

3. They saw Puruṣottama pleased and with a smiling look. He had the conch, the discus and the iron club in his hands. He had come for granting them boons.

4. They got up with joyous hearts and came out of their

houses. With due reverence, they took their holy baths in the sacred waters of Svāmipuṣkariṇī in accordance with the injunctions.

5. After duly performing all those rites that had to be performed in the morning all of them returned to their abodes to propitiate Lord Acyuta.

6. Seeing the good omen indicated by the birds on the way conducive to instant welfare, they thought that the favour of the Lord was within their reach.

7. Then they worshipped Janārdana, the maker of the three worlds. They eulogized him with different holy prayers described in the Vedas.

8. At the end of the prayers, O son of Kuntī, the excellent Pot-born Sage (Agastya) repeated the eight-syllabled Mantra of Hari (Oṁ namo Nārāyaṇāya) along with Śaṅkha.

9. An extremely mysterious brilliant light manifested (itself) in front of those persons who had thus dedicated their minds to Acyuta, the Lord of the universe.

10. It was stationed in the sky like the splendour of many crores of Suns, Moons and fires unified together in one place.

11. On seeing that brilliance all of them were immensely surprised. They meditated upon divine Nārāyaṇa, the embodiment of the greatest bliss.

12. The Lord was beyond the ken of speech and mind. He was shining with well renowned prosperity and glory. He had thousand, (innumerable) eyes and was equipped with a thousand arms and feet.

13. He was charming with a lustre that was as brilliant as that of molten gold. He was terrific with curved teeth. He was too dazzling to be seen properly, (as) he emitted masses of flames of fire.

14. He shone with the Kaustubha jewel. He held Śrī on his chest. He was incomprehensible, without beginning or end.

15-17a. He inspired excessive fright (in everyone). He was omnipresent. He revealed the entire Cosmic Egg within himself. On seeing the Lord all of them with Agastya and Śaṅkha as their leaders, became delighted in their minds.

On seeing the Lord of the universe they bowed to him again and again.

The weapons of Hari that were wandering for the sake of protecting the worlds, came back to serve him, equipped with their own respective splendour and strength.

17b-23a. (The weapons were) the discus that had the lustre of the Sun, the divine mace, the sword Nandaka, the Puṇḍarīka (white lotus), (the conch) Pāñcajanya of terrific sound having the lustre of the Moon. It filled the entire Cosmic Egg. The sound of Pāñcajanya was extremely terrifying unto all the Asuras.

On hearing the sound of Pāñcajanya which was extremely mysterious and terrific all the Devas came there riding on their respective vehicles.

Brahmā, Rudra, Indra, the Yogins beginning with Sanaka, the sages chief of whom was Vasiṣṭha, Gandharvas, serpents and Kinnaras, Viṣvaksena, Garuḍa, the servants of Viṣṇu beginning with Jaya and those who are permanently of the same form (as that of the Lord) and residents of the Śvetadvīpa (all these came).

A wonderful shower of flowers from the celestial (Kalpa) tree fell thick over all of them delighting everyone's mind through the excessive fragrance.

23b. The celestial damsels of beautiful eyes danced; the leading Kinnaras sang.

24-25. Suras, Gandharvas and Cāraṇas who were delighted and thrilled, eulogized. On seeing the Lotus-eyed Lord, who is fond of his devotees, pleased, they bowed down to him with eight limbs touching the ground and propitiated him with different kinds of hymns.

Brahmā and others said:

26. Be victorious, O Viṣṇu, O ocean of mercy. Be victorious, O lotus-eyed one. Be victorious, the sole bestower of boons in all the worlds. Be victorious, O suppressor of the agony of devotees.

27. Who knows you (fully), the endless one, the imperishable one, the quiescent one, one who is beyond the ken of speech and mind and is of the nature of consciousness and bliss?

28. They consider you minuter than the minutest; stouter

(grosser) than the stoutest (grossest), the immanent soul. The scriptures call you Acyuta, Puruṣa and one beyond Prakṛti.

29. Among the embodied souls subject to the wiles of Māyā who is competent to describe you who are the embodiment of the essence of the Vedāntas and who are stationed within and without everything?

30. On seeing this extremely frightening form of yours all of us are shuddering with fear. Do adopt a calm and graceful form.

Bharadvāja said:

31. On being eulogized by Viriñca and others thus, the Garuḍa-emblemed Lord spoke earnestly in words and tones resembling the thunder of clouds.

The Lord Adopts a Gentle Form at the Request of Brahmā and Others

Śrī Bhagavān said:

32. I shall shed off this terrifying form. I shall assume a pleasing and quiescent form. Look at me without being agitated.

33. After saying this the Lord vanished and within the same moment he reappeared in a pleasant form, in an aerial chariot studded with gems and jewels.

34. His face resembled the disc of the Moon. He was quiet and calm. He had a lustre like that of the petals of a blue lotus. His robes were golden-coloured. He was adorned with ornaments set with gems and jewels.

35. In his four hands shone the conch, the discus, the mace and the lotus. On seeing that lover of Ramā all of them saluted him again and again.

36. The Lord made Brahmā and others satisfied by granting them what they desired. He then spoke to Agastya, the prominent sage who stood there in humility:

Śrī Bhagavān said:

37. O eminent sage, you have become strained and fatigued on account of the arduous holy rites performed now with me as

the object (of worship). I shall grant you all desired boons. Tell me.

Bharadvāja said:

38. On hearing the words of the Lord of Śrī, the Pot-born Sage bowed down to him again and again. With hair standing on end all over the body (due to thrill of joy) he spoke these words:

At the Request of Agastya the River Suvarṇamukharī was Granted Superiority over Everything

39. "The *Homas* that I have performed, the penances that I have practised, (the Vedic Mantras) that I have studied, whatever I have heard—everything has become fruitful, because I have been honoured by you.

40. I am the only righteous-souled person, O Lord, in all the three worlds, because even as I am in search of you, you have come in search of me.

41. Even before your (formal pronouncement of your) favour I have realized all my desires, O Mādhava. Even after thinking deeply I do not see anything that remains to be attained (by me) now.

42. Still out of fickleness this is being submitted, O Lord. May my devotion unto you be like this always.

43. Remember this that it was at the request of Suras that the river Suvarṇamukharī (was brought) by me. It destroys the mass of sins of those who take their bath therein.

44. That river has come very near the ridge of your mountain. Do make it blessed, O Lord of the worlds, by means of your blessings and favour.

45. Those who take their bath in the waters of Suvarṇamukharī and visit you stationed on the Veṅkaṭa (Hill) shall be the recipients of worldly pleasures and salvation.

46. Foolish persons of short span of life, who have slipped (dropped) down from the path of knowledge and yogic practice, are not competent to see you through holy rites, study of the Vedas and other sacred activities.

47. O Sire of the universe, be always present on this moun-

tain. O Lord, grant your favours to everyone with beaming face. Bestow on them whatever object they may desire."

Śrī Bhagavān said:

48. O Brāhmaṇa, what has been requested by you shall certainly take place. Indeed, an act of devotion to me, that is matchless in the entire world, has been performed by you.

49. Like the river Gaṅgā, O sage, this river Suvarṇamukharī shall be worthy of being sought after. It shall cause all desired prosperity even to the Suras.

50. Svāmipuṣkariṇī shall become united with the form of the river. It shall pass over to that divine river which is the resort unto all the Tīrthas.

51. O sage, due to your request I shall take up my residence for ever from now onwards on this mountain named Vaikuṇṭha.

52-54. Those who have washed all the dirt of the mass of sins by means of holy bath in Suvarṇamukharī and then visit me on this Vaikuṇṭha mountain with great concentration, shall become richly endowed with sons and all types of prosperity and glory on the earth. After death they will enjoy the pleasures of heaven till the end of the Kalpa. Thereafter they will attain my region shining with (divine) bliss alone. From that region they will not return (to the earth). In this matter there is no doubt at all.

55. O sage, out of deference for your request I shall look after all those who come here to visit me. I shall always grant them all the auspicious things desired by them.

56-57. I shall grant many sons to those who seek sons, riches to those who seek riches, complete quelling of all ailments to those who desire good health, redemption from misery to those who are assailed by acute adversity and all rare enjoyment of pleasures (to everyone) at all times.

58. There is no doubt about this that everyone will attain all those desires seeking which he or she has come and visited me.

59. Wherever they may stay, all those excellent men who remember me shall get the fulfilment desired by them by my favour.

The Lord Grants Boons to King Śaṅkha and then Vanishes

60. After saying this to that sage, the Lord glanced at Śaṅkha, the king. He spoke these words even as Brahmā and others were listening:

Śrī Bhagavān said:

61. O Śaṅkha, I am delighted at your devotion. Choose a boon desired (by you). I shall grant it. I shall be the bestower of boons on you who have become very emaciated on account of the penance.

Śaṅkha said:

62. O mighty one, I do not request for anything other than service unto your lotus-like feet. I request for that excellent goal which your devotees attain.

Śrī Bhagavān said:

63. O Śaṅkha, what is requested by you, shall certainly be so. What is it that cannot be obtained by those people who have become very excellent and meritorious on account of their service unto me?

64. You will be in the world of Indra till the end of the Kalpa. You will be attended upon by multitudes of celestial damsels. After enjoying various kinds of pleasures you will attain my world.

65. Thus, O king, Nārāyaṇa, the origin of the universe, a wish-yielding tree unto those who worship him, granted desired boons to Śaṅkha.

66. Then the Lotus-eyed Lord bade farewell to everyone beginning with Brahmā. Being eulogized by them with devotion the Lord vanished there itself.

Conclusion of the Description of the Greatness of Śrī Veṅkaṭācala by Bharadvāja

Bharadvāja said:

67. The power of Veṅkaṭādri has been recounted to you, O

Arjuna. On hearing this sanctifying story men are liberated from sins.

68. On being requested by Brahmā Hari cast off the form of Boar. Enchanting the universe with his Māyā the Lord of wonderful features rejoiced here.

69. Afterwards on being requested by Agastya and Śaṅkha the Lord granted them (i.e. assumed before them) a physical body fit for enjoyment of pleasures, a body that was pleasing to look at, extremely graceful and calm.

70. By remembering Nārāyaṇa, Veṅkaṭādri, Svāmipuṣkariṇī and this narrative people become liberated from sins.

71. In the whole of the Cosmic Egg there is no other holy spot on a par with Veṅkaṭādri. A Lord equal to Veṅkaṭeśa has never been before nor will there ever be.

72. A holy spot equal to Veṅkaṭādri has never been before, nor will there ever be. There is nothing anywhere on a par with the Lake Svāmitīrtha.

73. If people remember Veṅkaṭeśa everyday on getting up in the morning, the glory of salvation comes within their reach. There is no doubt about it.

74-75. Those who take bath in Svāmipuṣkariṇī Tīrtha with perfect restraint and visit Hari, the immanent soul of everyone, residing on Varāhācala, obtain the full benefit of a thousand horse-sacrifices and a hundred Vājapeyas. There is no doubt about it.

76-77. The excellent men who listen to the greatness of Veṅkaṭācala will enjoy great pleasures here in this world and hereafter in the other world, and then will attain salvation.

The greatness of Veṅkaṭācala has been briefly recounted to you. Henceforth the power of the great river will be described, O Arjuna.

CHAPTER THIRTYNINE

Añjanā's Penance for Getting a Son

Śrī Sūta said:

1-2. Formerly, Añjanā who had no son became distressed and therefore engaged herself in a penance. On seeing her Mataṅga, a tiger among sages and a devotee of Viṣṇu, spoke these words to (the lady) named Añjanā who was engaged in a very severe penance.

Mataṅga said:

3. Get up, O gentle lady Añjanā. Why are you engaged in penance? Tell me, O highly fortunate gentle lady of excellent countenance, your purpose and aim (of performing penance).

Añjanā replied:

4-7. O Mataṅga, O tiger among sages, listen to my words. My father, a Rākṣasa named Kesarī, is a devotee of Śiva. He performed a severe penance to please Śiva. It was a very difficult penance for the sake of a son. Accompanied by Pārvatī and seated on his Bull, Lord Śaṁbhu appeared before him and granted him an auspicious boon.

Śaṁbhu said:

Listen, O King, soniessness in this birth has been ordained for you by your fate. Still I grant you another thing.

8. Your daughter will be well-known in all the worlds. Her son of great intelligence will cause delight unto you.

9-14a. After granting this boon to him, Hara vanished there itself.

On getting me (as a daughter), O Brāhmaṇa, my father became centented. Then, after some time, O Brāhmaṇa, the great monkey named Kesarī[1] requested my father to give me (in marriage) to him. Thereupon, my father gave me to him. As a wedding present he gave a hundred million cows and a hundred thou-

1. Keasarī is the name of Añjanā's Rākṣasa father and monkey husband.

sand elephants. (My father) of lofty mind gave a hundred million horses and an equal number of chariots. He gave garments and jewels in plenty and a thousand men and women servants. O highly intelligent one, along with me he gave many women to work in the inner apartment. They were experts in dance and music. He gave a thousand clothes too. For many years, O sage, I sported with my husband.

14b-18. I was extremely distressed, O Brāhmaṇa, because I had no son. There in the city of Kiṣkindhā many kinds of holy rites were performed by me. In the months of Māgha, Vāiśākha and Kārttika, O eminent Brāhmaṇa, holy ablutions, charitable gifts, holy rites etc. were performed. The holy observances extending over four months (in the rainy season) were performed. Prostrations as well as excellent circumambulations were performed, O Brāhmaṇa. Various kinds of charitable gifts were given, viz. gift of Śālagrāma, of food, lights, cows, gingelly-seeds, garments, O great sage, gift of land, water, flower etc. All the important holy rites pertaining to Viṣṇu were performed by me with a desire for the benefit of (begetting) a good son.

19-23. The holy rites suggested by the noble-souled Brāhmaṇas to be performed in Śrāvaṇa and other months have been performed by me, O great Brāhmaṇa, for the propitiation of the Slayer of Madhu.

All the chief varieties of fruits of various kinds have been gifted by me with a desire for having a good son. Innumerable holy rites (observances) of various kinds have been performed by me. Still I did not get a son. I am distressed thereby. So I am engaged in a penance.

How will a son famous in the three worlds be born, O Brāhmaṇa, after bowing down in front of you. O excellent Sage, I request you. Do tell me, O tiger among sages, distressed that I am and engaged in the penance.

Śrī Sūta said:

24-28. As she said thus, Mataṅga the excellent sage spoke:

"Listen to my words, O gentle lady. (They are) conducive to the attainment of sons and grandsons. Ten Yojanas (i.e. $10 \times 12 = 120$ kilometres) to the southern side from here there is the residential abode (shrine) of Nṛsiṁha well-known as Ghanācala. There is the charming Brahmatīrtha in it, O lady of good fortune. Ten Yojanas to the east of the same is the most excellent river named Suvarṇamukharī. To the north of it there is a mountain named Vṛṣabhācala. On its summit there is a splendid lake called Svāmipuṣkariṇī After going there and seeing the auspicious waters your mind will become purified.

29-35. Take your holy bath there in accordance with the injunctions. Bow down to the deity Varāha (Boar). Then go ahead, O lady of excellent countenance, after bowing down to Veṅkaṭeśa. A Tīrtha well-known as Viyadgaṅgā shines on the northern side of Svāmitīrtha. It is a place full of lions and tigers. Different kinds of splendid trees of great merit are found there, such as mango, Punnāga, jack tree, Mimusops Elengi, Embylic Myrobalan, Sandal, Agallochum, margosa, palm trees, Hintāla trees, Butea frondosa, Feronia Elephantum, holy fig tree, Marmelos and Iṅgudas (Terminalia Catappa).

O gentle lady Añjanā, take your holy bath there with all requisite preliminary rites of *Saṅkalpa* etc. After the bath drink the (water of the) auspicious Tīrtha. Standing facing the Tīrtha, O gentle lady of excellent countenance, perform a penance with the Wind-god as your object of worship. As a result of your penance, your son will be one who cannot be killed by Devas, Rākṣasas, Brāhmaṇas, human beings, excellent sages, black bees, birds, missiles and weapons of many splendid varieties."

Śrī Sūta said:

36. On being told thus, the gentle lady Añjanā bowed down to him again and again. Accompanied by her husband she quickly went to (the mountain) named Veṅkaṭācala.

37. After reaching the Kapila Tīrtha and taking her holy bath with the mind free from impurities, she climbed the mountain Veṅkaṭa and went to Svāmipuṣkariṇī.

38. After bathing there and bowing down to the deities Varāha and Veṅkaṭeśa, she remembered frequently the words of Sage Mataṅga.

39. The sweet-voiced Añjanā hastened to Viyadgaṅgā. She took her bath and drank the holy water. She then performed penance by standing on its banks and facing it.

40. With the Vital Breath (Prāṇavāyu) as her object of worship the lady of holy observances began the penance. First she subsisted on fruits, then on water and then she abstained from taking any thing.

41. With her eyes fixed on the tip of her nose she performed penance for a thousand years. Her splendid friend named Vipulā rendered service to her.

42-44. At the end of a thousand years the Wind-god of great intelligence appeared before her. The highly intelligent one spoke to her, O excellent sages, when the Sun had his transit to the Zodiac Aries on the meritorious Full-Moon day in conjunction with the constellation Citrā:

Vāyu said:

I shall grant you what you desire, O lady of holy rites; choose your boon.

On hearing his words thus the chaste lady Añjanā said:

45. "O Lord, Wind-god of exalted magnificence, of great intelligence, grant me a son."

On hearing her words the Wind-god said:

46. "I shall become your son. O lady of splendid countenance, I shall grant (bring to) you good reputation."

After granting her the boon thus, the mighty one remained there itself.

47-49. Then all these came to see her engaged in penance; Brahmā and other Devas, the Guardians of the Quarters, Indra and others, noble-souled (sages) like Vasiṣṭha and others, Yogins like Sanaka, eminent Brāhmaṇas Vyāsa etc., the Lord of the universe along with Lakṣmī, the wives of Devas and the wives of sages. Those noble-souled ones came there riding on their respective vehicles accompanied by wives, servants, sons and others.

50. Saying "Oh (How) wonderful! Oh wonderful!" all the groups of Devas, Brahmā and others stood far away in the firmament looking at her. All those (gods), the chiefs of whom were Brahmā and Maheśa, stood there looking from a distance.

CHAPTER FORTY

The Proper Time for Sacred Bath in Viyadgaṅgā

Śrī Sūta said:

1-3. After receiving the boon Añjanā rejoiced in the company of her husband. On seeing Brahmā and others come she became wonder-struck. But in the company of her husband the sweet-voiced Añjanā retained normalcy.

Permitted by Brahmā and others, Vyāsa, the most excellent one among those conversant with the Vedas, spoke to Añjanā in a voice as majestic in tone as the rumbling sound of clouds:

Vyāsa said:

4-7. O Añjanā, listen to my words which are beneficial unto the worlds.

On listening to the words of Sage Mataṅga you had gone to Veṅkaṭa with a mind free from impurities. You performed a very difficult penance. A heroic son with the greatest exploits in all the three worlds will be born to you.

Hence on the day of your perception (delivery) all the Tīrthas of the three worlds beginning with Gaṅgā will come into this excellent Tīrtha.

In the whole of this Cosmic Egg there is no other Tīrtha equal to Veṅkaṭādri. There too the splendid Svāmipuṣkariṇī is exceedingly meritorious.

8-11. Better still is this Tīrtha on the day of your perception (of your child?).

Listen, O gentle lady, of good holy rites. I shall recount to you the benefit of those who come for the sake of their holy bath to this Tīrtha on the auspicious Full-Moon day in conjuction with the constellation Citrā when the Sun has his transit into the Zodiac Aries. O lady of excellent countenance, they will have definitely that benefit which one derives by taking holy bath in all the Tīrthas beginning with Gaṅgā for a period of twelve years.

Listen to the height of benefit of those persons who make charitable gifts. O gentle lady of excellent countenance, know that their benefit will be what is mentioned in the appropriate place (*sthāne*).

Añjanā said:

12. O eminent Brāhmaṇa, most excellent among those conversant with the Vedas, tell me about all those charitable gifts that should be given on Veṅkaṭādri, the most excellent one among all the mountains.

In Praise of the Charitable Gifts[1] to be made on Śrī Veṅkaṭācala as Explained by Vyāsa

Vyāsa said:

13. The two gifts, viz. of foodstuffs and garments and the Śrāddha unto the Manes in particular (offered) on Veṅkaṭādri, the most excellent one among mountains, are praiseworthy.

14. Those who give gold for the pleasure of the Slayer of Madhu attain all the worlds and rejoice, O excellent sages(?)

15. He who makes the gift of a Śālagrāma stone on the excellent mountain is not reborn. He obtains perfect knowledge.

16. He who makes a gift of cow to an eminent Brāhmaṇa with a large family, shines in the world of Viṣṇu for as many (years) as there is hair on its (the cow's) body.

17. Who in heaven or on the earth is competent to recount the meritorious fruit of that person, O gentle lady, who gives land to a Brāhmaṇa with a large family?

18. He who gives a girl (in marriage) to a Brāhmaṇa well-versed in the Vedas, attains the world of Viṣṇu and rejoices along with the Pitṛs.

19. It is impossible even for Śeṣa to recount the meritorious benefit of those persons who construct free-water booths, O gentle lady, storing cool water (for travellers).

20. He who gives gingelly seeds to a Brāhmaṇa well-versed in the Vedas and having a large family, shall be rid of all sins and he goes to the world of Viṣṇu.

1. VV 13-25 state what gifts should be given and the fruit of the *Dāna*.

21. The Brāhmaṇas, the most excellent ones among those conversant with the Vedas, praise the charitable gift of foodgrains. Those who make gifts of foodgrains will have many sons.

22-25. He who gives to a Brāhmaṇa sweet scents, Campaka flowers etc., an umbrella, a fan, chowries, betel-leaves, camphor etc. enjoys worldly pleasures for a long time and then goes to heaven. For a thousand years according to the reckoning of gods he enjoys many pleasures there. Then he is born as an Emperor and enjoys the earth for a long time. Then he becomes a Brāhmaṇa and master of the Vedas and Vedāntas. Thereafter, by the grace of the Discus-bearing Lord he attains liberation. Thus, O gentle lady, the greatness of Veṅkaṭācala has been described.

26-28. He who always listens to this, he who glorifies it, shall be rid of all sins and he goes to the world of Viṣṇu.

He who listens to or reads this, originally spoken by the noble-souled Vyāsa, shall become contented and blessed. All the persons born in his family attain salvation. There is no doubt about it.

:: End of Veṅkaṭācalamāhātmya ::

INDEX

ERRATA

Page	Line	Incorrect	Correct
34	5	straight away	straightaway
99	2 (from bottom)	humanbirth	human birth
123	last	inde ed	indeed
130	5	Puṇyaśila	Puṇyaśīla
195	14	Devaṛṣipitṛtīrtha	Devarṣipitṛtīrtha
207	16	Kāśyapa	Kaśyapa
222	4 (from bottom)	centented	contented